Liberal Education and the Small University in Canada

Small liberal arts institutions whose focus is the undergraduate student have previously received little attention in the literature on higher education in Canada. Contributors to this collection of essays look at the present situation in such schools, discuss how best to preserve the values and integrity of liberal arts teaching, and make a case for the important role liberal education at the small university plays in higher education in Canada.

Whatever the goal of a liberal education, whether acquiring a core body of knowledge, a style of thinking, or the development of character, these essays suggest the importance of the academic community, characteristic of the small university, in the shaping and survival of liberal education. Contributors argue that small classes, a sense of community, and personal dialogue between students and faculty are best provided by the small university and make a unique contribution to students' intellectual development.

CHRISTINE STORM is professor of psychology and former director of research administration, Mount Allison University.

Liberal Education and the Small University in Canada

EDITED BY
CHRISTINE STORM

McGill-Queen's University Press
Montreal & Kingston • London • Buffalo

ISBN 0-7735-1424-4 (cloth)
ISBN 0-7735-1512-7 (paper)

Legal deposit first quarter 1996
Bibliothèque nationale du Québec

Printed in Canada on acid-free paper

McGill-Queen's University Press is grateful to the Canada Council for support of its publishing program.

The authors are grateful to the Social Sciences and Humanities Research Council through its Aid to Small Universities grant for support of the research reported here and for assistance with publication.

Canadian Cataloguing in Publication Data

Main entry under title:
Liberal education and the small university in Canada
Includes bibliographical references.
ISBN 0-7735-1424-4 (bound) –
ISBN 0-7735-1512-7 (pbk.)
1. Education, Humanistic – Canada. 1. Small colleges – Canada. 1. Education, Higher – Canada. 1. Storm, Christine, 1940–
LC1024.C3L52 1996 378'.012'0971 C96-900343-9

Typeset in Sabon 10/12
by Caractéra inc., Quebec City

Contents

Preface

The priority of Mount Allison University has always been the undergraduate student. As an institution of higher education it has never, in this century, aspired to be a multiversity dedicating major portions of its resources to post-graduate programs. Since World War II, at least, it has striven to offer the best in a liberal education, and to ensure that those undergraduate professional programs it does offer are thoroughly integrated into a liberal-arts context. It has not only accepted but embraced limitations on its size, inviting comparisons with the tradition of small, four-year liberal arts colleges in neighbouring New England. Like Mount Allison, many of these colleges grew out of the desire of a religious denomination to provide higher education not only for the children of its parishioners but for those of the local population generally.

Research in higher education is an active field. In addition to the work of individual scholars, many institutions have centres or institutes for research devoted to this area. There has been no such tradition of systematic self-examination or research at Mount Allison. John Reid's excellent two-volume history of the university from its inception in 1839 to 1964 was a substantial step towards establishing the historical record of the institution in the Maritime context. Yet there are many aspects to research in higher education that are relevant to the small university and to which research at Mount Allison might have something distinctive to contribute. Small liberal arts institutions have received little attention in the literature on higher education, particularly in Canada. When the Social Sciences and Humanities Research Council invited the small universities to submit a three-year plan for development of research under the Aid to Small Universities Program, the University Research Committee at Mount Allison, chaired by the director of Research Administration, submitted a proposal for the development of research in higher education. This plan seemed ideally suited not only to Mount Allison's mission but to the goals of the Aid to Small Universities Program: it was multidisciplinary; it could be used to augment the current library holdings; it was peculiarly suited to the institution; and potentially it filled a need in the Maritime provinces.

This volume is the product of the plan. Few of the contributors had previously conducted research or published in the area of higher education. The project encouraged research of any type by researchers from any discipline so long as the topic was relevant to higher education. Contributors asked their own research questions according to their interests. Although most of the chapters centre on Mount Allison University, we did not set out either to define the specific goals of liberal education at this institution or to evaluate the extent to which any such goals had been achieved. However, as the project progressed, certain common themes emerged in the different studies. One such theme is the contribution of smallness – both of the institution and of the town in which it is located – to the educational process. Another theme is the difficulty of reaching consensus on the essential goals of a liberal education in the contemporary context of diversity and proliferation of knowledge. Whatever the goals of a liberal education (whether a core body of knowledge, a style of thinking, or the development of character), these studies suggest that they are most effectively pursued in an environment where the academy pervades the lives of students and faculty and where the educational process continues outside the classroom as well as within it, in frequent and close encounters among the members of the community.

A variety of disciplines are represented in this volume – philosophy, economics, religious studies, sociology, classics, education, psychology, physics, English, and fine arts. Chapters 1 and 2 address the liberal arts. J. vanderLeest discusses how the concept of liberal arts has evolved from its classical origins, and Tom Storm and Christine Storm compare the contemporary arts and science curriculum in a sample of Canadian and American institutions. Both chapters raise the issue of what is the essential core of a liberal education and what means of instruction are central to its definition.

Chapters 3 and 4 are concerned with the origins, educational experience, and post-graduate careers of Mount Allison students. Berkeley Fleming and Brian Campbell compare the socioeconomic backgrounds of students at Mount Allison to students at other Maritime universities; Christine Storm, Tom Storm, and Michelle Strain report on graduates' perceptions of Mount Allison from 1960 to 1984. These two chapters show that the Mount Allison student body is socially distinct as a community from other Maritime student populations and that the small, tightly knit academic community is believed by several generations of graduates to have enhanced the quality of their education at Mount Allison.

The next four chapters examine particular fields of curricular and extracurricular activity from an historical viewpoint. Paul Bogaard reviews the development of science teaching in the Maritimes as an integral part of liberal education. The history and contemporary status of fine arts, drama, and religion, both as academic programs and extracurricular influences, are reviewed in turn by Virgil Hammock, Mark Blagrave, and Mark Parent. These chapters contribute to the impression gleaned from student surveys of an academic community extending beyond the classroom.

The last four chapters examine contemporary issues of technological innovation, learning assistance, and university financing. Paul Cant, Bob Hawkes, and Nancy Vogan describe the development of a centre for course development using computers. Jane Drover, Brian McMillan, and Lex Wilson describe the programs they have developed for helping students to learn. The developments reported in these two papers indicate the role of a small academic community in nurturing innovation. Frank Strain's two contributions address the impact of the economic and political environment on the financing of Canadian universities in general and Mount Allison in particular, using a simple dynamic economic model.

The history and philosophy of university governance and academic decision making, the early development of teaching in the humanities and social sciences, and the more recent history of developments in the formal curriculum are particularly significant topics for further research. More specific to Mount Allison is the absence from the present volume of a chapter on music, which, along with fine arts and drama, has been a conspicuous part of the universities history. A second phase of the higher-education project is currently underway and some of these topics are being addressed. It is too early to say that a tradition of research has been established, but several of the authors have continued the research reported here and some have initiated new lines of inquiry in higher education. It is our hope that, ultimately, research in higher education will indeed become a tradition at Mount Allison.

My thanks to the authors for their contributions and cooperation. I am grateful to the participants and discussants at a conference on Liberal Education at the Small Canadian University for their comments and ideas, particularly John Reid. The Social Sciences and Humanities Research Council Subcommittee on Research originally proposed the project. Its members were Sheila Brown, Bill Godfrey, Thaddeus

Holownia, Michael Tucker, and myself as Director of Research Administration. My husband, Tom Storm, made many useful contributions to the original proposal. Margaret Whitla supervised the preparation of the final manuscript which Charlotte Purchy typed. Both worked inconvenient hours to meet our deadlines without complaint. Finally, of course, a major debt is owed to the Social Sciences and Humanities Research Council and the Aid to Small Universities Program, which provided the funding for the project. This is the third volume of research that the Aid to Small Universities Program has supported, and we believe it is a vital and productive contribution to research in the social sciences and humanities not only at the small universities, which benefit directly, but to Canadian scholarship as a whole.

Christine Storm
Sackville, NB

PART ONE

Conceptions of a Liberal Education

CHAPTER ONE

The Purpose and Content of a Liberal Education

J. VANDERLEEST

But consideration must be given to the question, what constitutes education and what is the proper way to be educated. At present there are differences of opinion as to the proper tasks to be set; for all peoples do not agree as to the things that the young ought to learn, either with a view to virtue or with a view to the best life, nor is it clear whether their studies should be regulated more with regard to intellect or with regard to character.[1]

Writing in the fourth century BC, Aristotle raised questions about education that have been repeated in various forms from ancient to modern times. Several approaches to education have been developed in response; one of the most prominent approaches is the process known as liberal education. The term has a long history, and there are significant differences in the definitions that are applied to it. In part these variations are a matter of individual inclination and the period in which a scholar or commentator is active. But they raise the question whether what is meant by liberal education can ever be universally decided and accepted.

The *purpose* of a liberal education, however, elicits widespread agreement: it is a process designed to produce a fully educated person by providing knowledge that develops character and prepares individuals to be active citizens within their own societies. The knowledge imparted by a liberal education thus transcends individual interests or specific skills. It builds on the basic tools of reading and writing to teach students to think critically and logically, judge independently, provide leadership, and understand their culture and its historical context.[2] In short, it seeks "nothing less than the transformation of the individual, a conversion, as it were, to one's own humanity."[3]

The real problem of definition is that, as society becomes more complex and the realms of knowledge expand, it becomes more difficult to agree on what elements can best achieve the purposes of a liberal education. Hence there is great uncertainty about the content of the liberal education curriculum. As a result, while every institution of learning should be making a clear statement about itself through the curriculum it offers, faculty and students at institutions that profess to offer a liberal education often find great confusion both in the mission statements and in the programs of instruction. This situation seems to be the result of circumstances created in the twentieth century, but its origins can be traced to the educational ideas of ancient Greece and Rome.

Early Greek education had the simple goal of achieving *arete*, a particular and very concrete type of virtue. The ideal was embodied in the actions of Homeric heroes and a thorough knowledge of Homer, especially through recitation of his epics, was the main element of education.[4] As Greek society became more complex, particularly with the emergence of democracy in fifth-century Athens, the goals of education began to change. There were at the time three main theories of education.[5] Socrates and Plato took the philosophical approach, seeking for "truth" and believing that knowledge would lead to virtue. The sophistic approach, embraced by such figures as Gorgias and Hippias, had as its primary goal practical success through political persuasion. It sought to achieve this by teaching the skills of composing, delivering, and analyzing speeches. Finally, there was the oratorical approach, championed by Isocrates, who saw the sophistic method as reducing the role of the traditional principles associated with virtue while concentrating on public performance. To him rhetoric was a science that required above all the study of eloquence and political wisdom, which should be used as the means to practical knowledge and virtue.[6] In the fifth century these three approaches were clearly separate. The various elements that were later identified as the *artes liberales* were taught, but the various Greek schools, which were highly critical of each other, emphasized different *artes* and taught them in different ways. From this, one thing is clear: there was no standard curriculum in ancient Greece that can be identified with an early version of liberal education.[7]

For centuries the early Romans were primarily an agricultural nation, conservative and practical. From the beginning of Rome (traditionally 753 BC) well into the second century BC, two aspects dominated Roman education: *mos maiorum* (ancestral custom) and *patria potestas* (paternal authority). The power of the head of the household was absolute: he could decide whether to let a newborn child die through exposure; he could legally order his children to be flogged, imprisoned, or sold into slavery; he could even put his children to death.[8] The ideal situation, as described in the ancient sources, was that a mother would look after an infant during its earliest years, but the father would soon take over responsibility for the training of a son. The passing on of ancestral customs depended largely on the son accompanying his father everywhere. He assisted him in religious ceremonies, attended political assemblies, and observed the running of the household. Since the early Romans were frequently involved in military action and the army was drawn from the entire populace, fathers also put their sons through physical training to prepare them for fighting. This continued until, at about the age of sixteen, the son formally assumed the toga of manhood and began a military and political career of his own. Even so, as long as the father was alive, he exercised *patria potestas* over his son; Cato the Elder, who lived in the second century BC, is the most famous examplar of this tradition.[9] Thus, Roman education at the time was based in family tradition and national custom and sought to impart agrarian, political, and military skills. It involved a minimum of literary training and was even further from the concept of liberal education than the early Greek model.[10]

But after the Punic wars in the third century BC, Rome controlled all of Italy and Sicily and soon after became involved with Greece itself. Rome was soon inundated with Greek culture. The impact on Roman education was immense. It began with the use of Greeks, both slaves and free men, for much of the early instruction of Roman children. The goal of such primary education was to achieve competence in reading and writing, preferably in both Greek and Latin, and to pass on the basics of grammar and arithmetic.[11] The early Romans might have thought that this sort of education, especially the acquisition of Greek, was all that they needed to become as civilized as the Greeks. But Rome was not yet a great centre, and in the next seventy years the evidence suggests that few prominent Greek scholars visited the city. This changed only with the war against Mithridates which occupied the Romans for twenty-five years starting in 88 BC. During this war Athens and other Greek centres of learning were sacked, and Rome became a safe haven from the seemingly unending disruptions throughout the eastern Mediterranean. Other intellectuals came to Rome as prisoners. By the time the war was over, several eastern courts had lost their prominence or ceased to exist.[12] Rome now had the wealth to attract notable scholars and an upper class that was ready to take advantage of the new opportunities. Consequently it was the Greek scholars of the first century BC who were largely responsible for bringing higher education to Rome. But by this time, instead of the three systems that had been found in fifth-century Greece, a clear preference had developed for the oratorical approach of Isocrates. This had evolved more fully in the fourth century through the work of the notable Athenian speakers Demosthenes and Aeschines but did not yet present a set program.

A second aspect of later Greek education would also assume great importance. Even in the age of Socrates, some of the Greeks, particularly those who were interested in dialectic, had begun to create divisions and subdivisions within certain subjects. The tendency to categorize was developed more fully in the Hellenistic age when scholars began to collect information and ideas in handbooks. The Romans, with their logical minds, seized upon this organized way of thinking as a key element in their attempt to acquire culture. The transformation that resulted is apparent, for example, in the contrast between the elder Cato's *De Re Rustica*, a practical work about agriculture written in the second century BC, and the *Res Rusticae* of Varro, addressing the same topic but dating from the first century. The former suggests a disorganized collection of information, while the latter is very carefully structured, as are all Varro's written works.[13] This attempt to organize was a crucial moment in the development of the *artes liberales*, for the Romans decided that only those subjects that could be organized into handbooks were properly considered *artes*, or *technai* (the equivalent Greek term). Thus, in the work of first-century authors one finds discussions of the existing *artes* but also a connection between such *artes* and education.

One striking example can be found in the work of Cicero, many of whose writings have survived. In 55 BC, when he was still in his prime, Cicero completed *De Oratore* (On the Orator). Formulated as a dialogue between the leading speakers of Rome in 91 BC, it considers the question what constitutes a proper education for an orator and the principles that affect the discipline of rhetoric. As the participants consider whether rhetoric can in fact be classified as an *ars*, Cicero's own definition emerges: "If however the actual things noticed in the practice and conduct of speaking have been heeded and recorded by men of skill and experience, if they have been defined in terms, illuminated by classification, and distributed under subdivisions ... I do not understand why this should not be regarded as an art, perhaps not in that precise sense of the term, but at any rate according to the other and popular estimate."[14] This is a decidedly broad definition, but elsewhere Cicero discusses more precisely six of the fields that were developed as *artes* in his time: music, geometry, astronomy, arithmetic, grammar, and rhetoric.[15]

Four of these *artes* – arithmetic, astronomy, geometry, and music – had been linked as the mathematical disciplines from the time of the schools in classical Greece. But in the Roman world, despite the respect accorded these subjects by the Greeks, they were quickly relegated to secondary status. They were taught at the elementary level, along with reading and writing, but only insofar as they were seen to be of practical value: arithmetic was important for dealing with money, geometry for land surveying, and astronomy for the calendar and navigation. Too much interest in music was seen as morally corrupting, a point of view well illustrated by the censure that attached to such emperors as Nero who chose to perform in public. To go beyond basic study in these fields, Roman youths would have to find specialist Greek teachers and pay extra fees. Another factor that allowed the Romans to reduce these subjects to minor *artes* was that there were no great Greek mathematicians in the first century BC; the mathematical disciplines were left to a handful of philosophers who were drawn to them.[16]

Of the three remaining *artes*, the study of grammar was seen as the foundation for all education beyond the most basic level. This was not grammar in the modern restrictive sense. Cicero defines it as "the study of poets, the learning of myths, the explanation of words and proper intonation in speaking them."[17] Varro saw in it a broad knowledge of the poets, historians, and orators that was to be used for reading, writing, understanding, and evaluating.[18] Thus, it encompassed the study of language and literature. This formal discipline developed largely in the fourth and third centuries, particularly among the Stoic philosophers of the Greek world, who classified the letters, words, and parts of speech. From that point on all literature was analyzed to assess the correctness of the Greek used and the accuracy of the texts that survived. Since the second and first centuries produced a number of renowned Greek grammarians who were among the early influential figures in Roman learning, it is not surprising that grammar was an early area of interest in Roman higher education. Roman scholars who took up this discipline clearly began with Greek, which always maintained its place as a literary language, but their interest soon embraced the early Latin poets as well. By the middle of the first century BC, the study of grammar had advanced sufficiently for Varro to publish his *De Lingua Latina*, an examination of grammar and the Latin language in twenty-five books. The result of such studies is evident in the transformation that occurred from the awkward archaic Latin of the second century to the refined language used by the great writers of the Augustan age.[19]

With a proper grounding in grammar, Roman students were ready to move on to rhetoric, and during the age of Cicero it is clear that this was the most important of the *artes*. Instruction in the schools of rhetoric shifted from the study of language to the use of language in making speeches. In the early days grammar, literature, and rhetoric could all be taught by the same teacher, and preliminary rhetorical training was always left to the grammar schools.[20] This encompassed exercises that led to the composition of simple sayings, narratives, and arguments. But the goal of rhetorical education was the ability to plead cases in court or to speak in public assemblies, and the skills to accomplish such full-scale speeches had to be acquired through training under specialists. Rhetoric was confirmed as an *ars* in Rome with the production of two formally structured handbooks early in the first century BC: *De Inventione* by the young Cicero, and *Rhetorica ad Herennium* by an unknown author. Both observe that any speech should contain six parts – *exordium* (preface), *narratio* (narrative), *divisio* (classification of matter to be treated), *confirmatio* (proof), *confutatio* (refutation of opponent's case), and *conclusio* (conclusion). They also divide the art of speaking into five parts: *inventio* (devising the subject matter and the argument), *dispositio* (organization), *elocutio* (style), *memoria* (memory), and *pronuntiatio* (delivery). The speaker needed to be competent in each but especially in the use of style, since the success of any speech was to be found not only in the basic rules of organization, but also in the way it was put across and embellished. This was the art of literary prose, and the works of prose authors were now examined both for their content and for their refinements.

The seventh *ars* was dialectic, the discipline of logic, which led to proper organization of material and the knowledge of how to argue well; this art became closely associated with a rhetorical education.[21] It was the use of dialectic that had led Romans in the first place to the classification of subjects into *artes* through their organization into handbooks. Yet while the Romans took to the application of dialectic, few devoted themselves wholly to it and it was left largely to the Stoic philosophers to pursue it in detail. In his discussions of education, Cicero did not isolate dialectic as he does the other *artes*. Instead, he took the much broader view that education required the learning of "proper conduct," which was to be acquired through the study of all aspects of philosophy.[22] But this opinion seems to have developed over the course of his career. He himself devoted much of his life to the pursuit of rhetoric and only gradually shifted, in his later years, to a concentration on the study of philosophy. He observed that in early Greece philosophy and rhetoric had been taught by the same masters and noted with regret that the two disciplines had become separated.[23] The philosophy that reached Rome came as part of the teaching of several distinctive schools – the Stoics, the Epicureans, the New Academy – and the discipline as a whole never achieved the status of an *ars*. Cicero's writings emphasize that the pursuit of philosophy was something to be taken up after studies in the other *artes* had been completed. Varro makes the distinction even more explicit: although he did write a work on philosophy, it was separate from the *Disciplinae*, his handbook on education.

From the works of Cicero and Varro one can see that, by the end of the Roman republic, scholars were coming to recognize that certain *artes* were suitable for a proper education. But the program for a liberal education was not yet fixed. Varro's discussions included *artes* that would later be discarded, and other authors of the age are known to have put together different combinations of *artes* as the basis of education. Cicero, who seemed at times to be moving towards a coherent program, added to the uncertainty later in his career when he attempted to have education include all knowledge through the study of philosophy. His ideal was pursued by only a very few wealthy Romans who travelled in Greece. Thus, it was left to later Romans to pin down the curriculum for a liberal education.

Both Cicero and Varro lived at the end of an age. The former was killed in the civil upheavals that marked the transition in Rome from republic to empire; the latter died soon after the new settlement. The political changes at this time also had an effect on Roman education. The system that Cicero had in mind when writing *De Oratore* to guide the education of an orator was one that required public performance. But public assemblies were no longer held, and no meaningful debates occurred in the senate; opportunities for public speaking were limited. There were still the law courts, but now oratory was practised there as a profession, for fees, and by a different class of people. Rhetoric was still the most important of the *artes liberales*, but it became much more of an academic exercise. Practice speeches known as *suasoriae* and *controversiae*, which had always formed a part of the training for rhetoric, now were made primarily for display. They dealt in imaginary themes that were normally as fanciful as possible; the orator was left to invent all the details, and he would win praise for adding original material.[24] No longer were orators competing to persuade the senate or a jury but merely to outdo rivals in the extravagance of their creations and to show off the benefits of a rhetorical education. Some Romans at least found this troubling. About the middle of the first century AD the younger Seneca wrote to a friend, "We educate ourselves for the classroom, not for life: hence the extravagances with which we are troubled, in literature as in everything else."[25]

The decline of civic participation can be seen as a bad effect of the shift from republic to empire, but there were positive changes as well. Under the emperor Augustus literature and art received great support. Benefiting from the scholarship of the first century BC, which had refined the Latin language, the new writers produced the first great

Latin literature. At the same time many newcomers arrived in Rome from the provinces, and more and more of them were granted Roman citizenship. These people, whether businessmen or imperial bureaucrats, replaced the old aristocracy as the most important element in Roman society, and in their pride as new Romans they often looked first to Latin literature. Thus, commentaries were written on the works of Latin authors, who now found a significant place in the grammar schools.

The first century of the Roman Empire saw one further change that was significant for the development of liberal education. At this time philosophers developed new schools and modified older ones to put more emphasis on moral conduct. The obligations involved in pursuing this ideal required changes in one's way of life and separated the philosophers more completely from ordinary Romans. With this, there could no longer be any attempts such as Cicero had made to include philosophy as a part of the *artes liberales*. This can be seen in the letters of the younger Seneca, who rejected each of the *artes liberales* (with the exception of rhetoric, which he does not mention at all) because they did not teach moral excellence.[26] For him their only use was to prepare children for the study of philosophy. With such views the philosophers became almost totally isolated and were mistrusted by most Romans, including the emperors. As a result philosophy was placed outside the main program of education, which was developing around the *artes liberales*.

This separation is evident at the end of the first century AD, when Quintilian produced his *Institutio Oratoria* (The Education of an Orator). In his preface he noted that a proficient orator must also show virtue and good character, although some view these attributes as belonging solely to the realm of philosophy.[27] Quintilian looked to Cicero for the main outline of his teaching, but there is a difference in perspective. Whereas Cicero had written about oratory in an age when public speaking was of political importance for members of the aristocracy, Quintilian was a professional teacher who wrote for the upper classes in an age when political oratory no longer existed.

Education as outlined by Quintilian contained the various stages we have already seen: elementary school, grammar school, and school of rhetoric. Both Greek and Latin were to be taught, but by then the place of Latin in the schools was firmly established, and Quintilian assumed that Virgil's poetry would be among the first works read.[28] Most of the *Institutio Oratoria* deals with the theory and study of rhetoric. Quintilian recognized the weakness of the shift that had turned speeches into public display and commented that "the subjects chosen for themes should, therefore, be as true to life as possible, and the actual declamation should, as far as may be, be modelled on the pleadings for which it was devised as training."[29] In the last part of his work, Quintilian dealt with studies that should be pursued after the skills of rhetoric had been mastered. Such disciplines as philosophy and law were included but with so little enthusiasm that Quintilian might have been paying reluctant lip service to Cicero.[30] Far more important to Quintilian was the continued study of literature, both Greek and Latin. Since rhetoric was no longer used in the political arena, its main role was to serve as a literary exercise and as such it was to be based on the finest foundation – a wide knowledge of the best literature.

Quintilian was very well-regarded, with a much higher status than ordinary teachers. After arriving in Rome from Spain, he became closely connected to the imperial court and was rewarded with a chair of Latin rhetoric and a substantial salary. Later imperial scholars produced works on grammar or rhetoric, but they neither spoke with the same authority nor discussed the whole program of the *artes liberales*. Thus, it is not surprising that Martianus Capella, who in the fifth century AD sought to produce a handbook for his son, harked back to Quintilian. In a work called *De nuptiis Philologiae et Mercurii* (The Marriage of Philology and Mercury), Martianus Capella presents the allegory of the god Mercury taking a bride whose handmaidens are personifications of the seven *artes*. Capella devotes individual books to describing the characteristics of each *ars*: grammar, logic, rhetoric, geometry, arithmetic, astronomy, and music. This was a significant point in the development of liberal education; for here the *septem artes liberales* are found for the first time as a well-defined group. Martianus Capella's reliance on Quintilian meant that his work embraced fully the oratorical approach and the tradition that can be traced back to Cicero and Isocrates.

It was in the Middle Ages that the standard curriculum of a liberal education was set as the *trivium* (logic, grammar, rhetoric) and the *quadrivium* (arithmetic, geometry, astronomy, music). Since the work of Martianus Capella was used as the main source in schools during this period, the continued stress on the oratorical approach was ensured. The *trivium* contained the primary arts, and the content relied on Latin texts, particularly Quintilian and those cited by him, as the basis of study. The prominence of this oratorical tradition based on classical authors was maintained by humanists throughout the Renaissance and the Reformation, and it was this tradition that could be found in the early colleges of colonial North America.

But in the thirteenth century, with the rediscovery of various Greek works, particularly those of Aristotle, scholars attempted to integrate the new-found philosophical ideas with the works of classical authors already within the oratorical tradition. For the most part these attempts failed, and the result of disputes between scholars of that age was the development of a more philosophical approach to liberal education in addition to the traditional oratorical one. This new philosophical approach placed more emphasis on the role of logic while downplaying that of rhetoric. Although the *trivium* and the *quadrivium* still played a part, they were reduced in favour of three categories of philosophy: natural (physics), moral (ethics), and metaphysical (mental).[31] From that time to the present the development of liberal education would occur within two traditions.

The division between the two became more pronounced in the eighteenth and early nineteenth centuries. The Enlightenment brought new interest in experimental science and philosophy and with it, new ideas that affected the definitions underlying the concepts of liberal education. The term liberal was now equated by many with the ideas of freedom and open-mindedness, and the Socratic search for truth was more important than the development of the ideal citizen. The new emphasis on philosophical approaches stressed freedom and intellect, the preeminence of individual will, and egalitarianism.[32] The early influence of these ideals was largely felt outside the universities and was found most readily in the various scientific societies of the age. But another factor would soon enhance the stature of this approach; for the American Revolution led to a new stress on the concepts of equality and liberty. The set program, the contents, and the standards of the classical curriculum based in the oratorical tradition of Cicero and Quintilian now began to be seen as suspect. Although the traditional curriculum continued to dominate within the colleges, one also saw the first attempts to introduce new subjects and to reduce the importance of Latin and Greek.

Several elements in the late nineteenth century combined to set the stage not only for the continued confrontation between the oratorical and philosophical approaches to liberal education in North America but also for more radical changes. Prominent among these were the trends in Germany, where universities in the nineteenth century began to place great emphasis on specialized scholarship and research. As the North American colleges and universities embraced these ideas, they assumed that students were receiving the basics of a liberal education in the school system, much as German students did in the *gymnasium*. But the high schools in North America had never had that role, and there was no effort to ensure that they were ready and able to undertake it.[33] At the same time the Morrill Land Grant Acts promoted the teaching of disciplines with clear and immediate utility, with the result that vocational subjects such as engineering and agriculture acquired new status.[34] In the same period the number of people seeking higher education ballooned, and the backgrounds of those people were much more varied than ever before. Finally, the introduction of the elective system by Charles William Eliot, president of Harvard, placed further emphasis on the individual and freedom of choice.[35]

The results of this are clear: the twentieth century lost any unified concept of liberal education. Some still argued for the traditional oratorical or philosophical approaches, but many now sought some middle ground that combined aspects of the two.[36] Since there was no easy agreement on a single philosophy for liberal education, questions about the content of such an education tended to be set aside. Instead, the focus in this century has turned primarily to the structure of the curriculum and methods of instruction. The major became an integral part of any undergraduate degree, and, since individuals were encouraged to choose what to study, specialization became acceptable. The extremes to which this could be taken can be seen in the growth of clearly vocational programs, such as commerce and education, within institutions that professed to offer a liberal education.[37] With individual courses, as long as one could argue that a subject involved critical thinking and led to learning for its own sake, it could now be brought under the umbrella of liberal education.

Various approaches were used to try to ensure a liberal content. Some colleges turned to introductory survey courses in the first two years of a program. While these tried to provide a breadth suitable to liberal education, the fact that there was no integration meant that normally the emphasis turned more to the preparation of students for a major.[38] A second group resorted to special courses in general education. Designed to provide a part of the program that was common to all students, these courses emphasized breadth, skills for life-long learning and cultural understanding, and synthesis. The term general education is often equated with liberal education because the core of such courses is to be found within the traditional program of liberal studies. But in its narrowness the general-education approach diverged from the ideals of the classical liberal education, as did the emphasis on individualism and equality. General education usually amounted to trying to balance the depth of a major with some broader learning and variety. Colleges and universities that tried neither survey courses nor general education tended to rely solely on distribution requirements to achieve the same goal.

Each of these approaches attempts to introduce the liberal ideal through breadth, but none achieves the completeness and integration of a traditional liberal education, which grew out of the substance rather than the structure of the curriculum. Some may argue that this dilemma is the inevitable result of the information explosion of the twentieth century. But it is important to note that while the pace of discovery may have increased in the modern world, there has been too much available knowledge for educators to manage comprehensively since the Hellenistic age of Alexander the Great. Yet in all earlier ages there was an acknowledged content that was accepted, that achieved the aims of liberal education, and that was complete for this purpose.

I would suggest that the uncertainty surrounding the content of a liberal education today results instead from an inconsistency that has crept into educational thinking in recent years. While people still maintain that the purpose of a liberal education is the preparation of citizens for participation in society, they fail to acknowledge that historically, this was achieved by recognizing a core content. Consequently the various attempts during this century to modernize liberal education have sought to make the notions of freedom of choice and individuality central to the program. These concepts, however, are tied much more directly to specialization than to the development of character and do not lend themselves easily to the achievement of the traditional purpose. Appearing first on the educational periphery in the nineteenth century, they have been entrenched in the last hundred years by the structure of universities in North America, in which the faculty members are tied closely to specialized departments and research is clearly rewarded. Since curriculum reform is largely undertaken by scholars working within this system, the new directions continue to be strengthened while the concept of a single curriculum, such as that found in the earlier oratorical or philosophical traditions, has been lost entirely.

Few, if any, would argue that the content of a liberal education must still be sought in the regimen of the oratorical tradition that dominated from Roman times until the Enlightenment, or in the philosophical practice that accompanied it during the last six hundred years. There is certainly a need to face up to a world in which technology and specialization play key roles in determining educational directions. If liberal education is to be incorporated in these new directions, methods of instruction are not enough. There must be an underlying core of knowledge in literature, history, science, and values. Although the exact composition of this core needs constant adjustment, it is based on a tradition that goes back to the earliest days of liberal education. Once this base has been assured, ways can be sought to renew liberal education by joining to it the new knowledge of modern disciplines and technology.

NOTES

1 Aristotle *Politics* 8.1337a, trans. H. Rackham, Loeb Classical Library (Cambridge, MA: Harvard University Press, 1932).

2 A sample of statements concerning the purpose of liberal education may be found in Clarence H. Faust, "The Problem of General Education." In N.a. *The Idea and Practice of General Education*, no editor (Chicago: University of Chicago Press, 1950), 6; A. Whitney Griswold, *Liberal Education and the Democratic Ideal and Other Essays* (enlarged edition, New Haven, CT: Yale University Press, 1962), 1, 13, 19–20; Christian E. Hauer, "The Nature and Purpose of Liberal Arts Education," *Liberal Education* 49, no. 2 (1963): 204–17; Maurice Bowra, "The Idea of a Liberal Arts College," *Liberal Education* 50, no. 2 (1964): 187; Geoffrey Partington, "The Disorientation of Western Education," *Encounter* 68, no. 1 (January 1987): 14; John W. Chandler, "Higher Education in the 1990s," *Liberal Education* 76, no. 2 (1990): 17. For a summary of various modern statements of the goals of liberal education see David G. Winter, David C. McClelland, and Abigail J. Stewart, *A New Case for the Liberal Arts* (San Francisco, CA: Jossey-Bass Publishers, 1981), 9–13.

3 Bernard Murchland, "The Eclipse of the Liberal Arts," *Change* 8 (November 1976): 22.

4 On these early ideals see W. Jaeger, *Paideia: The Ideals of Greek Culture*, trans. G. Highet. (New York: Oxford University Press, 1945), volume 1, chapters 1–3, and A.W.H. Adkins, *From the Many to the One* (Ithaca, NY: Cornell University Press, 1970), chapter 2.

5 For this period see H.I. Marrou, *A History of Education in Antiquity*, trans. G. Lamb (New York: Sheed and Ward, 1956), chapters 5–7.

6 Isocrates *Against the Sophists*, trans. George Norlin, Loeb Classical Library (Cambridge, MA: Harvard University Press, 1929).

7 Bruce A. Kimball, *Orators and Philosophers* (New York: Teachers College Press, 1986), 15–29. This factor is often overlooked by modern educators, who readily link the concept of liberal education with the philosophy of Socrates, while ignoring the historical reality.

8 Dionysius of Halicarnassus *Roman Antiquities* 8.79, trans. Earnest Cary, Loeb Classical Library (Cambridge, MA: Harvard University Press, 1945).

9 Plutarch *Cato the Elder* 3, trans. Bernadotte Perrin, Loeb Classical Library (Cambridge, MA: Harvard University Press, 1914).

10 Stanley F. Bonner, *Education in Ancient Rome* (London: Methuen, 1977), chapters 1–2.

11 Bonner, *Education*, 165–88.

12 Elizabeth Rawson, *Intellectual Life in the Late Roman Republic* (Baltimore: Johns Hopkins University Press, 1985), 3–15.
13 E. Rawson, "The Introduction of Logical Organization into Roman Prose Literature," *Papers of the British School at Rome* 46 (1978): 13–18.
14 Cicero *De Oratore* 1.109, trans. E.W. Sutton and H. Rackham, Loeb Classical Library (Cambridge, MA: Harvard University Press, 1942).
15 Cicero *De Oratore* 1.8–12; 187.
16 Bonner, *Education*, 77–9; Rawson, *Intellectual Life*, 156–69.
17 Cicero *De Oratore* 1.187.
18 Rawson, *Intellectual Life*, 118.
19 Bonner, *Education*, 47–64; Rawson, *Intellectual Life*, 117–31.
20 Bonner, *Education*, 250–61.
21 Rawson, *Intellectual Life* 132–42.
22 Cicero *De Oratore* 1.20.72; 2.5; 3.57.
23 Cicero *De Officiis* 3. 58–60; trans. Walter Miller, Loeb Classical Library (Cambridge, MA: Harvard University Press, 1913).
24 Example: The law requires that children should support their parents or be imprisoned. A man has slain one of his brothers as a tyrant and another because he was taken in adultery, though his father begged for mercy. The man is captured by pirates, who write to the father for a ransom. The father answers that he will pay them double if they will cut off his son's hands. The son is released by the pirates and refuses to support his father (Seneca *Controversiae* 1.7, trans. Michael Winterbottom, Loeb Classical Library (Cambridge, MA: Harvard University Press, 1974).
25 Seneca *Epistles* 106.12, trans. Richard M. Gummere, Loeb Classical Library (Cambridge, MA: Harvard University Press, 1925).
26 Seneca *Epistles* 88.
27 Quintilian *Institutio Oratoria* 1. pr. 4–20, trans. H.E. Butler, Loeb Classical Library (Cambridge, MA: Harvard University Press, 1920).
28 Quintilian *Institutio Oratoria* 1.8.5; 10.1.86; Tacitus *Dialogue on Oratory* 12, trans. Sir W. Peterson. revised by M. Winterbottom, Loeb Classical Library (Cambridge, MA: Harvard University Press, rev. ed. 1970).
29 Quintilian *Institutio Oratoria* 2.10.4.
30 Quintilian *Institutio Oratoria* 12.3.9; A. Gwynn, *Roman Education* (New York: Oxford University Press, 1926), 222–4.
31 Kimball, *Orators*, chapters 3 and 4; see also Frederick Rudolph, *Curriculum, A History of the American Undergraduate Course of Study Since 1636* (San Francisco, CA: Jossey-Bass, 1977), chapter 2.
32 This has been labelled the "liberal-free ideal" by Kimball; see in particular *Orators*, 115–23.

33 Ibid., 146–7, 161–2; Rudolph, *Curriculum*, 10–11.
34 Kimball, *Orators*, 181; Lewis B. Mayhew, *The Smaller Liberal Arts College* (New York: The Centre for Applied Research in Education, 1962).
35 Kimball, *Orators*, 166–7; Rudolph, *Curriculum*, 131–8.
36 Kimball, *Orators*, 215–26.
37 Leon Botstein, "A Proper Education," *Harper's* 259, no. 1552 (September 1979): 33–7; Kimball, *Orators*, chapters 6 and 7; Rudolph, *Curriculum*, 215–20.
38 Kimball, *Orators*, 184–5; Murchland, *Eclipse*, 24–5.

CHAPTER TWO

Theme and Variations in the Arts and Science Curriculum

THOMAS STORM AND CHRISTINE STORM

A thorough review and discussion of the curriculum in institutions of higher education in the United States was published in 1987 by the Carnegie Foundation for the Advancement of Teaching.[1] It covered the full range from two year colleges to major research universities, public and private, and examined student attitudes, and college mission statements as well as degree requirements and course content of the curriculum. In the case of four year liberal arts colleges, where specific professional training is disavowed as part of the educational mission, the report distinguishes three components of the curriculum: general education, the major (and in some cases minor), and electives. The general education component is embodied in distribution requirements, in specifically designed courses of a general nature – that is, not simply introductions to one of the academic disciplines – or in interdisciplinary courses generally at the first or second year levels, as opposed to electives, which are simply courses offered by departments that the student chooses out of personal interest and to complete the required total of credits for the degree.

Study, discussion, and controversy about the liberal arts curriculum has been continuous since that time. There are sharply divergent views about the appropriate content and structure of an undergraduate curriculum for a liberal education in the contemporary world. The most public form of this debate has come from those who believe there is a canon of respectable knowledge, largely the product of Western civilization, extended historically to its classical and Hebraic origins – if not literally the "great books," something close to and based upon them. The purpose, as expressed by such proponents as Allan Bloom and William Bennett, is to provide a core of knowledge and reference common to the educated citizenry that supports political and cultural dialogue within the framework of Western values.[2] They criticize the long-term trend, documented by Frederick Rudolph in his history of the American liberal arts curriculum, towards an increasingly elective curriculum.[3] Over the past century less and less has been prescribed, while more and more has been offered outside the boundaries of the canon.

Opposition to this position is too diverse to carry a single label. As stated in one recent article, debate focuses on whether a common core of courses should be required, and, if so, whether that core should reflect the Western humanities tradition or should be designed to support diversity, economic growth, and global interdependence.[4] If Bloom and Bennett represent the cultural (and political) right, there is no single cultural left. The version of liberal education just described, however, is seen even by curricular centrists as an attempt to politicize higher education. If one can characterize the centrist position, it is to keep things pretty much the way they are, accommodating (slowly) such changes as are demanded by the evolution of disciplines, the changes in undergraduate demography and student interests, and the occasional invention or innovation undertaken in the spirit of educational adventure. Most faculty are moderates, ready for change in the abstract but easily wearied by any suggestion of another round of curricular debate. Like Stuart Smith, they feel that everything is pretty much all right with higher education, given a little tinkering around the edges.[5] The gradual changes whose cumulative effect arouses conservative wrath have been in the direction of fewer requirements, increased choice, and, latterly, the addition (in the form either of independent departments or interdisciplinary programs) of courses that recognize the existence of groups whose distinctive cultural heritage and perspectives are not adequately reflected in the European white male perspective.

Finally, universities have recognized in varying degrees that there is a great deal to know that is not represented in the traditional curriculum, at least some of which is extremely important in a world where national boundaries and the cultural differences once correlated with them are less and less important. There are other great civilizations. There is much about ordinary life, contemporary and historical, whose study may provide new insights and understanding. To the liberal left, it is not nearly as clear as the conservatives pretend that our own history has chosen adequately what is more and what is less worthwhile learning, teaching, and studying.

In spite of the debate and the efforts of curriculum committees and university senates, there has been little actual change over the postwar period in the undergraduate offerings. There has been a change in undergraduate requirements, however. For example, in the early

1950s, candidates for the BA or BSc at one large institution were required to take a second language through the second year; math through calculus, or a general math course specifically designed for the non-science students; two years of English, including expository writing as well as literature courses; one year of history; and a semester course in either public speaking or formal logic. This was a city university specifically catering to the working and lower middle class and part-time students, with relatively low entrance standards and tuition. Except for English, all of these have disappeared as requirements from most arts and science curricula, supplanted by much more general and elective distribution requirements. To the conservatives this general change is seen as a lowering of standards. To liberals it is seen as a broadening of accessibility. These changes were brought about, in most cases, by the inability of faculty to provide compelling arguments why these particular requirements were, or why this particular knowledge was more important than other candidates for inclusion in the core.

In the United States, organizations and foundations[6] concerned with liberal education have sponsored studies, working groups, and publications attempting to define the goals of a liberal education in contemporary society, to evaluate current curricular practices in the light of these goals, and to design specific innovations to remedy perceived deficiencies.[7] No such process has taken place in Canada, but of course those concerned with liberal education are aware of the American discussions and have occasionally participated in them.[8]

THE CURRICULUM IN A SAMPLE OF COURSE CATALOGUES

There is no recent study comparing the structure of arts and science curricula in various Canadian institutions and no study at all comparing the Canadian to the American liberal arts colleges. We decided, therefore, to examine a sample of course catalogues representing three types of institutions: large and small Canadian universities and small American colleges devoted exclusively to the liberal arts. Our purpose was to determine what seemed to be common in the contemporary liberal education as defined by programs leading to the BA or BSc degree.

We were also interested in the ways small Canadian universities differed from large Canadian research universities and small American ones. The latter group seemed particularly relevant for two reasons. First, they were selected from those universities that represent the purest version of the North American notion of a liberal education. Second, at various points in its history Mount Allison has regarded itself as the Canadian representative of the pure liberal arts tradition and does so to a considerable extent today; on occasion, it has explicitly cited the élite, small American colleges as models for its own development.[9]

We asked what the universities currently regard as essential for any student graduating with a BA or BSc degree. That is, we examined the constraints on students' choices in proceeding towards their bachelor degrees. Regardless of these constraints, we also wanted to know what range of choices was available to the student. In most cases this boils down to the questions what disciplines or areas of learning are represented, how many different courses they offer, and how many faculty are available to teach them.

We examined recent course catalogues for thirteen small universities in Canada, including most of those regarded by the Natural Sciences and Engineering Research Council and by the Social Sciences and Humanities Research Council of Canada as "small" – all the anglophone instances in the Maritimes and a number from elsewhere. Our sample included eight large Canadian universities and nine smaller American liberal arts colleges.[10]

American research on higher education generally follows a classification of institutions devised by the Carnegie Council, which uses three major categories: doctorate-granting institutions; comprehensive universities and colleges; and liberal arts colleges. All of our Canadian universities would fall into one of the first two categories. All of our large Canadian universities would fall into one or another subdivision of the first category; all of our small Canadian universities would fall into the second category, because each of them offers at least one degree program other than liberal arts, such as engineering, business administration, and education. All of the American colleges we looked at would meet the criteria for the most selective subdivision of the liberal arts colleges. This classification is based on the size and variety of degree programs on offer, the presence and importance of graduate work at the institution, and the total size of the student body and faculty. Another distinction that is often made in research on American higher education is that between public and privately funded institutions. By either type of criterion, higher education in Canada is far less diverse than in the United States.

General Requirements

Some things that have remained constant throughout the post-war years and that seem to be common to all contemporary North American versions of a liberal arts education – operationally, programs for the BA and BSc degrees – are the emphases on both breadth and depth and on general as opposed to vocational education.

The emphasis on general as opposed to vocational or professional education is represented explicitly in mission statements and other rhetorical forms. Courses with a vocational and professional emphasis are rare or absent in liberal arts programs. This emphasis is also reflected in student surveys. Only thirty-six percent of students in liberal arts colleges in the Carnegie Foundation survey, for example, said that training or skills for a profession was an essential part of their education – a much lower percentage than among students at any other type of institution. Fifty-three percent said that "detailed grasp of a special field" was essential – somewhat lower than in any other student sample, but seventy percent, the highest of any group, selected a well-rounded education as essential. More recent surveys of college students indicate similar differences between BA and BSc students compared to others.[11]

A large proportion of students rated "getting along with others" and "formulating the values and goals of my life" as essential parts of their education. Students at liberal arts colleges did not differ much from others in this respect. The perceived salience of these goals is more characteristic of a developmental stage than a type of educational institution. However, personal growth may indeed be more a concern of the small liberal arts college. At least rhetorically, mission statements of some small American institutions often suggest this.[12]

Breadth

The notion of breadth has been operationalized in distribution requirements and the consensus seems to have been reached that breadth in a liberal education is achieved by requiring a certain number of courses from each of the three groups of disciplines represented by the natural sciences, the social sciences, and the rest, most commonly labelled humanities or arts. The placement of some disciplines varies – for instance, mathematics, history, geography, and psychology. The consensus is really quite remarkable given that there are other, equally cogent kinds of breadth (e.g., cultural breadth, breadth of expression). It is also remarkable in that the rationale for this division is typically methodological. Some descriptions ascribe to these groups of disciplines distinctive styles or modes of thought, generally without specifying the distinctive differences.

It would be difficult to demonstrate that the variations or distinctions within these groups, or even within individual disciplines, are less than the variations between them. For example, language departments offer courses that teach the language (as a medium of communication), teach about the language (its history, its structure, its relation to other languages), and teach the culture and literature of the peoples who use that particular language. Similar variations in content and method exist within other disciplines commonly represented as academic departments.

Anyone who has had to advise students and make sure that they meet the general degree requirements in a timely way so that they do not run afoul of some regulation in their graduating year knows that it is not a straightforward matter for many faculty, let alone students, to interpret calendar descriptions. We cannot characterize the general education requirements of our sample of institutions as a consensus with any statistical confidence, but it does seem to us that the pattern – requiring of every student something from each of these three groups of disciplines – is discernible in every case. Additions to these – most commonly a language and literature course, or English and another of the humanities; sometimes a second language – are present. The most difficult to compare are the cases where core courses designed specifically to meet a general education purpose, and not simply introductory courses to one of the standard disciplines, are required of all students *in toto* or in some set of alternative combinations. Usually, though, even when the titles are opaque or ambiguous, the course descriptions suggest an attempt to include approaches or content representative of these disciplinary groups, whether or not that is central to the course conception.

The American colleges are more idiosyncratic, differing from each other as well as from the Canadian institutions. Some institutions have attempted to separate the administrative divisions of faculties and departments from the teaching divisions relevant to distribution requirements. Middlebury College, for example, requires each student to take at least one course in seven out of eight categories: literature, the arts, philosophical and religious studies, historical studies, physical and life sciences, deductive reasoning and analytical processes, social analysis, and foreign language. Many departments have courses that fall in more than one of these categories. Colby College has a rather similar distributional requirement. Changes at both colleges are recent and reflect attempts to deal with the issues raised in the various curricular workshops and reports referred to earlier.

Depth

The notion of depth is written into regulations by requiring a minimum number of credits in a single discipline and by requiring that a minimum number of these be classified at the third or fourth year levels. There is considerable consensus on this implementation of the depth desideratum, once again subject to the complexities of the calendar. In this case the complexities arise from the existence of three year and four year degrees, honours and otherwise, and "general" degrees with no official major; differences in the units (e.g., semester, trimester, quarter, or year courses); and differences in whether introductory courses are included in the minimum cited for the major or not. We took the four year degree with a major as a standard.

In our sample the minimum requirements for a major were in the range from thirty percent to forty percent of the credits required for the degree. There did not appear to be systematic differences between the three groups of universities in this respect. The Carnegie Foundation review of curriculum gave a figure of thirty-three percent for this depth component in 1975 and found no change from an estimate a decade earlier.[13] This proportion would fairly represent what we found. The maximum concentration of credits, either stated explicitly or constrained by the other requirements, was about fifty percent.

Another much more recent study of the American curriculum attempted to quantify the notions of breadth and depth, taking into account the courses actually taken by undergraduates within the broad structure imposed by the regulations.[14] This was a study conducted by the Center for the Study of Higher Education at the University of Pennsylvania and commissioned by the Association of American Colleges. Their measure of breadth was based on the same three disciplinary groups already discussed. They found that institutions of all types required breadth and the vast majority of students fulfilled the requirements, although they conclude that not nearly enough students have substantial exposure to science and math. They used three measures related to depth that drew on more information than simply the number of courses required for a major and tried to capture more of the meaning of the concept. These measures are of some interest because of the attempt to specify more precisely what might be meant by depth and because of the general conclusions they reached with the use of these measures.

One measure of depth was based on the homogeneity of classes, that is, the percentage of students in a class who were at the same stage in their university career; another was based on the sequencing of courses, the number in a discipline or disciplinary group that had three or more prerequisites; the third was based on the percentage of students in a course who had at least three other courses in the same field, prerequisite or not. The criterion based on prerequisites was the most demanding, but all three involved the notion that the more background students have in a course area, the more intensive the treatment of the course's subject matter could be.

In some ways the attempt to quantify seemed to obscure more than it revealed, but the generalizations that were supported were more or less what one would expect. They found, by their criteria, that the humanities were broad but not deep; that the sciences were the reverse; and that the social sciences were intermediate. These generalizations applied to all BA and BSc programs regardless of the type of institution.

The kind of structure that makes sense within a discipline or a domain of knowledge otherwise defined is not addressed in this study, which discusses its results as though the kind of structure found in the sciences should be applicable to the humanities as well. It seems clear that the relationship between different aspects of knowledge within a domain differs from discipline to discipline.[15]

It does seem that the rationale for prerequisites for advanced courses within the discipline or for the placement of courses at first, second, third, or fourth year is rather arbitrary. Often the structure seems really to be based on a funnel principle – first year courses treat many topics in a superficial way; each of these is then treated later on in a more intensive way, sometimes with a third level of intensity and specialization added for honours students. The primary purpose, or at least the effect, of prerequisites often seems to be to discourage less-able or less-motivated students from enrolling in upper level courses rather than genuinely to supply knowledge or skills necessary to advanced study.

The report by the Association of American Colleges on the arts and science major suggested a number of characteristics for a well-designed major to achieve depth in at least one discipline.[16] The curriculum for the major should have a coherent design. It should involve sequential learning directed towards explicit goals. All parts of the curriculum should incorporate a critical perspective. Finally, the curriculum should communicate the relationships between the disciplines and other fields, potential careers, and the students' own personal lives.

Lisa Lattuca and Joan Stark analyzed the responses from ten disciplines to this report and found that they corresponded roughly to the natural sciences, social sciences, and humanities, the first two being most receptive to the recommendations, the third the least.[17] They suggest that this reflects the more paradigmatic knowledge structure of the scientific compared to the humanistic disciplines.

Size and Composition

Obviously the number of students and the type of university affects both the number and variety of courses offered and the number of faculty. The total number of undergraduates at the eight large Canadian universities included so far in our database ranged from about 10,000 (Dalhousie) to about 25,000 (the universities of Alberta and British Columbia). The number of BA students ranged from about 3,000 (Dalhousie) to about 8,000 (UBC), and the number of BSc students from 1,000 (Brock) to 4,500 (Alberta and UBC). Arts and science students were about forty-five percent of the total undergraduate body, ranging from thirty-five percent (Alberta) to fifty-four percent (Brock). This is very close to the proportion at the large research universities in the Carnegie study.

These numbers and ratios affect the context in which students are taught and, in some respects, the shape of the curriculum itself. When there are large numbers of students enrolled in bachelor programs in education, commerce, nursing, engineering, forestry, agriculture, and social work, the liberal arts disciplines must provide courses that meet these students' general education requirements. Disciplines especially relevant to the professional school must accommodate students who are required to take specific courses as part of their professional program. This means that not only are courses, particularly first and second year courses, larger than they would be if only liberal arts students were present but the mix of student interests, values, and abilities may be different. At the large universities, moreover, the presence of significant numbers of graduate students is liable to mean that faculty members have less time for, and often less interest in, the undergraduate courses.

The total number of undergraduates at the smaller Canadian universities in our sample ranged from 1,800 (Bishop's) to 6,000 (Winnipeg); the number of BA students ranged from 400 (Cape Breton) to 4,500 (Laurentian), and BSc from 115 (Lakehead) to 1,300 (Winnipeg). The ratio of arts and science students to total undergraduates is greater than at the large universities. The average is about sixty percent.

In contrast, the nine American colleges we selected are almost entirely arts and science. The lowest percentage is above eighty percent – higher than any of the Canadian institutions. The total number of undergraduates ranged from 1,000 (Earlham) to 2,800 (Oberlin). Of course, we deliberately selected small, élite colleges that were known to focus exclusively on liberal arts or nearly so. The only point of note about this contrast is how far any Canadian universities are from that particular American model.

These colleges made no distinction between BA and BSc students. Bachelor of Arts students were about seventy percent of the arts and science total at the small Canadian universities, slightly less on average at the large, and went as high as eighty-five percent of the total.

Departments and Programs

Those disciplines that were listed in the catalogues as separate departments with the requirements for a major potentially met by courses within the department listings were recorded with the number of full-time faculty listed as members and the number of courses entered under the department. (Courses were converted to half year, semester, or one-fortieth of the total credits for the degree.) In any one year, not all of the faculty are necessarily teaching and not all courses are available, so these numbers cannot be used as a reliable guide to teaching loads, for example, but they are a rough guide to what is potentially available to students and in what subject.

The average number of departments at the large Canadian universities was twenty-six (range 20 to 30), at small, eighteen (range 13 to 28), and at the American colleges, twenty-one (range 19 to 24). The larger number of departments at the large universities derives primarily from the division of more-inclusive into two or more less-inclusive departments – zoology and botany, in some instances physiology, biochemistry, or microbiology, rather than a single department of biology; departments of computer science or statistics, in addition to mathematics. As well, there are basic disciplines in the larger universities that are rarely represented in the smaller (e.g., linguistics) and a variety of departments focusing on particular cultural and geopolitical areas (e.g., Near Eastern studies, Asian studies, Slavonic studies). There are more languages offered at larger universities and they are less often combined in departments of related languages.

Thus, the larger universities offer the full range of courses and a possible major in areas that are represented at the smaller universities only in occasional courses within a more inclusive department. They also offer departmental majors in areas that are not represented at all in the curricula for the small universities.

There are eleven disciplines that are represented at the departmental level at all the institutions in our current sample. French and German are also offered at all the sample universities but are often combined at the small Canadian universities in a single department of modern languages and elsewhere in various combinations with related languages. There are a few other departments that are represented at all the large universities and the American colleges and at the majority, but not all, of the small Canadian universities. These include classics, geology, and religion, or religious studies. Finally, geography is represented at most, but not all of the Canadian universities, large or small. The difference between the small Canadian and American colleges is mostly the latter's inclusion of more of these somewhat less common departments. Some have separate anthropology and computer science departments. Some colleges in both groups include one or another more professionally oriented departments – business administration, education, music, art – in their listing of arts and science departments.

The large universities, of course, have many more faculty and offer many more courses in each discipline than the corresponding disciplines in the smaller institutions. In this respect the latter are impoverished versions of the former. To the extent that a university, for its undergraduates, is a representation of, and an opportunity to explore freely, a wide range of knowledge, and to the extent that a student's motivation is one of pure intellectual curiosity, the major research universities provide the opportunity. A student at UBC, for example, could take courses in Bengali language and poetry, Polish literature, the urban geography of the Soviet Union, and linguistic theory on his or her way to a BA degree. On the other hand, the students at the large universities like UBC must receive their education in the earlier years, and in the most popular disciplines in the later years as well, often in very large classes that are not uncommonly taught by graduate students or by faculty whose major attention and investment is elsewhere.

The curriculum is only one determinant of the nature and quality of higher education.[18] The quality of the faculty, its commitment to undergraduates, the quality of the students, and the context in which all these components interact are just as important, if not more so. Potentially, a student at a small college can get to know several of his or her professors personally, could easily make friends with an assortment of students from other disciplines who share a variety of interests, participate in drama or other extracurricular activities, and, in the absence of graduate students, have the opportunity to work on a research project during the summer months.

The nine American colleges usually have larger faculties in those departments that are also represented in the small Canadian universities and offer fewer courses, but these differences are small. A major difference between the American and Canadian universities is in the much larger number of programs of study on offer that include courses not linked to any of the departments, together with an interdisciplinary mix of related courses. There was an average of nineteen interdisciplinary programs specified at the American colleges. In this respect, they exceed even the large Canadian universities, which offer an average of fourteen. The small Canadian universities list an average of seven.

We made no attempt to discriminate among programs that clearly offered enriched possibilities to the undergraduate, for either elective or concentration purposes, and it is clear that in some instances these programs are moribund. Enrolment figures from the American colleges make it clear, however, that the majority of the interdisciplinary programs are active and vital parts of their undergraduate curriculum.

A variety of types of study is included in the category of programs. The common element is that they do not provide the possibility of a self-contained concentration without incorporating courses from regular departments related to the program. They do not have an independent faculty complement – at most, they have a single faculty member, or a committee with a director or coordinator.

One type of program that is represented at all the colleges in our sample encompasses studies of national, regional, or ethnic cultures related to the composition or location of the university offering the program. Canadian studies programs are ubiquitous at the Canadian colleges; American studies at the American. Many of the Canadian universities, large and small, have programs like Native studies, Celtic studies (St Francis Xavier and University College of Cape Breton), or Mennonite studies (Winnipeg). Several of the American colleges have Black studies. Somewhat different, but very common, are women's studies programs. All of the large Canadian universities in our sample, six of the small, and eight of the nine American colleges have such programs and list faculty and courses that indicate they are clearly actively developed and well subscribed.

Other types of programs found particularly at the American colleges are those in the language, culture, and history of specific foreign areas, like Latin America or the Middle East; such programs are often represented at the large universities by full-scale departments. Still other types present at the small Canadian university but more common at the American colleges are those that are specifically interdisciplinary like comparative literature, environmental studies, medieval studies, neuroscience and cognitive science, peace and war, and labour studies. Finally, there are programs in the creative and performing arts – drama, dance, film studies, creative writing, popular culture, as well as music and fine arts. The American colleges could be said to offer a considerably enriched version of the small Canadian liberal arts programs.

Of course, the American colleges are enriched in a very literal sense. They have been generously endowed and they charge high tuitions, compensated only modestly by programs of financial aid. Nevertheless, they seem able to tolerate more diverse subject matter and to generate more experimentation and innovation, not only in programs such as these but in the organization of courses. For example, the block program at Colorado College divides the academic year into eight three-and-a-half-week segments. Students take one course per segment, meeting every day for variable amounts of time. Several American colleges have added a short term to the normal two semesters devoted to independent study projects or intensive, innovative courses. Another interesting trend is the introduction of low enrolment first year seminars in which a specialized, often quite imaginative and advanced topic is offered by each department. The rationale is to provide at the outset of the student's university career a more stimulating and involving experience than the usual introductory courses, as well as a setting in which frequent writing assignments can be expected.

Small universities in Canada provide readier access to higher education for local populations. In smaller centres or rural areas they may provide a richer and more accessible extracurricular life. They often have special traditions to which students and alumni are attached. They allow more contact and familiarity with faculty and smaller classes with more personal instruction. With their dependence on provincial governments, the stringent financial constraints of recent years, and the often short sighted response of some administrations, the genuinely educational advantages they offer are being lost. Information technology will make education at all levels both more effective and more efficient in the future, but the best environment for intellectual development remains frequent and active contact with a sensitive and intelligent teacher who is knowledgeable and enthusiastic about an academic subject. Liberal education works best where there is an institutional culture, including peers, in which learning and intellectual engagement have been made the norm.

However, it is clear that the prototype of the liberal arts college – small, highly selective, with a national rather than a local student body, limited to arts and science programs, and privately funded – is simply absent from the Canadian scene. In terms of mission statements, degree programs offered, and the proportion of BA and BSc students to the total, Mount Allison, Bishop's, and Trent are most similar to the prototypical liberal arts college in the United States. This is particularly true if size, location (small town), and a largely residential student population are added to the comparison. Nevertheless, in terms of selectivity, source and magnitude of funding, and degree of focus on the liberal arts, they are clearly not in the same league.

Although it does seem strange that private wealth in Canada is unwilling to support even one undergraduate liberal arts university comparable to the best small colleges in the United States, not all the deficiencies of Canadian small universities are financial in origin. Faculty tend to emulate the multiversities. Academic administrators use the multiversity criteria in hiring. They rarely set themselves to do a different job, to diversify, experiment, or exploit the special opportunities of smallness or location or to pursue the special purposes of liberal education.

Departments cultivate their majors and, more particularly, their honours students as though their main purpose was the preparation of professional researchers and their primary success the admissions to graduate school. To a significant extent Canadian science departments in particular, even at the undergraduate level, see themselves as training scientists rather than educating students. The insidious distinction between the BA and BSc programs contributes to this attitude in Canada, which is fundamentally contrary to the concept of a liberal education. It also tends to be associated with differential teaching loads for science and other faculty.

THE NATURE OF THE LIBERAL EDUCATION

The evidence from the American liberal arts colleges suggests that in the matter of curriculum the advocates of diversity have won over the advocates of a traditional Western canon as the core of a liberal education. There should really be no need to resolve the issue in principle. There is room for a college emphasizing the great books of the Western tradition as well as institutions that encompass broader and more diverse domains of knowledge. Canadian higher education, in particular, lacks this kind of diversity.

One goal of a liberal education is the acquisition of a body of knowledge; another is the development of intellectual skills; and a third is the development of personal qualities of character and judgement. Most university statements of their mission mention, in one way or another, all three of these goals and indeed they are not independent. Intellectual skills such as critical thinking, logical analysis, and conceptualization require a solid foundation of knowledge. The more one knows about a topic, the better one can think about it.

So far as the essence of a liberal education is concerned, there is common agreement on breadth and depth. We have found no compelling arguments, and we believe there are none, for selecting one particular domain of knowledge as more essential than another to producing an educated person. Breadth should imply access for the students to the widest possible range of knowledge outside the very practical – understanding of the domains of knowledge, alternative ways of classifying and organizing knowledge, and the relations among separate domains. Breadth is clearly only very approximately and inadequately met by the distribution requirements among humanities, social sciences, and natural sciences. Liberal education must include the study of some portion of the universe of knowledge in sufficient detail to require, develop, and practise advanced intellectual skills and a mature style of thinking under the guidance of critical and sympathetic faculty. This is the criterion of depth. Academic departments and their majors are not the only, nor are they likely to be the best, way of defining the pursuit of depth.

Institutions of liberal education will continue to strive to define the relevant content and the best curricular means of achieving breadth and depth. Formal lectures, technological aids, and examinations are only adjuncts to a genuine liberal education. The central features are dialogue, inquiry, and criticism and personal interaction among peers and between students and scholars. A setting that is small enough to be a community and in which the distractions of other faculties, pursuing other goals, are not present is most conducive to this style of learning. In such an environment, the student can pursue a personally chosen but expertly guided program of study.

NOTES

1 Carnegie Foundation for the Advancement of Teaching, *Missions of the College Curriculum. A Contemporary Review with Suggestions* (San Francisco, CA: Jossey-Bass, 1977).

2 See Allan Bloom, *The Closing of the American Mind* (New York: Simon & Schuster, 1987), and William Bennett, *To Reclaim a Legacy* (Washington, DC: National Endowment for the Humanities, 1984). Bennett became secretary of Education in the Reagan administration partly as a result of his forceful argument in this book. Recently, Harold Bloom in *The Western Canon* (New York: Harcourt Brace, 1994) has given his version of the works that belong in such a canon.

3 Frederick Rudolph, *Curriculum. A History of the American Undergraduate Course of Study since 1636* (San Francisco, CA: Jossey Bass, 1987).

4 Lisa R.Lattuca and Joan S. Stark, "Will Disciplinary Perspectives Impede Curricular Reform?" *Journal of Higher Education* 65, no. 4 (1994): 401–24.

5 Stuart L. Smith, *Report. Commission of Inquiry on Canadian University Education* (Ottawa: Association of Universities and Colleges of Canada, 1991).

6 In addition to the various reports of the Carnegie Foundation for the Advancement of Teaching, the Association of American Colleges (AAC) has published two volumes on the arts and science major: *Liberal Learning and the Arts and Science Major*, vol. 1, *The Challenge of Connecting Learning*; vol. 2, *Reports from the Fields* (Washington, DC: The Association of American Colleges, 1991). Another AAC report was concerned with the general education portion of the college curriculum –

Strong Foundations: Twelve Principles for Effective Education Programs (Washington, DC: The Association of American College, 1994). The National Endowment for the Humanities, in addition to Bennett's book *To Reclaim a Legacy*, sponsored a book by L.V. Cheney, *Fifty Hours: A Core Curriculum for College Students* (Washington, DC: National Endowment for the Humanities, 1989). The Lilly Endowment Workshops on the Liberal Arts held at Colorado College, Colorado Springs, have also been an important influence on the curricular philosophy of the liberal arts and the origin of several common curricular innovations.

7 Colby College, for example, adopted ten precepts to guide both curriculum reform and the course choices of contemporary students (*Colby College Catalogue 1994–95*, 27). These precepts include the development of critical thinking; knowledge of American culture; familiarity with other cultures, including a foreign language; learning "how people different from oneself have contributed to the richness and diversity of society" and "how each individual can confront intolerance;" understanding one's own and other's values; becoming "familiar with the art and literature of a wide range of cultures and historical periods;" exploring a scientific discipline; studying the use of quantitative methods; studying one discipline in depth and exploring the "relationships between academic work and one's responsibility to contribute to the world beyond the campus."

8 So far as the liberal arts are concerned, Mount Allison has to some extent been an exception. It was the site of a conference on the Past and Future of Liberal Education in 1989. Mount Allison was also the first Canadian university to participate in a Lilly Foundation Workshop in 1993.

9 See, for example, New Brunswick, Legislative Assembly, *Report of the Royal Commission on Higher Education in New Brunswick* (Fredericton, NB: Queen's Printer, 1962).

10 The large universities were Alberta, British Columbia, Brock, Dalhousie, Manitoba, Queen's, Saskatchewan, and Toronto. The small Canadian universities were Acadia, Bishop's, Brandon, Cape Breton, Lakehead, Laurentian, Mount Allison, Mount Saint Vincent, Saint Francis Xavier, Saint Mary's, Trent, and Winnipeg. The nine American colleges were Bates, Bowdoin, Colby, Colorado College, Earlham, Emory, Middlebury, Oberlin, and Reed.

11 For example, E.L. Dey, A.W. Astin, W.S. Korn, and E.R. Riggs, *The American Freshman: National Norms for Fall 1992* (Los Angeles, CA: University of California at Los Angeles Higher Education Research Institute and the American Council on Education, 1992), and Clark, *The Class of '86*. Our own survey of Mount Allison graduates reported in

this volume found similar differences between graduates of different degree programs.

12 The Carnegie Foundation for the Advancement of Teaching, *Missions*, 136.

13 Ibid. The change that the Carnegie Foundation report did find, and deplored, was a decrease in the general education requirements as a proportion of the total and an increase in the proportion of electives.

14 Robert Zemsky, *Structure and Coherence: Measuring the Undergraduate Curriculum* (Washington, DC: American Association of Colleges, 1989).

15 Disciplinary differences in the structure of knowledge and, consequently, the structure of departmental curricula have been noted and classified by various authors. See, for example, D.A. Kolb, "Learning Styles and Disciplinary Differences," In A. Chickering (editor), *The Modern American College* (San Francisco, CA: Jossey-Bass, 1981).

16 Association of American Colleges, *Liberal Learning*, vol. 1.

17 Lattuca and Stark, "Disciplinary Perspectives," 401–24. The responses analyzed in this article were contained in Association of American Colleges, *Liberal Learning*, vol. 2.

18 Some institutions (e.g., Hamilton College) design programs deliberately intended to foster extracurricular intellectual activities. See Mike De Braggio, "Making Connections," *Liberal Education* 80, no. 1 (1984): 46–9.

PART TWO

Students and Liberal Education

CHAPTER THREE

Perceptions of the Undergraduate Experience: Graduates of a Small University 1960–84

CHRISTINE STORM, THOMAS STORM, AND MICHELLE STRAIN

The nature of the undergraduate population has changed considerably over the past thirty-five years. The society into which graduates emerge from the university has also changed in ways that may affect their expectations of a university education and the criteria by which they judge whether those expectations have been met.

One major change in the student population, clearly, has been in its gender composition. The majority of students in the arts and humanities, and in many science programs, are now women. With the increased accessibility that accompanied the expansion of university education that began in the sixties, a larger proportion of undergraduates had parents who were not university graduates. All students now see a university degree as a minimum requirement for a middle-class career rather than a luxury. An increasing number, maybe the majority in arts and science, have anticipated the need for additional training beyond the undergraduate degree. In terms of expectations, once again, perhaps the major change is gender related. In recent years women in universities have expected to enter the workforce and to qualify for a wider range of careers than the traditional female occupations of teaching, nursing, and other helping professions.

The research reported here was intended to examine changes in graduates' perceptions of their undergraduate experience at Mount Allison University. Mount Allison is not typical of Canadian universities. It is small. It has had a relatively high ratio of faculty to students, a high percentage of students living in residence, a small-town environment where the university is the dominant institution, small classes, at least at the upper levels and, to a considerable extent, at the introductory levels as well. These characteristics are part of the North American prototype of the liberal arts university. Mount Allison views itself and is viewed by others as exemplifying the liberal arts ideal, even though in many respects it has always differed from the prototype in significant ways. A large part of its original mission seems to have been to provide the surrounding communities with an opportunity for higher education that was otherwise lacking. Throughout its history it has offered professional programs, which are not part of the pure liberal arts tradition, such as engineering, commerce, and secretarial studies. In its curriculum it bears a closer resemblance to other small Canadian universities than to typical exemplars of American small liberal arts colleges.

John Reid, in his history of Mount Allison and elsewhere, suggests that Mount Allison's self-image as a small liberal arts institution dedicated to excellence is an invented tradition that dates only from the early 1960s and arose out of debates within the university.[1] When Mount Allison was integrated into the provincial university system, it was described as "an undergraduate liberal arts college of limited enrolment."[2] The myth, however, took hold. The university most recently described its mission as the provision of "a rigorous liberal education of high quality primarily to undergraduate students in a coeducational, intimate, residential environment."[3] Using rhetoric that is characteristic of the mission statements of institutions professing the primacy of the liberal arts, it goes on to describe the meaning of liberal education in terms of "both breadth and depth in academic programs as well as the development of the whole person." In recent years, the myth has been reinforced by the publicity given to the university in the annual rankings of Canadian universities by *MacLean's* magazine.[4]

In our research we surveyed members of the graduating classes from 1960–84. We wanted to survey graduates who were at least a few years beyond their bachelor's degree. More recent graduates, of course, may be quite different, given lowered expectations since the recession and the "global restructuring" that is said to have changed forever the occupational structure of Canada and other Western nations. It will be particularly interesting to see the effect of these changes on the more recent cohort when we survey them in the next few years.

This chapter focuses on graduates' perceptions of the quality of the undergraduate education they received at Mount Allison and of the factors contributing to it. We also examine the characteristics of courses and faculty members mentioned by graduates as significant in their educational experience. We are particularly interested in differences between cohorts, genders, and degree programs.

THE QUESTIONNAIRE AND THE SAMPLE

The questionnaire contained four sections.[5] The first asked for background information on the graduates including gender, year and place of birth, high school, marital status, current and previous employers, and parents' education and occupations. The second asked why they had attended Mount Allison, what degree program and major they had chosen, what their year of enrolment and graduation had been, and what their subsequent educational experience had been, including post-graduate degrees. Section three asked to what extent they were satisfied that their education had met a number of potential objectives and also asked them to indicate how various factors in the university environment had contributed to the quality of their undergraduate experience. The questions in the final section attempted to identify the characteristics of particular courses and faculty that had been in some way memorable to the individual graduates.

This questionnaire was mailed to 901 graduates. Fifteen percent of those graduating at each convocation from 1960–84 with a bachelor's degree in arts, science, commerce, fine arts, or music were randomly selected to receive the questionnaire. Forty-one percent (367) returned completed questionnaires. The rate of return was lower in more recent graduating classes. This rate of return is fairly typical of response rates to mailed questionnaires. However, we compared the characteristics of those graduates who returned questionnaires to all the graduates for the same period in terms of gender, degree program, and post-graduate degrees – information that is maintained in the files of the Mount Allison Development Office.

The major difference between our sample and the population from which it was drawn was with respect to post-graduate degrees. Although the percentage receiving any particular advanced degree is small in both the sample and the population, it is much larger among those who returned questionnaires. For example, eight percent of our sample has received PHDs compared to less than two percent of the more than 6,000 graduates. There are similar discrepancies with every other post-graduate degree, including law and medicine. In interpreting the results we report here, it should be kept in mind that our sample is somewhat unrepresentative of Mount Allison graduates as a whole in terms of numbers that have received advanced education.

Characteristics of the Sample

We grouped the sample into five cohorts: 1960–64, 1965–69, 1970–74, 1975–79, 1980–84. There was indeed an increase in the percentage of women from the earliest to the latest cohort. The proportion of women is approximately 40 percent in the three earliest cohorts and 58 percent in the last two. Fifty-one percent of our sample were BA graduates, 27 percent BSc, and 14 percent Bachelor of Commerce (BComm.). Degree program was clearly related to gender. Sixty percent of women but only 40 percent of men took a BA degree. A greater proportion of men took a BSc or BComm. degree. There is some increase in the number of women who went into commerce or science programs over this period, a trend that would be more marked if the years since 1984 had been included.

There is a smaller proportion of BSc and a larger proportion of BA graduates in the earliest cohort and a higher proportion of BComm. graduates in the most recent cohort than in the corresponding convocation lists. Otherwise, the proportion of our sample in each degree program is comparable to the entire population of graduates. Wherever possible, our analyses took account of differences between the cohorts and between men and women in degree programs.

The most common major area of concentration was English with 61 graduates, followed by biology (42), commerce (42), and psychology (35). History (29), math (22), music (19), and chemistry (18) were other areas with substantial numbers.

Seventy percent of our sample came from the Atlantic Provinces, eighteen percent from Quebec and Ontario; eight percent from outside Canada; and only four percent from the western provinces. This distribution is roughly characteristic of the entire post-World War II period.[6] Two-thirds graduated from high school in the place where they were born.

We asked for the occupation of each parent while the graduate attended Mount Allison. The majority of our graduates' mothers worked at home and of the forty percent who had other occupations, they were overwhelmingly stereotypical female occupations. Fathers were managerial or professional (thirty-nine percent), sales or office workers (twenty-six percent), or manual workers (twenty-four percent). The remainder were dead or retired. Thirty-five percent of the fathers had less than grade twelve education; an additional twenty-six percent had no education beyond grade twelve; seven percent had some additional formal education short of university; seventeen percent were university graduates but went no further; and fifteen percent had post-graduate training, including medical or law school. A larger percentage of the mothers were high school graduates or had some education beyond high school, but fewer went on to university or post-graduate training.

Not surprisingly (since by definition all of our respondents are university graduates), both men and women in the sample showed considerable upward occupational mobility, compared to their parents. Eighty-six percent of the men and sixty-nine percent of the women are in management or professional positions. The largest single occupation for the women in this category continues to be teaching. Only twelve percent describe themselves as house-spouses compared to sixty percent of their mother's generation. Twelve percent of the men and fifteen percent of the women are in office and sales positions. None of the women and two percent of the men are in manual work. There are no notable differences among the cohorts.

Altogether, the graduates in our sample were assiduous earners of degrees, reporting a total of 291. Sixty-one percent received at least one other degree and nineteen percent received at least two.[7] Fifty-six of these degrees (nineteen percent) were earned at Dalhousie and another thirty from the University of New Brunswick (ten percent). Otherwise, there was no noticeable concentration of post-graduate institutions attended, although only a few were outside Canada.

We classified each person in our sample according to the highest degree received. Cohort differences were not significant, although some respondents, particularly in the 1980–84 cohort, may not yet have completed their post-graduate degrees. For those respondents who went on to a PHD (eight percent of the sample, twenty-four men and six women), the median time between graduating from Mount Allison and obtaining the doctorate was about seven years. The thirty doctorates were pretty well distributed across disciplines and across universities, although these were largely Canadian. Three percent obtained an MD (eight men and two women). Twenty-three percent of our sample of graduates received a master's degree (thirty-seven women and forty-three men). These were fairly evenly distributed between arts, science, and education with a sprinkling of masters in divinity, social work, and business administration. Women were much more likely to receive an MA and men an MSc. Finally, twenty-six percent received a second bachelor's degree, most commonly in education, and most commonly by women.

Eighty percent of the sample were married; sixteen percent had never married; and five percent were widowed, separated, or divorced. The modal number of children was two for all the cohorts except the youngest, where the largest number of respondents had not yet had children.

All of the samples were asked why they had chosen to attend Mount Allison. More than eighty percent of the graduates indicated that the small size, academic reputation, and liberal-arts program offered by Mount Allison were somewhat or very important. These three reasons are correlated and reflect the image of Mount Allison. Geographical proximity, the availability of financial aid, and similar reasons represent a second factor, involving cost or convenience of attending Mount Allison. Geographical proximity was somewhat or very important for fifty-five percent and financial aid to forty percent. The third set of items that were highly intercorrelated involved personal influence of a family member, friend, or high school teacher. These factors played an important role in a smaller but still substantial number of cases. The influence of a family member who had attended Mount Allison, for example, was very or somewhat important to thirty-four percent. Similar but lower percentages were obtained for the other variables in this group. There were no differences between men and women nor between graduates of various degree programs, but there was a tendency for academic reputation to be more important in the later cohorts.

We also asked the graduates in our sample to give their reasons for choosing their particular field of concentration, offering ten alternatives. Interest in the subject matter and interest in furthering their education were rated as important or very important by over ninety percent of the sample. Next in the percentage assigning some importance were the prospect of good employment, preparation for a particular occupation, and the prospect of an interesting career. Social respect and prospects of a high income were given some importance by about one-third. Twenty-eight percent said that their parents had some influence and seventeen percent were willing to say that they could not think of anything else to do and that this had played a role in their choice of their field. Only eight percent assigned any importance to friends' influence. Women assigned more importance than men to furthering their education or interest in the subject matter and commerce graduates assigned more importance than arts and science graduates to the more career-oriented reasons.

Satisfaction with Undergraduate Education

We asked five questions about our graduates' satisfaction with their undergraduate education and experience. They were first asked to rate the quality of the education received at Mount Allison in overall terms, from excellent to very poor. This overall rating was followed by four questions intended to tap four different conceptions of the goals of an undergraduate liberal education. We asked: "Did Mount Allison provide you with the knowledge and skills required for your subsequent career"(the vocational objective); "Did Mount Allison provide you with a thorough understanding of an academic discipline" (the depth-of-learning objective); "Did Mount Allison provide you with a broad background of cultural knowledge and the ability to read with understanding and communicate effectively" (the breadth-of-learning objective); and "Did Mount Allison provide you with a satisfying and enriching social experience" (the personal- and social-fulfilment objective). Respondents answered by checking one of four alternatives: yes, to a large extent but not completely, not really, or not at all. Two of these questions, those concerning depth and breadth of learning, are nearly universal elements in statements of the objectives of a liberal arts education. A third, vocational relevance, is not a typical objective of the pure liberal arts education. In fact, the lower priority on occupational training is often regarded as a defining characteristic. Development of character, "the whole person," and similar phrases, are used to distinguish the liberal arts from other approaches to higher education.

Ratings on all five questions dealing with the quality of Mount Allison education were positively intercorrelated, indicating that if alumni rated their overall experience very positively they also tended to rate the achievement of specific objectives highly and vice versa. The correlations are not so high, however, as to make these questions simply alternative measures of the same thing. For BA graduates, the two commonly recognized liberal arts objectives of understanding an academic discipline and broad cultural knowledge were most highly correlated with the overall rating of the quality of education. For BSc students, these relationships were positive but not so strong, especially the measure of broad cultural knowledge. Instead, the rating of the social experience at Mount Allison was most predictive of the overall quality.

Table 1 shows that, for the sample as a whole, ninety-four percent of the respondents rated the education that they received at Mount Allison as excellent or good, about equally split between the two positive alternatives. Of the more specific objectives, the most positive collective result was that Mount Allison had provided a satisfying and enriching social experience. Sixty-four percent agreed that it had, with no qualifications; ninety percent said at least "to a large extent." There is really little to choose between this item and the questions about breadth of cultural knowledge and understanding of a discipline. Basically, responses to all three were overwhelmingly positive. The largest number of negative responses were given to the question concerning preparation for a career, where twenty-five percent felt that this had not really been achieved. Three-quarters, of course, felt that to a large extent it had been.

The concentration of responses to these questions about the quality of educational experience limits the possibilities for differences among subgroups in the sample. Nevertheless, we examined the distribution of responses and did statistical analyses of differences between cohorts, BA, BSc, and BComm. graduates, men and women, and combinations of these. There was no evidence of any differences among cohorts in

Table 1
Satisfaction with Undergraduate Education

Overall quality	*Excellent*	*Good*	*Fair*	*Poor*
	45% (165)	49% (178)	5% (18)	1% (2)
Did Mount Allison provide you with:	*Yes*	*To a large extent*	*Not really*	*Not at all*
a thorough understanding of an academic discipline	47% (174)	44% (160)	8% (29)	1% (4)
a broad background of cultural knowledge and the ability to read with understanding and communicate effectively	51% (187)	37% (136)	11% (40)	1% (3)
the knowledge and skills for a subsequent career	25% (90)	51% (187)	21% (75)	4% (13)
a satisfying and enriching social experience	64% (233)	26% (94)	10% (35)	1% (4)

their perception of the overall quality of their Mount Allison education, i.e., there was no change over the years in the tendency to perceive that quality as excellent or, at least, good. The percent who rated it as excellent or good varied from ninety-one percent to ninety-eight percent but in no systematic way. There was a significant difference depending on the degree program. BA graduates were considerably more favourable than BSc or BComm. graduates, who did not differ from each other. BMus. graduates were the most favourable of all and BFA graduates the least favourable, but given the small number of each, any comparison of these to the other degrees is unreliable. There was no significant difference between women and men in their view of the overall quality of their education, but there was an interaction of gender with degree program. That is, women in the BSc program were less favourable than men in the same program, but women BA or BComm. graduates were more favourable than their male counterparts. Given the restricted range of responses to this item, the result should not be overinterpreted, but it suggests that the BSc program was more oriented to male undergraduates.

We did similar analyses of the responses on knowledge and skills for a subsequent career. In this case, there was a clear and significant trend from the earlier to the later cohorts, which were less likely than the earlier to indicate that this objective had been achieved. The trend was not continuous: the significant contrast was between those graduating during the 1960s (who gave high ratings to Mount Allison in this respect) and all three later cohorts (who gave lower ratings). There were also significant differences between graduates of different degree programs. Perhaps obviously, the BComm. graduates felt that they were better prepared for their further career than BA or BSc graduates.

There were no differences among cohorts, between men and women, or between graduates of different degree programs in the extent to which they felt they had acquired a thorough understanding of an academic discipline. As one might expect, BA (ninety-one percent), BFA, and BMus. graduates were most likely to feel that they had acquired a broad background of cultural knowledge, compared to "only" eighty percent of BSc and BComm. graduates. There were no differences between cohorts or between men and women. Finally, the only significant difference in ratings of the value of the social experience at Mount Allison was between men and women. More women answered this question with an unqualified "yes."

Differences between graduates in different areas of concentration in ratings of overall quality were relatively minor, although statistically significant. There was a predictable difference in ratings of the degree to which they had obtained knowledge relevant to their future careers, commerce and music graduates giving higher ratings than the others. Mean ratings for understanding of a discipline also differed significantly among graduates with different majors, but since these differences are more likely to reflect the particular departments rather than the disciplines they represent, they are of little general interest. There were no significant differences among the graduates in different fields in the degree to which they felt they had obtained a broad background of cultural knowledge or an enriching social experience.

Summarizing the results of these questions on the quality of the undergraduate experience, the dominant impression is one of positive evaluation in all respects. The graduates experienced both breadth and depth in a social atmosphere that was perceived to be enriching. Learning that was specifically helpful in their subsequent careers was noticeably less likely to occur, although the majority were still positive in their evaluation of this factor. Graduates of any university are generally positive about the value of their education. It is, after all, an important part of their life history and personal identity. Even when this is taken into consideration, however, the results of our survey are very positive.[8]

The differences found in the more detailed breakdowns are minor compared to the favourable consensus on all items. The differences that were found are largely obvious and serve, perhaps, to confirm the validity of the results. The difference between the cohorts of the sixties and graduates from the seventies and eighties may be more worthy of attention since we find a similar contrast in some other results. For this particular result, it seems that either the earlier cohorts were less demanding or less aware of the preparatory potential of their education, or the Mount Allison education was actually somewhat more oriented towards future careers during the years of their attendance.

Factors Contributing to the Quality of Education

We listed sixteen factors that might contribute in one way or another to the quality of an undergraduate education and asked respondents to indicate the degree and direction of influence each had had in their experience. Most of these factors were selected for their particular relevance to Mount Allison University and to other universities to the extent that they share a similar mission. Table 2 presents the graduates' responses.

Over ninety percent of our sample indicated that small classes and personal relationships and discussions with other students made an important contribution. These were the only two characteristics whose contribution was rated as very important by a majority of respondents; only one person indicated that they were in some way a disadvantage. These are the features that Mount Allison advertises. They are clearly the features that its graduates consider most valuable about their undergraduate experience and the reason for their satisfaction with their choice of university.

The quality of the faculty and the quality of the students also ranked very highly; about a third of the graduates indicated that these made a very important contribution while only three percent suggested that they detracted from the educational experience. The quality of lectures belongs with this pair, although somewhat fewer rated them as very important. Clearly a strong faculty and a carefully selected student body can create a good environment for education. Mount Allison is currently the most selective among the primarily undergraduate universities, according to *MacLean's*,[9] and this may well have been the case in the years when our graduates attended. It is not at all clear whether the faculty is, or has been, exceptional in quality and it is difficult to compare the smaller institutions in this respect. However, they were obviously of sufficiently high quality to produce, in combination with the small classes and intimate environment, a high level of satisfaction with the quality of the education provided.

Other characteristics associated with the small size and location of Mount Allison that were regarded as important positive factors by substantially more than half the respondents were the experience of living in residence, personal relations and discussions with faculty,

Table 2
Factors Contributing to the Quality of Education (percentage)

What was the contribution of: *Rank*	*Very important*	*Somewhat important*	*Not important*	*Disadvantage*	*Major disadvantage*	
1 small classes	58	37	4	0	1	a
2 personal relations with other students	54	41	5	0	0	a
3 quality of the faculty	34	57	6	2	1	
4 quality of lectures	21	66	11	2	1	a
5 quality of the students	26	59	14	1	1	a
6 experience of living in residence	36	42	16	5	2	
7 personal relations with faculty	31	44	22	2	1	c,e
8 cultural events on campus	22	52	25	1	1	a,e,f
9 opportunities for social life	17	52	27	4	1	a
10 small town location	21	47	22	10	1	a
11 homogeneity of student body	10	33	47	8	1	d
12 student government	7	28	63	2	0	
13 intramural sports	7	28	67	1	1	b
14 working with faculty on research	13	18	68	1	1	c,e
15 intercollegiate athletics program	10	17	70	2	1	b
16 selection of courses offered (limited)	1	9	53	33	5	g

a: more important to women
b: more important to men
c: more important to those with MA, MSc, or PHD
d: less important to those with MA, MSc, or PHD
e: less important to commerce graduates
f: less important to more recent graduates
g: more disadvantageous to more recent graduates

cultural events on campus, the small-town location, and opportunities for social life. Of these, only one, the small-town location, was regarded as a disadvantage by a substantial number (eleven percent). A large number also regarded the homogeneity of the student body, the experience of working with a faculty member on research, intramural or intercollegiate sports, and student government as important contributors to the quality of their undergraduate experience. A minority (nine percent) regarded the homogeneity of the student body as a disadvantage. The only characteristic that was seen as a disadvantage by a large number (thirty-eight percent) was the selection of courses offered, although fifty-three percent felt that this made no difference to their own education.

We examined these data for any differences among the cohorts, between women and men, or between graduates of different degree programs. We also compared graduates who went on to obtain advanced degrees (PHD, MA, or MSc) with all the others. The factors on which we found significant differences are indicated in Table 2. The rank order of factors is essentially the same for all these subgroups. Nevertheless, women were more likely than men to rate factors associated with the social environment as more important and factors involving sports as less important. Safety, security, and intimacy appear to be more significant to the women graduates. Personal relations with faculty were less important to commerce graduates. Cultural events on campus were less important and the limited selection of courses more disadvantageous according to more recent graduates. Finally, the only differences between those who received advanced research degrees and others were personal relations with the faculty and working with the faculty on research. Whether these closer contacts with faculty influenced the graduates in the direction of post-graduate work or whether their more serious academic interests led them to seek more contact with the faculty cannot, of course, be determined.

Most of our respondents took advantage of the opportunity to elaborate on positive and negative aspects of their undergraduate experience. For the most part, their remarks reinforced the overall results. More than half emphasized the small size of the university and the small classes as the single most positive aspect of their education. Other common responses were variations on this theme. For example, the family or friendly atmosphere was volunteered by forty-four people, caring attitudes and student-professor relations by thirty and twenty-one people respectively. The quality of the education, the faculty, and the program were also commonly mentioned but clearly were secondary to the first group of comments. Fewer people commented on negative aspects of their experience and their remarks are more difficult to summarize. Remarks about particular departments or faculty members who were deficient in one way or another were most common. Limitations in course offerings or resources were next and a few people mentioned insularity or similar negative consequences of smallness.

Courses and Faculty

In addition to our interest in the graduates' evaluation of the overall quality of their education and the factors that were important contributors, we were interested in the characteristics of specific courses and of individual faculty members that stood out in their memory of their undergraduate experience. The respondents were asked to list up to three courses that had been most important and up to seven faculty members whom they best remembered.[10]

A total of 973 courses were listed. Seventy-six percent of the graduates listed the maximum number of three. Sixty-one percent of the courses listed were third or fourth year; sixty-three percent of the courses listed had enrolments of less than thirty (and nineteen percent less than ten). Of the lower level courses listed, those with low enrolments were mentioned disproportionately. This confirms the importance graduates assigned to small classes in their overall ratings. More than two-thirds of respondents indicated that the quality of the instructor was the primary factor contributing to the quality of the course, the intrinsic interest of the subject and the quality of the lectures following closely in importance for the majority. Ratings of other factors – the quality of the other students, active discussions, friendly atmosphere – varied considerably. Laboratory work was rated as moderately important in science courses with a laboratory component. The quality of the students and class discussions were rated as more important for upper level classes. These factors were also rated more important in humanities than in other courses.

It is not surprising that a good instructor teaching an interesting topic is a prerequisite to a memorable undergraduate course. Smaller and more advanced courses were more likely to be memorable. The importance of other factors depended on the nature of the subject matter in understandable ways. For example, in a language course, it seems clear that the level of instruction depends very much on the quality of the other students in the class, whereas this is not so clearly true of other disciplines.

There were no differences among the cohorts in the type of course listed or the ranking of factors contributing to its quality. BA students, however, were more likely and BComm. graduates less likely to choose upper level courses. BA students also ranked the interest of the subject matter, the quality of the students, and the role of active discussion more highly in the courses they chose to mention than did either BSc or BComm. students. Finally, women listed very small courses more often than men and large courses less often.

One of the advantages of a small university is supposed to be the possibility for more contact and closer relationships between students and faculty. The final section of the questionnaire was intended to assess this. Respondents were asked to name up to seven faculty members whom they best remembered and to answer a set of questions for each.

Almost all of the respondents listed at least one faculty member whom they remembered well and thirty-five percent listed the maximum of seven. Altogether, 289 faculty members in twenty-four different departments were named at least once. The calendars for the twenty-five years encompassed by our sample list a total of 574 different faculty members. Thus, sixty-two percent of the faculty teaching for at least a year during this period were actually well remembered and mentioned by at least one of the graduates in the survey. The faculty members' chances of being mentioned, of course, depend on the number of students they've taught, which in turn depends on their particular discipline, the number of years they've spent teaching, the level of the courses they teach, and their reputation. Obviously there are a variety of factors and processes affecting a faculty member's salience in the alumni's experience. The number of graduates listing a particular faculty member was not, in fact, significantly correlated with the number in the sample that had majored in the faculty member's discipline. This number, however, was highly correlated with the number of years on faculty.[11] Women faculty were less likely to be cited than were men, but women were also far likelier to have held temporary or short-term appointments. More than three-quarters of the women and only half of the men were on faculty for four years or less.

Of those sixty-two percent of the faculty who were mentioned at least once, the overwhelming majority were mentioned only once. Even the most frequently mentioned individual was mentioned by no more than ten percent of the sample. No more than six faculty members were mentioned by more than five percent of the sample. What these data suggest, at least, is that there are a few stars, but they are very few and even the most prominent affect only a small minority of students, while on the other hand a sizeable majority of faculty affect at least one student to the extent that they are remembered as an important part of the undergraduate experience after a period ranging from five to thirty years. Every faculty member is memorable to at least some students although only a few are memorable to a large number.

In general, the first faculty member mentioned was the one with whom the respondent had the most personal experience. The number of courses taken with the faculty member decreases from the first faculty member mentioned to the last. Eighty-eight percent of respondents indicated that the first faculty professor listed had an especially important influence on their interests or attitudes. Thus, for the most part, these faculty members are people who were not only memorable but important and influential in the undergraduate experience of our sample. On the other hand, only thirty percent considered these same professors to be personal friends.

We asked the graduates whether they had worked with the professors they named on research, either their own or the faculty member's. We also asked whether they were or had been aware of the research interests or writings of these professors. One index of close contact between faculty and students with particular potential for educational value is collaboration or familiarity with the research of the faculty. Forty-two percent of our sample said that they knew something about the research interests of the first faculty member they cited and seventeen percent had worked with the professor on research. There is a decline in the percentage of graduates who are familiar with the faculty member's research from the forty-two percent who claimed such knowledge for the first faculty member named to thirty-four percent for the second named, all the way to sixteen percent for the seventh (based on 129 cases). There is a similar decline in these percentages with the question regarding collaborative research from seventeen percent to thirteen percent with the second person named to six percent with the seventh.

As one might expect, there are large differences between graduates of different degree programs on these research questions. Thirty-five percent of the BSc graduates, as opposed to twelve percent of the BA graduates, had worked with a faculty member on research. There is also a regular increase with year of graduation in the percentage that had worked with faculty on research, from twelve percent in the oldest cohort graduating from 1960–64 to twenty percent in the graduating years from 1980–85. Finally, the percentage that had experience working with a faculty member on research is much larger for those who went on to a research degree, i.e., MA, MSc, or PHD.

SUMMARY

To the extent that our sample is representative, the graduates of Mount Allison in the years from 1960 to 1984 came to the university primarily because of its academic reputation, the type of program it professed to offer, specifically the emphasis on a broad general liberal arts education, and its small size. These three reasons are consistent with Mount Allison's self-presentation. However it originated, Mount Allison's image as an institution dedicated to the liberal arts and to close personal student-faculty relationships (as opposed to the impersonal instruction supposedly characteristic of larger institutions) has become increasingly well defined over the years and appears to be more important in attracting students to Mount Allison than to other institutions in Canada.[12]

Images, even if they are only partially accurate, traditions, even if they are invented, are certainly important – they affect alumni loyalty and identification with the institution, for example. They can have a self-fulfilling influence if the image attracts better students or students more suited to the kind of education the institution projects publicly. It can only be maintained, however, if the institution remains substantially true to its image.

The majority of our sample experienced their undergraduate education, at least retrospectively, in a manner consistent with that image. They report a high degree of satisfaction with the education they received and with their experience as they received it. Graduates of institutions of higher education are generally satisfied with their educational experience. It is not surprising, therefore, that these graduates were similarly satisfied. It is true, however, that they were markedly more unanimous in their satisfaction than students and graduates in other Canadian surveys.[13]

Whether in their reasons for attending Mount Allison or for choosing a particular field, or in their assessment of the quality of specific aspects of the Mount Allison education, practical considerations were rated relatively low. In this respect, our sample conforms to the general profile of liberal arts students and graduates compared to those at larger universities or in professional programs. As for the two widely recognized goals of the liberal education, about half of our graduates were fully satisfied with the breadth ("broad background of cultural knowledge") and depth ("thorough understanding of an academic discipline") components of their education, features that were regarded as essential by about two-thirds of liberal arts students in the Carnegie survey but considered less essential by students at other types of universities.[14]

Even though there is little data that compares directly with our questions about courses and faculty, it is clear from other studies that small classes and interactions with faculty members at small universities, particularly the élite American colleges, are considered by students and graduates as very important contributors to the quality of their education and influences on their future life.[15] Our survey supports the same conclusion. If almost all small universities must provide less variety than the large multiversities in the disciplines and subdisciplines that they are able to offer, they can compensate through more active participation and interaction with their students in all aspects of academic endeavour. They can also compensate through imaginative approaches to the curriculum and courses of study.

The small undergraduate liberal arts college, of which Mount Allison is one of the few Canadian examples, may graduate satisfied alumni for reasons other than the educational value they provide – for example, because of the friendships that they foster, because of membership in a small group, or because of greater individuation. A high faculty/student ratio, small classes, and a faculty undistracted by graduate students allow for, but do not guarantee, the kind of individual and interactive development of knowledge and skills for which computer technology may ultimately provide a partial substitute in larger institutions. The promise can only be delivered by a faculty that is able and willing – because of their own knowledge and commitment to continued learning, their concern for students and their confidence that their efforts are appreciated, and the supportive conditions it is a university administration's responsibility to provide – to devote their energies and imagination to the task, in and out of the classroom.

NOTES

1 John G. Reid, *Mount Allison University: A History to 1963. Vol I: 1843–1914. Vol II: 1914–1963* (Toronto: University of Toronto Press, 1984).

2 New Brunswick, Legislative Assembly, *Report of the Royal Commission on Higher Education in New Brunswick* (Fredericton, NB: Queen's Printer, 1962).

3 Mount Allison University, "A Statement of the Institutional Role and Planned Capacity of Mount Allison University." Submission to the Maritime Provinces Higher Education Commission (1992), 2.

4 In 1991, *MacLean's* 104, no. 42 (21 October): 14–16 ranked the arts and science undergraduate programs of forty-six Canadian universities regardless of size and placed Mount Allison third, following McGill and Queen's. In its 1992 (9 November) and 1993 (15 November) rankings, after dividing the universities into three categories, *MacLean's* put Mount Allison first among those classified as primarily undergraduate. The criteria used, and their combination to provide an overall ranking, have been widely criticized, with considerable justification. These rank-

ings are perpetuating a reputation based on small classes and an emphasis on excellence that has been steadily eroded in recent years by a reduction in the teaching faculty and an increase in class sizes. A relatively narrow range of programs has been reduced even further in an attempt to deal with budgetary difficulties. Mount Allison's endowment, substantial in the Canadian context for a small institution, and its alumni/ae support are small by comparison with those small, private liberal arts universities in the United States whose liberal arts philosophy it espouses.

5 Copies of the questionnaire are available from the authors.

6 See Table 12 in Reid, *Mount Allison University*, vol. 2, 454.

7 K. Archer, "Political Science BA Graduates from the University of Calgary: Education and Career Paths," *Canadian Journal of Higher Education* 26, no. 1 (1986): 65–76, found that sixty-three percent of political science graduates at the University of Calgary continued their studies beyond the BA; D. Rennie, "Survey of York University 1976–78 Bachelor's Degree Graduates in Psychology Located in Greater Toronto," *Canadian Journal of Higher Education* 11, no. 1 (1981): 45–57, found that forty-two percent of psychology graduates at York pursued further studies; whereas H. Ralston, "The Uses of a Bachelor's Degree in Sociology: Careers of Recent Graduates of a Maritime University," *Canadian Journal of Higher Education* 8, no. 3 (1978): 47–66, found that seventy percent of sociology graduates from a Maritime university enrolled in studies beyond the BA.

8 A series of National Graduate Surveys conducted by Employment and Immigration Canada and Statistics Canada in 1988, 1984, and 1978 provides a context for the interpretation of the positive evaluation of their undergraduate education by our sample. The focus of these surveys is on employment experience of graduates of secondary institutions and there are no directly comparable items to ours, but in the 1992 survey of 1990 graduates (unpublished tables received from Statistics Canada) on all items that concern the achievement of personal objectives of one kind or another, average ratings are on the positive side on their four-point scale. This same general pattern is found with few exceptions in the earlier published surveys. See Warren Clark and Z. Zsigmond, *Job Market Reality for Post-Secondary Graduates: Employment Outcomes in 1978, Two Years after Graduating* (Ottawa: Supply and Services Canada, 1981); Warren Clark, M. Laing, and E. Rechnitzer, *The Class of '82* (Ottawa: Supply and Services Canada, 1986); and Warren Clark, *The Class of '86* (Ottawa: Supply and Services Canada, 1992).

9 *MacLean's* 106, no. 46 (15 November 1993): 35.

10 There was a clear tendency for respondents to remember courses from their own area of concentration. Courses in departments with larger numbers of majors were therefore more likely to be cited.

11 The relationship between the number of times a faculty member was cited and the number of graduates majoring in his or her discipline was +.13; the number of years on faculty (up to 1984) was +.64. The more years on faculty, of course, the more students who could have encountered the faculty member. Longevity also provides an opportunity for a reputation to be established and spread. Thus, one might expect, longevity to magnify the effect of whatever qualities make a teacher memorable.

An annual teaching award was instituted in 1984. All of the eleven recipients to date were on faculty at some time during the period 1960–84 (the most recent joined the faculty in 1980). Of these, three were among the most frequently cited in our survey. On the other hand, seven of the ten most frequently cited faculty members, all of whom continued on faculty beyond the institution of the award, were never formally recognized. It is characteristic of such awards that they create more resentment in those unrecognized than satisfaction in those recognized. They may be an effective public relations exercise, but they neither help to raise the net level of morale among devoted teachers nor to encourage better teaching.

12 A. Frizzle, *The Commission of Inquiry on Canadian University Education* (Ottawa: Carleton University Press for the Carleton University Survey Centre, 1991) found that only thirty percent of students gave the academic reputation of their institution as a very important reason for their choice.

13 We were unable to find very many reports of studies that are directly comparable to ours. The most extensive surveys on the quality of undergraduate educational experience have been done on samples of students enrolled in university at the time of the survey, rather than retrospective surveys of graduates. Some of these, however, have questions similar to some of ours (in fact, we based some of our questions on them), notably the very large surveys of American undergraduates conducted for the Carnegie Foundation, the latest of which was in 1984. The Carleton University Survey was less extensive but comparable. Statistics Canada reported the results of a national survey of persons who graduated in 1982 from any type of higher education and interviewed a sample by telephone. Although some of the studies we have seen inquire about the faculty in general and student relationships with faculty, we have seen nothing that is comparable to the section of our questionnaire in which specific courses and specific faculty were named and rated on various factors.

14 Frizzle, *The Commission of Inquiry.*

15 See K.A. Feldman and T.M. Newcomb, *The Impact of College on Students*, vol. 1. (San Francisco, CA: Jossey-Bass, 1969). J.G. Gaff, "Making a Difference: The Impacts of Faculty," *Journal of Higher Education* 44, no. 8 (1973): 605–22, also presents evidence on this point. This study is particularly interesting for the combination of faculty with student responses in attempting to assess the degree and the nature of faculty impact.

CHAPTER FOUR

Access to Excellence? The Social Background of Mount Allison Students as Compared to Four Other Universities in the Maritimes

BRIAN CAMPBELL AND BERKELEY FLEMING

In this paper, we explore the social background of university students at five institutions in the Maritimes. We examine three major social factors: parents' education, parents' occupation, and the social-class identity of students. A fourth social factor, gender, is used throughout our analysis. Our interuniversity comparative framework helps us to understand the situation of the individual institution. In addition, we extend our comparison to an analysis of the differences between the background of university students at these five institutions and that of the general population. The focus on Mount Allison is maintained throughout, but we gain an understanding of this institution through comparison. It will be shown that there is inequality among student populations, and that Mount Allison students are the most privileged.

UNIVERSITY DIFFERENCES AND ACCESSIBILITY

We begin this analysis with the idea that not all universities are the same. There is a long Canadian tradition, backed by government policies, of university differentiation in terms of religious denomination, language, ethnicity, gender, academic specialization, region, and size. In short, universities have reflected the diversity within Canadian society.

There is a difference between variation and rank. *Maclean's* magazine and other sources have recently given us hierarchical rankings of Canadian universities. In Canada, this popular and controversial focus on university inequality is relatively new. In the past, elevated university status has usually surfaced in relation to high-profile, often foreign, institutions: for example, Oxford and Harvard have long been lauded for their glories. Domestically, there has of course always been some lustre attached to the older established schools in the major centres, but the importance of institutional differences in terms of the quality and accessibility of university education for Canadian students has remained largely unexplored.

Given the differences among universities, it is curious that this has not been a major theme in the sociological literature on university participation. Students of university accessibility and participation seem to have assumed some kind of "generic" university. Porter and others,[1] for example, have studied large numbers of university students in Canada without regard to their individual university affiliation. Researchers have then drawn conclusions concerning participation and accessibility. Various social-background factors (wealth, education of parents, gender, and the like) and certain convenience factors (proximity to home, availability of program, region, and so forth) have been used to analyze student attendance at university.[2] Going to university has been treated in such studies as a generic issue. However, since universities differ, students may well choose between what they take to be "greater" and "lesser" institutions, between Roman Catholic universities and others, between larger and smaller places, and so on. Perhaps economically advantaged students tend to go to certain institutions. Perhaps university degrees are not all accorded the same respect. With these sorts of considerations in mind, we argue that the analysis of accessibility and participation must take into account university differences and hierarchy. This paper is part of such an analysis.

Our research on university students in the Maritimes considers individual institutions and how their distinctiveness might be linked to participation. In this preliminary paper, we analyze some of the ways that university student populations differ from each other and we discuss some of the possible reasons for these variations. When discussing individual institutions, we shall concentrate on the case of Mount Allison.

UNIVERSITY, ACCESSIBILITY, AND CREDENTIALISM

People from all social backgrounds attend university. In this sense, higher education is accessible to a broad spectrum of modern Canadian society. However, the participation rates of people from various social backgrounds are not equivalent. For example, the poor are less likely to attend university than wealthier members of our society. Similarly, people whose parents received higher education tend to participate at higher rates than the general population.

The university is a key institution of the middle class in industrial societies.[3] A university education is necessary for most modern managerial and professional positions. This is publicly recognized in a variety of ways. One of them is that access to university education is often discussed in the public arena as a way of giving opportunities to poorer individuals so that they may attain a middle-class lifestyle, an argument that seems oblivious to structural constraints on the size of the middle class itself. Another form of recognition is the contention that access to post-secondary education "pays off" in terms of better life chances (employment, health, lifetime earnings, etc.) for individuals.[4]

Also, in our culture it makes common sense that people should be trained formally to fulfil their occupational roles. Part of the logic here is that production systems and whole societies that employ well-trained and talented people successfully will have a productive advantage in the creation of wealth.[5] However, efficient societies may generate surpluses of talented and well-trained people. In addition, such highly trained people may actually create unemployment through their effectiveness, since highly rationalized and efficient systems may need fewer people. Paradoxically, education contributes to societal wealth and provides access to rewards but does not necessarily ensure rewards for all. Although it can help in the creation of wealth, education does not eliminate poverty. It might actually be part of the sorting-and-authority mechanism that establishes who will be poor. Inequality in the distribution of rewards and positions in society persists despite more broadly available education. An increased number of people with credentials chasing relatively few positions results in inflation of requirements and the need for more education and credentials.[6] If there is a surplus of university graduates, then other factors such as the status of the degree granting institution may have consequences.

In this paper we concentrate on whether there are differences in accessibility at five universities in the Maritimes. These institutions will provide a test of the extent to which institutions vary in their accessibility. We shall begin with Mount Allison.

FROM ACCESSIBILITY TO EXCELLENCE AT MOUNT ALLISON

Accessibility for students from all social backgrounds was an important feature of Mount Allison's self-definition in the early years, as evidenced by speeches made by certain prominent figures in the institution. However, more recently, Mount Allison officials have not made this kind of argument, at least not with the same degree of fervour, in their public pronouncements: "Debates over openness to students from all social and ethnic backgrounds, and over the maintenance of academic quality – or, as one federal government report glibly put it in 1988, 'access to excellence' – will force universities to review not only immediate priorities but also the more fundamental questions of why they do what they do and how far continuity with the past can or should be maintained."[7]

At Mount Allison, some have argued that "access" and "excellence" are mutually contradictory. Additional factors, such as limiting enrolment, increasing enrolment, serving the Maritime provinces, maintaining the connection to the United Church, widening the constituency, emphasizing selectivity, and offering "average" as well as "scholarly" students a solid liberal undergraduate education, have also often entered such discussions during Mount Allison's history.[8] Nevertheless, there is evidence that for certain institutional leaders, "openness to students from all social and ethnic backgrounds" was considered central in the first seventy or eighty years of the university's existence.

For example, Humphrey Pickard, the first president of Mount Allison, is thought to be the editorialist who in 1861 opined that higher education "should be accessible to all who may aspire to its attainment, and to all who, from position or profession, ought to have it in their possession,"[9] even if it were impractical to make it universally available. In 1870, David Allison, the second president, argued fervently that "the sons of the wealthy will be welcome ... [b]ut we are eager to help those needy youth whose souls are a glow [*sic*] with an ardent desire for a liberal education, who toil hard both mentally and manually for the attainment of the worthy object of their desire."[10]

In the late 1890s, the editors of the *Argosy Weekly* decried élitist recruitment to Mount Allison with the comment that "no one should be attending Mount Allison *simply* because his father or uncle, or some other relative attended before him."[11] After quoting that source, Mount Allison historian John Reid observed that "Mount Allison had purported from the beginning, and had earnestly striven, to make education available to all who sought it and could profit from it ... [b]ut by the turn of the century there was good reason to fear that this crucial element of what Mount Allison had always stood for was in serious jeopardy."[12]

Perhaps the most significant statement in support of accessibility can be found in the 1923 inaugural address of George J. Trueman, the fifth president of Mount Allison:

In a country like Canada, people of ability come from every group. In these Provinces, especially, a much larger per cent than the usual of the population is of good ability, and the available wealth is low. This creates a serious problem, for if the greatest possible progress is to be made, the higher schools of learning should be open for all who can enter them. In other words, whether a student gets a university education or not should depend on his ability, ambition, and character, and not upon the family income.[13]

Noble sentiments indeed. Trueman was by no means an egalitarian, but there were "liberal-meritocratic" and "human-capitalist" elements in his vision of Mount Allison as an educational institution that would provide fulfilment and uplift for Maritime youth and social improvement for Maritime society. There is even some evidence that Trueman advocated "affirmative action" *avant la lettre,* in favour of relatively deprived rural Maritime youth. When Mount Allison recruiter W.S. Godfrey assessed Trueman's contribution, he commented that "in the Maritimes generally there are many who have brains and personality but have no money. To these men and women he has rendered signal service. He has made it possible for many who would otherwise have found it altogether impossible to get an education."[14] Clearly, Trueman favoured "selectivity" in admitting students but was opposed to selectivity by wealth.

Apart from whether, to what degree, and how the sentiments quoted above were actually translated into practice, one can observe that since the 1960s invention of the tradition of "excellence" at Mount Allison,[15] the notion of "accessibility" has not been a dominant feature of the institution's self-conception, at least as articulated in various public documents. Still, on occasion one encounters in Mount Allison's official discourse some nods to accessibility. For example, in its 1973 brief to the Deutsch Commission, Mount Allison declared that "it is a selective University in the sense that, while *there are no barriers of race, sex, religion, or politics,* it chooses sparingly what it will teach, it chooses carefully who will teach, and it seeks to admit those students who will benefit from rather demanding programs of study and standards of performance."[16] Similarly, Mount Allison calendars and admissions brochures have, in recent years, consistently included the statement that "Mount Allison University ... does not discriminate against applicants and students on the basis of race, color [*sic*] and national or ethnic origin, and such a non-discriminatory policy ... extends to non-discrimination on the grounds of creed or sex."[17] A recent Mount Allison admissions brochure includes the information that "Mount Allison University has been dedicated ... to the cause of providing students *of all backgrounds* with a first-class liberal education" (emphasis added).[18] Thus, when making representations to government and when recruiting students, appropriate sentiments are expressed with respect to non-discrimination.

With respect to economic need, the same admissions brochure indicates that "Mount Allison policies have long maintained that *no academically deserving student should be denied a university education for reasons of financial need*" (emphasis added).[19] Two booklets issued in connection with the *Universitas* fund-raising campaign of the late 1980s do, in that limited sense, acknowledge a concern for accessibility issues. In one, it is asserted that "it is a tenet of Mount Allison that outstanding students should not be handicapped by financial need ... [I]f legitimate requirements for assistance are to be met, more funds are needed."[20] As the other booklet acknowledges, "so that outstanding students are not prevented from attending university as a consequence of financial need, additional scholarship and bursary funds are required."[21] It is important to note here that the deserving student is characterized as outstanding. There is no recognition of a need to support average, hard-working students. Accessibility is for the excellent. So, when seeking funds and when recruiting students, official notice is taken of accessibility issues, but only for a narrow range of students.

On the other hand, no such interest is discernible in internal debates. We see no evidence of a concern with accessibility in the written records of the "excellence" debates of the 1960s. Neither Mount Allison's most recent mission statement (1990) nor its present "Vision 2000" statement-in-the-works includes reference to accessibility. And although there is serious concern among students and faculty over the implications for accessibility of tuition-fee increases and changes in the federal and provincial governments' loan and bursary programs, this concern has not been addressed in any "official" announcements of tuition increases. Indeed, Mount Allison was recently singled out by the Maritime Provinces Higher Education Commission as a post-secondary institution unlike the others in New Brunswick and Prince Edward Island in that it does not "have a primary accessibility role."[22]

We draw two conclusions from this brief overview of public discourse concerning access to Mount Allison. First, there have on occasion been important individuals for whom accessibility has been a major concern, albeit one informed by a late nineteenth or early twentieth century Maritime Methodist perspective. Second, although on occasion in the late twentieth century there have appeared vague references to accessibility issues and glossy pronouncements concerning non-discrimination, such concerns do not appear to have the same official significance today as they seem to have had in the earlier period.

The question we now raise is, what do the results of our survey tell us about the actual social backgrounds of Mount Allison students when they are compared to other Maritime students and to the general population?

THE MARITIME UNIVERSITY STUDENT SURVEY

Three types of study have been done by Canadian sociologists on access to post-secondary education, particularly university education. Some researchers have done surveys of high school students, focusing on determinants of their levels of educational aspiration.[23] Others have examined historical changes in patterns of educational inequality in Canada by analyzing census data, focusing especially on cohort analysis of unequal probabilities of educational attainment.[24] Still others have conducted surveys of students actually attending university, at least implicitly comparing their social-background characteristics with the characteristics of others of their approximate age in the general population.[25]

Our work follows this third tradition but pays more attention to the significance of institutional differences. We have conducted two surveys that tell us a great deal about the social backgrounds and motivations of students in the Maritimes. The Mount Allison Student Survey (MASS), essentially an exploratory study, was conducted in 1990. All full-time and part-time students at Mount Allison were sent a questionnaire, and our response rate was approximately forty-two percent. The second study, the Maritime University Student Survey (MUSS), was conducted among a twenty percent sample of students at five Maritime universities – Mount Allison, Acadia, St Francis Xavier, St Thomas, and the University of New Brunswick (UNB), with a response rate of 55.9 percent. The first questionnaire (MASS) was a modification of the ones used in the National Post-Secondary Student Surveys conducted by Statistics Canada in 1974–75 and 1983–84.[26] Based on our experience with our MASS instrument, we developed an improved version for the MUSS study. The modifications and improvements we introduced in our two questionnaires were designed to allow us to tap certain variables, typically ignored in the existing literature, that we thought might be particularly relevant for the Maritimes and for smaller institutions such as Mount Allison. Our MUSS survey also allows us to compare the responses of students from different universities, something that to our knowledge has not been attempted before.

In considering the question of accessibility we focus our analysis on who participates in higher education. There are many ways to divide up the social landscape. Our interest is in social hierarchy, so we have looked at some of the major indicators of social inequality in our society. We compare students using three social background factors: parents' educational attainment, parents' occupation, and social class identity. As noted earlier, gender, an important factor in any comprehensive assessment of social inequality, is used throughout our consideration of these three factors. After analyzing each of these elements individually, we combine their effects into a composite measure.

The results show that there are differences in the social makeup of the student populations at the five universities in the survey. Mount Allison students in particular are consistently more privileged, as are the student populations of the other residential universities we looked at (Acadia and St Francis Xavier), but to a lesser extent. Further, important gender effects are evident in terms of the influence of parents on their same-sex and opposite-sex children.

Parents' Educational Attainment

It is clear from the literature that parents' educational attainment is related to the likelihood of their children anticipating and attaining post-secondary education.[27] Therefore, we begin our discussion of the social background of university students with family educational background. In doing this, we shall start with the analysis of differences among universities. Throughout this section of the paper, we report the results for mothers and fathers separately. This is in large part because gender differences in educational attainment have existed for a long time in Canada: although in recent years the participation rates for women, as measured particularly by undergraduate enrolment figures, have become more equitable,[28] men have historically attained much higher levels of education than women.

Figure 1 displays the educational attainment of the mothers of students by university of student. The first column in this figure shows the breakdown for all mothers of students in the MUSS survey. This indicates that 42.7 percent of MUSS mothers had some university education, 19.3 percent had some post-secondary non-university training, 18.8 percent had completed secondary education, and 19.3 percent had completed less than secondary. The remaining five bars give these distributions for mothers of students from each of the five universities. There are some clear differences. At one extreme is Mount Allison, with 56.9 percent of mothers with university education and only 11.9 percent of mothers with less than secondary. At the other extreme is St Thomas, with 36.6 percent of mothers with some university and 25.7 percent with less than secondary. This pattern of Mount Allison at the high end and St Thomas at the low end of a status distinction continues throughout the analysis of the data in this paper.

Figure 2 displays the educational-attainment distribution for fathers of students at the five institutions. It shows that, like Mount Allison mothers, Mount Allison fathers are relatively highly educated. Another

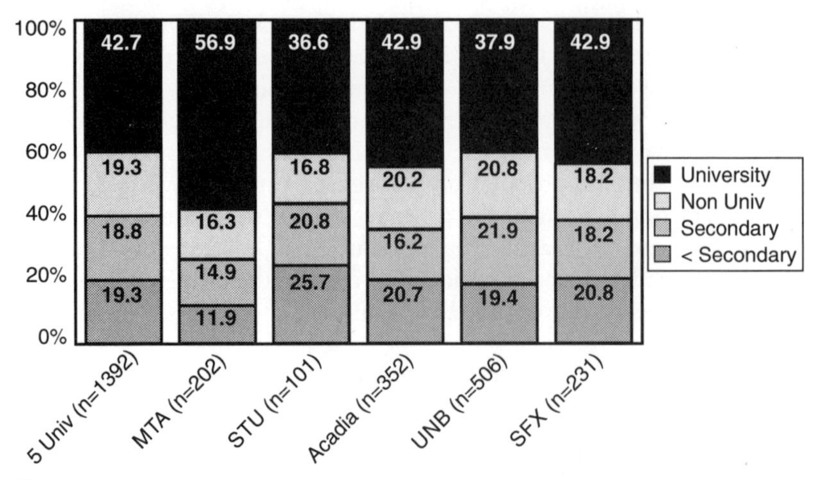

Figure 1
Educational Attainment of Students' Mothers by University

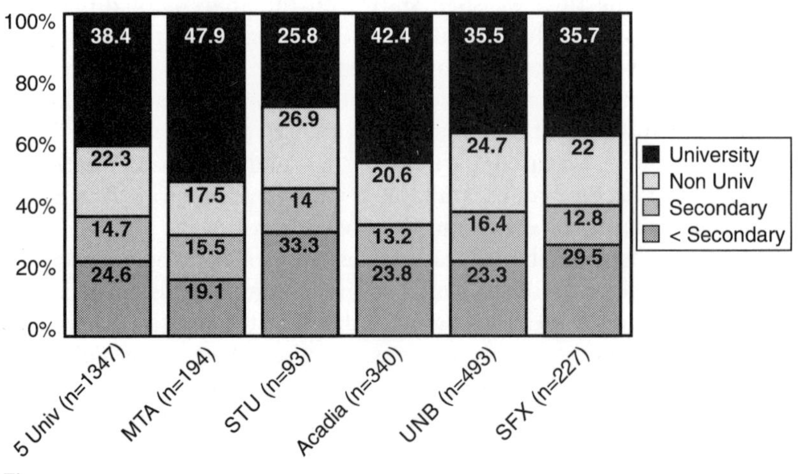

Figure 2
Educational Attainment of Students' Fathers by University

rather striking finding is that fathers are generally somewhat less formally educated than mothers, despite the historical pattern of women in the general population achieving less formal education. Mothers' education may be a more important influence on student educational attainment than fathers' education. We shall pursue some of the implications of this later. First, we shall combine the educational attainment levels for both mothers and fathers.

Figure 3 displays university attainment for mothers and fathers, shown for both men and women students by university. Mount Allison

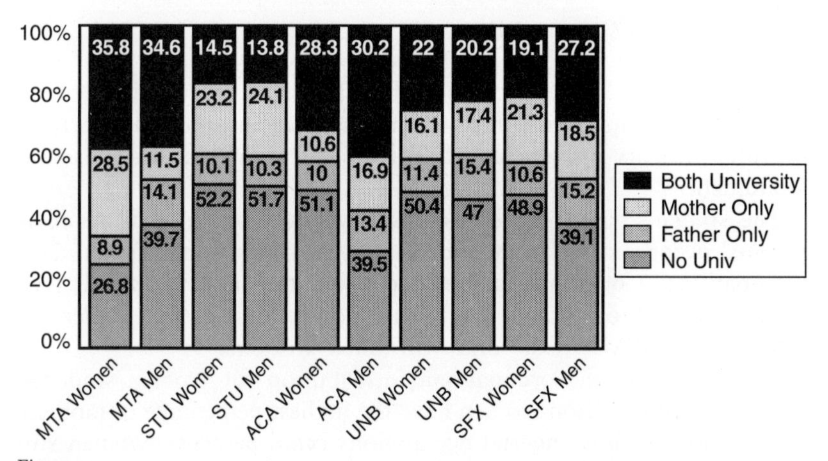

Figure 3
Parents' Combined University Attainment by Student Gender and University

stands out with the highest (and almost identical) percentages of students who have two university-educated parents, 35.8 percent for women students and 34.6 percent for men. In general, there is a great deal of consistency between men and women students at each university in the proportion of families with two parents who have attended university.

Let us look at Figure 3 in further detail. When we add down the columns, that is, look at the cumulative percentage of students with at least one parent with university education, additional patterns emerge. The primarily residential universities – Mount Allison, Acadia, and St Francis Xavier – have almost identical combined parent university attainment for men students. Men at Mount Allison, Acadia, and St Francis Xavier have families where at least one parent has some university in 60.3 percent, 60.5 percent, and 60.9 percent of the cases respectively. For women students, a different kind of consistency emerges: with the exception of Mount Allison, a similar percentage of women at all universities have at least one university educated parent. For St Thomas women, it is 48.2 percent, Acadia 48.9 percent, UNB 49.6 percent, and St Francis Xavier 51.1 percent. For Mount Allison women, the figure is much higher, at 73.2 percent. In this respect, Mount Allison women also deviate from the general tendency that can be observed in Figure 3 for men's families to have higher cumulative university attainment than women's families in each university. This Mount Allison female exceptionalism with respect to parents' education is quite dramatic and bears further investigation.[29]

In sum, although there are certainly some consistencies, our contention that universities are not all the same in terms of the social background of their students is borne out by this examination of the educational attainment of students' parents.

Parents' Occupation

In this section we extend our social-background analysis by looking at parental occupation, a factor that has been established clearly in the literature as influencing children's educational aspirations and attainment.[30]

The students' open-ended responses, when asked to indicate their parents' occupations,[31] were coded using Statistics Canada's Standard Occupational Codes and aggregated using the main census-derived categories of "Professional, Semi-Professional, Managerial," "Clerical, Sales," "Skilled Workers," and "Unskilled Workers."[32]

Table 1 shows the occupational distribution for women students' parents. Mount Allison women have the highest percentage of mothers with professional/managerial occupations (56.6 percent). Women students' mothers at the other four institutions have similar and lower values under this category, all close to 40 percent. There are negligible values for skilled and unskilled workers in all cases.

The differences between Mount Allison and the other universities shift when fathers' occupations are considered. The professional/managerial category remains high at Mount Allison (58.6 percent), but Acadia has a slightly higher value (59.3 percent). The other universities follow a similar pattern for fathers as for mothers, with professional/managerial values from 39.7 percent to 45.2 percent. Outside of the professional/managerial category, women students' fathers have a greater range of occupations than mothers. This reflects the actual range of male occupations, as opposed to the concentration of women in clerical and professional roles. The major differences among universities for fathers' occupations are that St Thomas University and UNB have higher values for skilled workers, 31 percent and 23.5 percent respectively. In sum, the professional/managerial status of parents' occupations is important for daughters, and we can see differences among universities in its distribution.

The case of male students is slightly different. Table 2 shows men students' parents' occupation. The table displays a roughly even split between professional/managerial and clerical/sales occupations for mothers. Unlike the situation for the mothers of women, specific university does not differentiate among males. Clearly, going to university is affected by mother's occupation but not by individual institution. This contrasts with same-sex influences where the particular university is important. A strong 66 percent of Mount Allison men students' fathers have professional/managerial occupations. Three other universities, Acadia, UNB, and St Francis Xavier, all have values very close to 50 percent. St Thomas is relatively low in this category

Table 1
Women Students' Parents' Occupations by University

	MTA		*STU*		*Acadia*		*UNB*		*SFX*	
	Mothers	*Fathers*	*Mothers*	*Fathers*	*Mothers*	*Fathers*	*Mothers*	*Fathers*	*Mothers*	*Fathers*
Prof/Manag	56.60	58.60	41.20	39.70	40.70	59.30	40.50	45.20	41.60	42.10
Clerical, Sales	40.60	17.20	54.90	15.50	53.80	16.00	53.30	20.90	48.50	20.60
Skilled Workers	0.90	13.80	2.00	31.00	0.70	14.80	1.40	23.50	1.00	19.00
Unskilled Workers	1.90	10.30	2.00	13.80	4.80	9.90	4.80	10.40	8.90	18.30
Total	100.00	100.00	100.00	100.00	100.00	100.00	100.00	100.00	100.00	100.00

All figures are percentages; errors are due to rounding

Table 2
Men Students' Parents' Occupations by University

	MTA		*STU*		*Acadia*		*UNB*		*SFX*	
	Mothers	*Fathers*	*Mothers*	*Fathers*	*Mothers*	*Fathers*	*Mothers*	*Fathers*	*Mothers*	*Fathers*
Prof/Manag	45.60	66.20	47.80	25.90	47.80	47.40	40.20	50.90	47.90	48.30
Clerical, Sales	49.10	17.60	47.80	40.70	44.90	20.80	56.00	22.50	50.70	21.30
Skilled Workers	0.00	6.80	0.00	18.50	0.00	16.20	1.60	20.30	0.00	15.70
Unskilled Workers	5.30	9.50	4.30	14.80	7.40	15.60	2.20	6.30	1.40	14.60
Total	100.00	100.00	100.00	100.00	100.00	100.00	100.00	100.00	100.00	100.00

All figures are percentages; errors are due to rounding

Table 3
Students' Social-Class Identity by University and Gender

	MTA		*STU*		*Acadia*		*UNB*		*SFX*	
	Women	*Men*	*Women*	*Men*	*Women*	*Men*	*Women*	*Men*	*Women*	*Men*
Upper	0.80	5.10	0.00	0.00	1.10	0.60	0.80	0.40	0.00	0.00
Upper Middle	25.00	26.60	10.00	10.30	24.70	21.20	17.50	17.50	18.70	22.80
Middle	43.50	36.70	30.00	51.70	48.10	44.10	50.20	46.60	43.90	50.00
Working	20.20	22.80	40.00	31.00	12.60	24.70	23.10	24.30	27.30	21.70
Lower	0.00	0.00	7.10	0.00	1.60	1.20	1.60	1.60	4.30	3.30
No such thing	7.30	5.10	11.40	6.90	7.70	7.10	5.20	7.70	2.90	1.10
Don't know	3.20	3.80	1.40	0.00	3.80	1.20	1.60	1.60	2.90	1.10
Total	100.00	100.00	100.00	100.00	100.00	100.00	100.00	100.00	100.00	100.00

All figures are percentages; errors are due to rounding

with 25.9 percent and a much higher proportion of fathers in clerical/sales.

Overall, parents' occupation has a great bearing on who attends university. The sons and daughters of professional/managerial and clerical/sales personnel are clearly advantaged in going to university.[33] In addition, our original contention that there are differences among universities is supported. These differences are strong for women students when both mother's and father's occupation are considered. For men, university differences show in the case of father's occupation, but not mother's.

Subjective Social-Class Identity

Social class is an important concept for the analysis of modern societies. There is much sociological debate on the precise nature of class structure and culture. In this paper we shall concentrate only on subjective class identity. In our survey we asked students, "What social class best describes your family background?" We gave the options of "upper," "upper middle," "middle," "working," "lower," "no such thing as class," and "don"t know."

There are no class-identity gender differences when we consider all of the students in the aggregate. At least middle-class identity is claimed by 66.4 percent of women and 66.6 percent of men. Subjective class differences involving gender only surface when we compare universities. Table 3 shows the results for men and women for all five universities. The greatest contrast is between Mount Allison and St Thomas. Mount Allison women have 25 percent claiming upper-middle identity as compared to 10 percent for St Thomas women. There are similar contrasts between the male populations of these two institutions. Overall, if the reader scans the pairs of figures in columns, it is apparent that women and men tend to resemble each other at the same institution. There are some notable exceptions.

St Thomas students have the highest elections for working-class identity with 40 percent for women and 31 percent for men. St Thomas women also make the highest claim to lower-class identity (7.1 percent), whereas no St Thomas men or Mount Allison students of either gender chose this identity. In addition, Acadia women have the lowest working-class identity (12.6 percent), half of the value (24.7 percent) for Acadia men. Looking at the identity profile of Acadia women in the middle and upper-middle categories, we can see a great similarity with Mount Allison women. This showed up in our other indicators discussed above.

Social-class identity tends to support the contention that universities differ in the social background of students. In general, women and men look like each other at the same institution. The main differences are between universities.

An Occupational/Educational/Identity Index

We have discussed the importance of parents' educational attainment, parents' occupation, and class identity. In this section, we shall combine these three elements to gain a more synthetic view of the nature of student social backgrounds. We have constructed three indexes. The first considers "family" background in that it blends occupational and educational characteristics of both mothers and fathers with the class-identity variable. In constructing this first index a "middle" Occupational Educational Identity (OEI) is attained if a student has at least one parent with a professional/managerial occupation, *or* at least one parent with some university education, *or* at least a middle-class identity. An "upper" OEI is attained when a student has at least one parent with a professional/managerial occupation, *and* at least one parent with some university education, *and* at least a middle-class identity. The results of this coding are displayed in Table 4.

Mount Allison women stand out from other university women with 48.8 percent in the upper OEI. No other group of women is over 40 percent for this category. The differences between Mount Allison and St Thomas women are shown clearly in the index. In addition to having the highest percentage of women in the upper OEI Mount Allison has the lowest percentage in the lower OEI (11.2 percent), while St Thomas has the lowest percentage of women in the upper OEI (16.9 percent) and the highest percentage in the lower OEI (28.2 percent).

Interuniversity differences for men are less pronounced. The percentage of men in the upper OEI at the smaller residential universities – Mount Allison, Acadia, and St Francis Xavier – is fairly constant, in the low forties. The main difference for men appears to be between these universities and St Thomas and UNB. The importance of specific university for participation and accessibility is supported, and we can see that this has some gender variation. However, this is not the final word.

In the previous sections we have shown that there is a difference between men and women in terms of the importance of fathers' versus mothers' educational attainment and occupation. In this section, we present some gender-specific indexes to explore these relationships as well.

The first gender-specific index we will discuss is a "mother-based" OEI. This index is constructed similarly to the family-based measure,

Table 4
Family-Based Occupational/Educational/Identity Index by University and Gender

	MTA		*STU*		*Acadia*		*UNB*		*SFX*	
	Women	*Men*	*Women*	*Men*	*Women*	*Men*	*Women*	*Men*	*Women*	*Men*
Upper	48.80	44.00	16.90	31.00	37.10	40.50	34.10	34.30	32.60	44.10
Middle	40.00	36.70	54.90	48.30	45.70	41.00	46.10	48.80	42.60	38.70
Lower	11.20	19.00	28.20	20.70	17.20	18.50	19.80	16.90	24.80	17.20
Total	100.00	100.00	100.00	100.00	100.00	100.00	100.00	100.00	100.00	100.00

All figures are percentages; errors are due to rounding
Upper = any parent professional/managerial occupation, plus any parent higher ed, plus at least middle identity
Middle = any parent professional/managerial occupation, or any parent higher ed, or at least middle identity
Lower = none of the above

Table 5
Mother-Based Occupational/Educational/Identity Index by University and Gender

	MTA		*STU*		*Acadia*		*UNB*		*SFX*	
	Women	*Men*	*Women*	*Men*	*Women*	*Men*	*Women*	*Men*	*Women*	*Men*
Upper	38.40	21.50	12.70	20.70	22.60	25.40	21.30	18.90	22.00	26.90
Middle	46.40	54.40	52.10	51.70	55.40	51.40	55.80	56.70	50.40	52.70
Lower	15.20	24.10	35.20	27.60	22.00	23.10	22.90	24.40	27.70	20.40
Total	100.00	100.00	100.00	100.00	100.00	100.00	100.00	100.00	100.00	100.00

All figures are percentages; errors are due to rounding
Upper = mother professional/managerial occupation, plus mother higher ed, plus at least middle identity
Middle = mother professional/managerial occupation, or mother higher ed, or at least middle identity
Lower = none of the above

Table 6
Father-Based Occupational/Educational/Identity Index by University and Gender

	MTA		*STU*		*Acadia*		*UNB*		*SFX*	
	Women	*Men*	*Women*	*Men*	*Women*	*Men*	*Women*	*Men*	*Women*	*Men*
Upper	32.00	36.70	9.90	10.30	30.10	27.70	22.90	23.60	21.30	29.00
Middle	51.20	44.30	46.50	62.10	50.00	47.40	53.10	52.00	46.80	50.50
Lower	16.80	19.00	43.70	27.60	19.90	24.90	24.00	24.40	31.90	20.40
Total	100.00	100.00	100.00	100.00	100.00	100.00	100.00	100.00	100.00	100.00

All figures are percentages; errors are due to rounding

Upper = father professional/managerial occupation, plus father higher ed, plus at least middle identity

Middle = father professional/managerial occupation, or father higher ed, or at least middle identity

Lower = none of the above

except that only the occupation and education of the mother are considered. In constructing the index, a "middle" OEI is attained when a student's mother has a professional/managerial occupation *or* at least some university education, *or* when the student has at least a middle-class identity. An "upper" OEI is attained when a student's mother has a professional/managerial occupation *and* at least some university education, *and* when the student has at least a middle-class identity. The values for this gender-specific index are lower than those for the family-based index since the social resources of only one parent are considered. The results of the coding are displayed in Table 5.

The table shows that mother's status is not important in differentiating among male university populations. A very different story applies to mothers of women. There are marked differences between Mount Allison women at the top (38.4 percent upper), Acadia, UNB, and St Francis Xavier women in the middle (22.6 percent, 21.3 percent, and 22 percent respectively), and St Thomas women at the bottom (12.7 percent).

In Table 6 the same type of calculation was done for fathers. Again, Mount Allison students come from more privileged backgrounds. Unlike the case with mothers, the same-sex influence does not seem to apply at the upper OEI category. Women and men tend to look like each other. Some difference occurs at the lower end since St Thomas and, to a lesser extent, St Francis Xavier women tend to have more fathers in the lower category than their male counterparts. In checking back with the family-based OEI, it appears that the trend for these two groups of women holds there as well; women at these institutions come from relatively disadvantaged backgrounds as compared to men.

From the above analysis we can conclude that individual university is related to accessibility. There are important differences among university student populations with respect to gender, parents' education, parents' occupation, and social-class identity. The differences hold for these factors individually as well as when they are aggregated. The social differences support the importance of individual university for the analysis of accessibility. In the next section we will connect one of these factors, parents' educational attainment, to the general population.

COMPARING STUDENTS TO THE GENERAL POPULATION

So far we have seen that student populations vary among universities. We have linked these differences to the issue of accessibility with the argument that universities with relatively privileged student populations are less accessible than other universities. However, no direct connection has been made thus far to the general population. We will now make such a connection with one of the factors discussed above, parents' educational attainment. We can do this because there is a similarity in the way we have measured educational attainment and the way it is measured in the Canadian census. Our findings reinforce the above analysis. In addition, as we consider the effects of individual university we also directly measure accessibility in relation to the general population.

We shall consider whether the differences in university populations are the result of variations in client populations. For example, if Mount Allison students have a higher educational background, maybe this is because the New Brunswick population has a higher educational background. Or perhaps women in New Brunswick have a higher educational attainment than men, and this could contribute to differences among universities. We shall explore these relevant general population differences, setting the stage for a calculation where we control for these variations in an analysis of university differences.

The Case of Parents' Educational Attainment

We have shown that students' parents at five universities in the Maritimes vary in their educational attainment. In this section we examine the relationship between university students' parents and the general population. The general population varies in its educational attainment in many ways. Some of the most important variables are age (older people have less education), gender (men have traditionally had more than women), and province (people from Ontario and the West have more than people from the Maritimes). These are the factors we shall control for in considering the differences in university populations.

Figure 4 shows the educational attainment of the New Brunswick population by age and gender as of the 1991 census. The pattern by age is clear. The older the population, the less formal education it has. There is also some minor variation between genders within each age category. We have restricted the analysis here to those thirty-five years old and up since virtually all of the parents of university students fall into this age range. Figure 5 shows the percentage of parents in each of the census age ranges. Mothers are younger than fathers. Clearly we cannot simply compare the educational attainment of students' parents to that of the general population without controlling for age.

There is yet another source of general educational-attainment variation: province of permanent residence. For example, Figure 6 shows the educational attainment for the largest age group, people of forty-five to fifty-four years in Atlantic Canada and in Canada overall. There

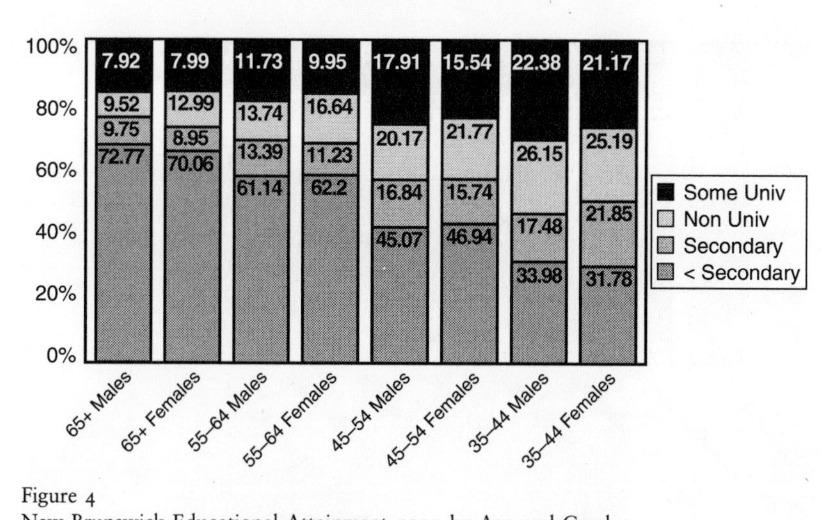

Figure 4
New Brunswick Educational Attainment 1991 by Age and Gender

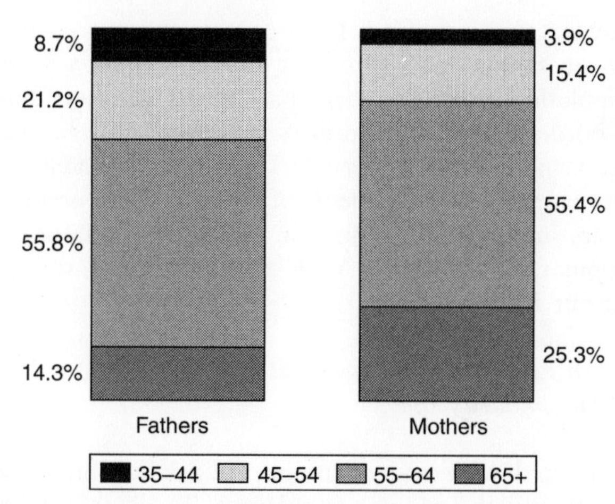

Figure 5
Age Composition of MUSS Parents by Gender of Parent

is provincial and regional variation. Atlantic Canada has a lower formal education-attainment rate than other parts of Canada. Within Atlantic Canada, Nova Scotia has the highest rate of educational attainment. This variation is important for our analysis since the students at the five universities come from different provinces and regions, so that variation in the educational attainment of parents may reflect provincial or regional origin.

Table 7 shows this variation in provincial origin for the five universities as indicated by our respondents. Both Mount Allison and St

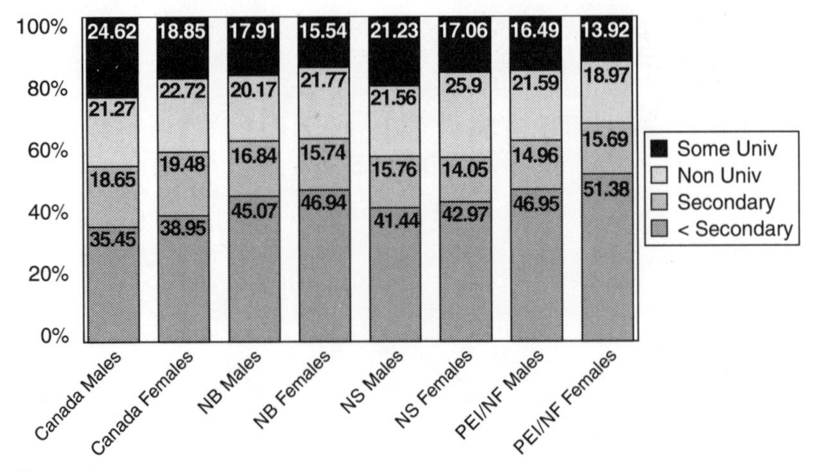

Figure 6
Atlantic Educational Attainment, 45 to 54 Year Age Range, 1991 Census, by Gender

Francis Xavier recruit students from outside the region. In addition, Mount Allison stands out for its New Brunswick/Nova Scotia split in student-population origins, due in part to its location close to the provincial border. For the purposes of this display we have amalgamated "other Canada" and "PEI/NF." The "other Canada" category is almost entirely made up of residents of Ontario and Quebec. It is clear that there are important variations in educational attainment for the general population whom we wish to compare to the parents of students at our five universities.

An Educational-Attainment Dissimilarity Index

We are still faced with understanding the relationship between students' parents and the general population. To do this we have constructed an index to take into account the variations in educational attainment outlined above and control for provincial origin, gender, and age.[34] Table 8 shows the steps in the construction of this index. We shall discuss these steps in some detail so as to reveal the logic and the method behind our approach.

We have created a general comparison population based on the 1991 census structured on the same age, gender, and provincial basis as MUSS population parents. We have taken the general population and looked at its educational attainment, but we have weighted this population to follow the age and provincial-origin characteristics of the

Table 7
Location of Permanent Residence by Gender and University

	MTA		*STU*		*Acadia*		*UNB*		*SFX*	
	Women	*Men*	*Women*	*Men*	*Women*	*Men*	*Women*	*Men*	*Women*	*Men*
PEI/NF	12.1	5.1	9.9	0.0	13.0	6.9	4.3	7.5	9.9	10.9
NS	33.1	28.2	2.8	6.9	64.1	67.6	5.4	5.5	68.1	60.9
NB	37.1	38.5	87.3	89.7	11.4	4.6	83.3	72.8	5.0	5.4
Other Canada	14.5	24.4	0.0	0.0	4.3	12.1	5.4	7.9	15.6	19.6
Outside Canada	3.2	3.8	0.0	3.4	7.1	8.7	1.6	6.3	1.4	3.3
Total	100.00	100.00	100.00	100.00	100.00	100.00	100.00	100.00	100.00	100.00

All figures are percentages; errors are due to rounding

Table 8
Census Mothers and MUSS Mothers Dissimilarity Index

	NB 35+ Women	*MUSS Census Mothers*	*5 Univ (n=1392)*	*Dissimilarity (MUSS Mothers – MUSS Census Mothers)*
Some Univ	14.41	17.71	42.7	24.99
Non Univ	19.64	22.9	19.3	–3.6
Secondary	15.15	16.48	18.8	2.32
< Secondary	50.77	42.9	19.3	–23.6
			Index	54.5

survey populations. We start off doing this for our survey population overall, and in the analysis below we do it for each of the institutions in our survey.

Table 8 shows the main steps in the calculation. The first column shows the educational attainment of the New Brunswick female population in 1991 that is thirty-five years of age or older. The second column shows the educational attainment of the general population structured in terms of the age profile and provincial origin of the MUSS mothers group as a whole. This comparison group for MUSS mothers, which we call MUSS Census Mothers, would have 17.71 percent with some university education, as opposed to the 14.41 percent for New Brunswick females in the 1991 census. The higher "university" value in this case comes from the fact that university students' mothers are younger than the general population over thirty-five, and the provincial origin of MUSS students is broader than New Brunswick, which has relatively low post-secondary educational attainment. The third column is the actual educational distribution of MUSS mothers.

The effect of this weighting exercise is to compensate for spurious demographic differences. Doing this has the effect of minimizing the dissimilarity among universities. If there is a systematic error here, it would be to understate university differences.

The Dissimilarity Index calculation is done by subtracting the MUSS census mothers' educational distribution from the actual distribution.[35] In the far right column, the value is the number of percentage points of difference. This will be a positive or negative value, reflecting whether the actual population "overrepresents" or "underrepresents" the comparison group.

The bottom of the right column has a summary index number, the Dissimilarity Index. This value is the sum of the absolute value of the differences, whether positive or negative. No differences would result

Table 9
Mount Allison Women's Mothers, Calculating Dissimilarity

	MUSS *Census Mothers*	MtA *Census Mothers*	MtA *Mothers*	*Dissimilarity (MtA – MtA Census Mothers)*
Some Univ	16.98	18.75	63.70	44.95
Non Univ	22.43	23.58	13.70	−9.88
Secondary	16.01	17.11	12.10	−5.01
< Secondary	44.27	40.56	10.50	−30.06
Summary Index				89.90

Differences are calculed using the age and provincial-origin census population weighted to mothers' ages, and provincial origin for Mount Allison women

in a zero, while the greatest Dissimilarity Index value would be 100. In the case of all MUSS students' mothers, the score is 54.5.

It is important to note a general pattern that is apparent in Table 8. The mothers of university students with "secondary" and "post-secondary non-university" training themselves closely represent the distribution of adults in the general population: the differences are only −3.6 and 2.32. The dissimilarity comes at the extremes, i.e., in the "less than secondary" and "university" categories. University education is highly oversubscribed by families with mothers with university backgrounds and considerably undersubscribed by families with mothers with less than secondary education.

Since we are interested not only in the general differences between student families and the population at large but also in the differences among universities, we have refined the analysis to create comparison populations for each relevant combination of university, gender of student, and gender of parent. A detailed example of these calculations is revealed in Table 9, where the case of Mount Allison women's mothers is shown. The first column shows MUSS census mothers for women students at Mount Allison. The second column shows the Mount Allison women's census mother distribution. Since Mount Allison mothers are younger than other university mothers, and since Mount Allison recruits more students from Ontario than the other institutions, the Mount Allison census-mothers reference population has an overall higher educational attainment than MUSS census mothers. Using this adjusted reference census population, Mount Allison women's mothers end up with a Dissimilarity Index of 89.9. This is the highest of all of the specific index calculations.[36]

Our method gives us a firm measure of the difference between student families and the general population. Clearly all family educa-

Table 10
Women's Mothers' Educational Attainment, Dissimilarity Index by University

	5 Univ	MTA	STU	*Acadia*	UNB	SFX
Some Univ	25.07	44.95	19.69	20.05	22.39	22.12
Non Univ	–1.84	–9.88	–8.04	2.73	2.92	–5.25
Secondary	–0.13	–5.01	5.34	–1.97	1.65	1.43
< Secondary	–23.00	–30.06	–17.08	–20.81	–23.47	–18.30
Summary Index	50.04	89.90	50.15	45.56	50.42	49.61

Table 11
Men's Fathers' Educational Attainment, Dissimilarity Index by University

	5 Univ	MTA	STU	*Acadia*	UNB	SFX
Some Univ	21.99	30.07	8.08	24.53	19.08	23.11
Non Univ	0.95	–5.99	13.04	–4.30	5.95	–0.48
Secondary	–0.29	1.97	–4.83	–1.50	1.22	–2.65
< Secondary	–22.63	–26.09	–16.27	–18.72	–26.17	–19.99
Summary Index	45.86	64.12	42.22	49.04	52.42	46.23

tional backgrounds are represented, but some are more represented than others. As we shall show, Mount Allison recruits from a more highly educated social base than the other institutions. In the remaining tables on dissimilarity, only the dissimilarity figures and summary indexes will be displayed.

Now we can broaden the use of the Dissimilarity Index to compare students at the five universities. Tables 10 and 11 display the patterns for women students' mothers and men students' fathers. In both cases, we can see that very little of the divergence from the educational attainment of the general population comes in the middle educational ranges. The ends of the educational-attainment spectrum, the some-university and the less-than-secondary categories, account for virtually all of the dissimilarity, 49.07 of the 50.04 for women's mothers overall, and 44.62 of the 45.86 for men's fathers overall. Differences among universities persist. Mount Allison students' same-sex parents are the most dissimilar from the general population, with a particularly dramatic situation for women's mothers. This is solid evidence of inequality in the student populations among universities and of the lack of opportunity in relation to Mount Allison in particular.

Our final table in this series on dissimilarity, Table 12, displays a summary of all of the gender and university combinations. Mount Allison parents have the highest Dissimilarity Index scores on three of the four possibilities. The exception is the case of men's mothers, where

Table 12
Dissimilarity Index by University and Gender

	5 Univ	MTA	STU	*Acadia*	UNB	SFX
Women's Mothers	50.04	89.90	50.15	45.56	50.42	49.61
Women's Fathers	41.72	53.92	28.00	49.23	43.76	25.91
Men's Mothers	60.54	58.61	44.10	63.04	60.27	25.50
Men's Fathers	45.86	64.12	42.22	49.04	52.42	46.23
Average Index	49.54	66.64	41.12	51.72	51.72	36.81

Mount Allison, at 58.61, is slightly under the Acadia (63.04) and UNB (60.27) index scores. We have displayed an overall average Dissimilarity Index for each institution. Here again Mount Allison, with a score of 66.64, is clearly the most dissimilar from its reference population. The least dissimilar are St Thomas and St Francis Xavier.

Such a table raises questions about the influence of parents' gender and educational attainment on student participation beyond the consideration of this analysis of university differences in accessibility. These data show a marked effect for same-sex influence on student enrolment in university, and generally a greater importance of mothers' educational attainment for both male and female students.

CONCLUSIONS

Our analysis has been limited to a few key social factors. We have not examined motivations, finances, ethnicity, religion, rural/urban differences, or other possibly important social contingencies in this paper. These other dimensions will have to await subsequent analysis. However, our inquiry has revealed clear and significant patterns.

Mount Allison University is not as accessible as the other four institutions in this study. Students at Mount Allison, especially women, come from more advantaged social backgrounds. Both this gender dimension to inequality and the extent of the interuniversity differences are quite striking.

At this point in our research, we are unable to identify the forces contributing to the apparently distinctive composition of the Mount Allison student body. However, in subsequent articles we shall be investigating such possible influences as Mount Allison's higher tuition and residence fees, its escalating academic reputation, and its relatively high academic admission standards.

At the beginning of this paper we discussed the history of the concept of academic excellence at Mount Allison and its relationship to accessibility. At the level of public pronouncements we have seen a shift from accessibility to excellence over the last hundred years, although these two goals have not been explicitly joined as a trade off in public debate. We cannot say, from the information we have presented, whether Mount Allison is more or less accessible or excellent now than before. We can say that Mount Allison is less accessible today than the other institutions in the study. We do not know whether the education at Mount Allison is more excellent than the education at these or other institutions. We can say that Mount Allison promotes itself as, and enjoys the popular reputation of, an institution that offers a superior education.

If the quality of education, or the value of a degree, varies among institutions, then the question of accessibility must be conceived in relation to these real and perceived institutional inequalities. Beyond the individual situation of Mount Allison it is clear that particular universities are important for the consideration of the general issues of accessibility and social inequality. Overall, gender, education of parents, occupation of parents, and social-class identity affect university participation. However, we have demonstrated in this paper that these factors are mediated by the particular university. This has significant implications for the study of education and social inequality.

NOTES

1 Two examples are John Porter, *The Vertical Mosaic: An Analysis of Social Class and Power in Canada* (Toronto: University of Toronto Press, 1965), and Marion Porter and Gilles Jasmin, *A Profile of Post-Secondary Students in Canada. The 1983–1984 National Post-Secondary Student Survey: Summary National Data* (Ottawa: Secretary of State Canada, 1987).

2 The individual university that a student attended was actually coded in the national surveys, although the names of particular institutions are protected in the data sets. We intend to use these data in a later analysis. As far as we know, this aspect of the national data has never been analyzed.

3 This has been argued very effectively with respect to Canadian universities in Paul Axelrod, *Making a Middle Class: Student Life in English Canada during the Thirties* (Montreal: McGill-Queen's Press, 1990).

4 See, for example, Harry Hiller, *Canadian Society: A Macro Analysis*, 2d ed. (Scarborough: Prentice-Hall, 1991), 83; Lucie Nobert, *Profile of Higher Education in Canada* (Ottawa: Secretary of State Canada, 1991), 27–8; National Council of Welfare, *Funding Health and Higher Education: Danger Looming* (Ottawa: Supply and Services Canada, 1991), 8; and Neil Guppy and A. Bruce Arai, "Who Benefits from

Higher Education? Differences by Sex, Social Class, and Ethnic Background," in James Curtis et al., *Social Inequality in Canada: Patterns, Problems, Policies* (Scarborough: Prentice-Hall, 1993), 221.

5 "Human capital theory" typically stresses the net benefits of wider and increased access to higher education for both the individual and society, or, as the economists put it, its private and public returns on investment. See, for example, Gary S. Becker, *Human Capital* (Chicago: University of Chicago Press, 1964); P. Bourdieu, "The Forms of Capital," in *Handbook of Theory and Research in the Sociology of Education*, edited by J.C. Richardson (New York: Greenwood Press, 1986); J.S. Coleman, "Social Capital in the Creation of Human Capital," *American Journal of Sociology* 94 (supplement): S95-S120; Clark Kerr et al., *Industrialism and Industrial Man* (New York: Oxford University Press, 1964), 18; and Keith Newton et al., *Education and Training in Canada* (Ottawa: Economic Council of Canada, 1992), 1–6.

6 Ivar E. Berg, *Education and Jobs* (New York: Praeger, 1970); Randall Collins, *The Credential Society: An Historical Sociology of Education* (New York: Academic Press, 1979).

7 John G. Reid, "The Excellence Debate and the Invention of Tradition at Mount Allison: A Case Study in the Generation of Mythology at a Canadian University," *Dalhousie Review* 69, no. 2 (1989): 190.

8 All of these themes emerged in the course of the so-called "Excellence Debate." See Mount Allison Faculty Association, *The Idea of Excellence at Mount Allison: A Study Prepared by the Committee on Excellence* (1962), and I.L. Campbell et al., eds., *Comment on the Idea of Excellence at Mount Allison* (1963).

9 John G. Reid, *Mount Allison University: A History to 1963. Vol. I: 1843–1914* (Toronto: University of Toronto Press, 1984), 83. The editorial in question first appeared in the *Provincial Wesleyan* and was subsequently reprinted in the *Mount Allison University Gazette.*

10 Ibid., 140–1. Reid, the chronicler of Mount Allison's institutional history, has further observed that "Allison's statements carried the undertone that it was questionable whether this professed openness of access which ... had been proclaimed from the beginning, was being maintained in practice at the college" (ibid., 141).

11 Ibid., 230.

12 Ibid.

13 John G. Reid, *Mount Allison University: A History to 1963. Vol. II: 1914–1963* (Toronto: University of Toronto Press, 1984), 60.

14 Margaret Norrie, *George Johnston Trueman.* BA thesis (Mount Allison University, 1954), 49.

15 Reid, "The Excellence Debate"; Mount Allison Faculty Association, *Excellence*; and I.L. Campbell et al., *Comment.*

16 Cited in Reid, "The Excellence Debate," 202, emphasis added.
17 Mount Allison University admissions brochure, 1992.
18 Ibid.
19 Ibid.
20 Mount Allison University, *Universitas: The Campaign for Mount Allison*, 1987, n.p.
21 Mount Allison University, *Universitas: The Campaign for Mount Allison. Case for Support*, 1987, 13.
22 Maritime Provinces Higher Education Commission, *Role and Planned Capacity Report No. 2: New Brunswick and Prince Edward Island Universities and General Regional Recommendations*, November 1993, 45.
23 For example, Paul Anisef et al., *Is the Die Cast? Educational Achievements and Work Destinations of Ontario Youth* (Toronto: Ministry of Education/Ministry of Colleges and Universities, 1980); Marion Porter et al., *Stations and Callings: Making It Through the School System* (Toronto: Methuen, 1982); and Dianne Looker, "Active Capital: The Impact of Parents on Youths' Educational Performance and Plans," in *Sociology of Education in Canada: Critical Perspectives on Theory, Research and Practice*, eds. Lorna Erwin and David MacLennan (Toronto: Copp Clark Longman, 1994).
24 For example, Neil Guppy et al., "Changing Patterns of Educational Inequality" in James Curtis et al., *Social Inequality in Canada*, 155–62, and Neil Guppy and A. Bruce Arai, "Who Benefits."
25 For example, Porter, *The Vertical Mosaic*, and Porter and Jasmin, *A Profile*.
26 For documentation on these surveys see Porter and Jasmin, *A Profile*.
27 We provide one example from each type of literature distinguished: Looker, "Active Capital," 169–72; Guppy and Arai, "Who Benefits," 222; and Porter, *The Vertical Mosaic*, 189.
28 See Neil Guppy and Krishna Pendakur, "The Effects of Gender and Parental Education within Post-Secondary Education in the 1970s and 1980s," *Canadian Journal of Higher Education* 19, no. 1 (1989): 49–62; Sid Gilbert and Neil Guppy, "Trends in Participation in Higher Education by Gender," in James Curtis et al., *Social Inequality in Canada*, 163–9; Alexander D. Gregor and Gilles Jasmin, *Higher Education in Canada* (Ottawa: Secretary of State Canada, 1992), 43–7; and Guppy and Arai, "Who Benefits."
29 Careful examination of Figure 3 reveals quite similar percentages of Mount Allison women and St Thomas women with mothers who are the only parents with university education (28.5 percent and 23.3 percent, respectively). This seeming similarity in parental background is more apparent than real. St Thomas students, and St Thomas women in particular, are considerably poorer than Mount Allison students. There

is a real difference between well-educated affluent mothers and well-educated poor mothers, a difference that one must be careful not to lose sight of when examining parental educational attainment. On the other hand, the finding of fairly close percentages for both parents having university education for female Mount Allison and Acadia students is meaningful, because of their also having fairly similar SES (socio economic status) backgrounds. We attend to some implications of such differences and similarities below.

30 Again, we provide an example from each type of literature: Porter et al., *Stations and Callings*, 57–61, 289–90; Guppy and Arai, "Who Benefits," 223–4; and Porter, *The Vertical Mosaic*, 183–91.

31 We did this both for the previous year (1991) and for each parent's "main occupation" in "adult life." In this paper we will discuss this longer-term view of the occupation of parents. One of the reasons for choosing to go with this measure is that it might be more sensitive to the occupational histories of women, who are more likely to interrupt their careers.

32 This is the same classification scheme used by Porter and Jasmin in their analysis of the 1983–84 post-secondary student survey.

33 We intend to engage in a detailed analysis of parents' occupation to establish the extent of this overrepresentation. This will appear in another paper.

34 We have been led to the notion of creating for each institution indexes of dissimilarity for parental educational attainment, having encountered the indexes of occupational dissimilarity for various ethnic groups in Canada at different times reported in E. Hugh Lautard and Donald J. Loree, "Ethnic Stratification in Canada, 1931–1971," *Canadian Journal of Sociology* 9, no. 3 (1984): 333–43. Lautard and Loree's analysis was a refinement of an earlier attempt by Darroch to develop a more sophisticated approach to what John Porter had called "over-representation" and "under-representation": see A. Gordon Darroch, "Another Look at Ethnicity, Stratification and Social Mobility in Canada," *Canadian Journal of Sociology* 4, no. 1 (1979): 1–25.

35 Since the survey was conducted in 1992, parents have been made younger by one year so that they can be compared directly to the 1991 census population.

36 Although this calculation shows a great dissimilarity between Mount Allison women's mothers and the general population, there is still a slight understatement as a result of the way we have computed the differences. The age structure used for comparing the population of university mothers to women overall does not take into account the interaction effects between age and province of origin. In the case of Mount Allison, mothers from Ontario are older than other mothers, but we used the younger average-age structure for Mount Allison in constructing

the index. If we had controlled for age by province of origin, we would have been comparing Mount Allison mothers from Ontario to an older, and thus less well educated, general Ontario population. This would have created an even greater dissimilarity-index value. We decided not to make this age adjustment by province since the small population fractions for many of the out-of-province student populations at the five universities would have made some of these age calculations suspect. As it happens, where we do have large fractions, as in the Mount Allison Ontario situation, we can actually see a strengthening of the university-differences argument we have made in this paper.

PART THREE

Science and Culture in Liberal Education: Historical Studies

CHAPTER FIVE

Science within the Liberal Arts: Mount Allison and the Maritime Universities

PAUL A. BOGAARD

Including science within the curriculum of the liberal arts has long been a challenge that requires some form of accommodation. As the character and demands of science have evolved the challenges have multiplied. A series of challenges and accommodations is evident in the adaptation of the liberal arts within Canadian universities, and this evolution will be elucidated in this paper through the particular case of Mount Allison University within its Maritime setting.

The colloquial usage of "arts and science" so common in our own day begs the question what place the sciences were thought to have within the liberal arts curriculum of our early colleges. Which sciences were expected to play a part? How was the study of science thought to contribute to the ideals of a liberal arts education, in these early- to mid-nineteenth-century institutions of higher learning?

Whatever image of science helped to resolve these initial questions, it could not have continued to do so for long. Through the second half of the nineteenth century the image of science was transformed, both by its subdivision into different fields and, especially, by the utility it demonstrated in an increasing number of technological applications. The role of science within our institutions of higher education was transformed in the process. As Laurence Versey proclaimed, "The closing years of the nineteenth century brought about the most sweeping transformation of American higher education ever thus far to occur."[1]

I shall attempt to isolate the impetus given to this transformation by changes in science, as evidenced by the accommodations that appear in the curriculum at Mount Allison and other Maritime universities. This process will be mapped out in two steps, the first showing a series of accommodations that arose in the last decades of the nineteenth century, and the second showing the final accomodation Mount Allison shared with most other universities just before and after World War I. I will describe Mount Allison's response to both the early changes in science and the way a continuing role for the multiple sciences within a liberal-arts institution was finally secured, but we must begin by setting the background against which these changes unfolded.

In their collection of essays on *Youth, University and Canadian Society*, Axelrod and Reid emphasized the conspicuous change from 1871, when the eight Maritime colleges shared a total of 286 students, to 1971 when tens of thousands of students attended the same institutions.[2] Though this paper focuses on curricular matters, it is nevertheless important to realize that only two dozen students attended Mount Allison in the 1860s. The same numbers were found at King's (still at Windsor), St Francis Xavier, and St Mary's, while Acadia and the University of New Brunswick (UNB) had somewhat more and Dalhousie more than twice that number.

By the years leading into World War I student numbers had grown by a multiple of five to over one thousand in Maritime universities.[3] But there are two important comparisons to be noted. The first, as observed by Axelrod and Reid, is that this accounts only for arts and sciences students at what we have come to call the undergraduate level. Graduate programs were as yet small, while other professional programs (in medicine, law, and engineering) had grown so dramatically in the preceding two decades that less than half the total student numbers in Canada were in arts and science.

The second point to note is that in the decades after World War I total student numbers ballooned not just by a multiple of five but by almost twenty-five. So the growth that was conspicuous throughout this hundred-year period was especially dramatic after World War I. The growth in student numbers during the nineteenth century was significant but not dramatic.

To characterize the liberal arts being taught to these Maritime students, we will turn next to the professors carrying this student load. We will find that the rate of growth in the professoriate was even slower in the nineteenth century than for students, and that it picked up by turn of the century but grew more rapidly only after World War I.

In the 1860s Mount Allison had one professor devoted to teaching science, one for mathematics, and three others. This total had varied from four to six professors through the preceding twenty years, when Mount Allison was still an "academy." At every other Maritime college during the middle decades of the nineteenth century the picture was the same. The number of professors totalled from four to six, and there was at least one devoted to teaching science (or sometimes two where one of these also carried the responsibility for math). The same was true for Victoria and Queen's colleges, for example, in Upper Canada.[4]

By the 1880s Mount Allison still had one professor of science in a faculty of five. So did all the other institutions in the Maritimes except Dalhousie, which by this stage had double that number of professors. By 1900 Mount Allison had also doubled its staff to ten, as had St Francis and Acadia, with Dalhousie again at twice the number. By World War I these numbers of professors had increased further, but only marginally. What was new was the addition of staff members specifically to teach engineering, though they were not listed as part of the faculty of arts and science. In fact there were typically as many engineers as there were professors of science, at least two or three at every institution.

As such, this provides only a sketch of student and professor numbers, but two points are already evident. One is the clear implication that the transformation Veysey said was so sweeping did not come simply by growth, which was modest to this stage. But once the transformation had taken place, it was apparently carried along by accelerating growth in the numbers of both students and professors. The other implication is that by World War I no Maritime university had enough science professors to devote one to each scientific field. The departmental structure with which we are now familiar was not yet in place; nor, therefore, was the structured curriculum we have come to expect. The role of growth, it would seem, was secondary to the changes in science itself and in the role science played in a liberal education. We will now turn back to examine these changes.

The Mount Allison University Archives still hold a single handwritten sheet announcing a series of public lectures to be given by the then principal, the Reverend Humphrey Pickard.[5] The date is 1851 and the topic is "natural philosophy." The individual lectures on pneumatics, hydrostatics, electricity and magnetism, and celestial mechanics are all representative of what we would call Newtonian physics. But in the mid-nineteenth century the common designation remained what Newton himself had entitled: The Mathematical Principles of Natural Philosophy.

Only rudimentary portions of these topics would have been taught within what was then called the Mount Allison Wesleyan Academy, but these public lectures are a glimpse of what Pickard wanted to teach at a full degree-granting college. A wide-ranging public debate grew out of the concerns of that decade to upgrade Mount Allison by provincial act. These concerns were not limited to Mount Allison. The King's College then in Fredericton was barely surviving its own struggles. Dalhousie actually closed for many years until political and financial support secured its reopening in 1863. By the time Dalhousie reopened, the King's in Fredericton had just been re-established as the University of New Brunswick and Mount Allison joined the two as a full partner in Maritime higher education.

John Reid's careful account of these years includes excerpts from a series of *Provincial Wesleyan* editorials, among them this plea (presumably from Humphrey Pickard himself):

> It might be *desirable* that vast collections of objects in all departments of Natural Science should be accumulated at Sackville; that magnificent and costly Chemical, Philosophical and Astronomical apparatus should be procured; and that a lofty, cloud-piercing observatory should be reared, whence young Newtons and Herschels might watch the unrolling of the Celestial mysteries. But what is *needful* to begin with is, a sufficient number of natural objects, and a sufficiently extensive apparatus to illustrate the leading principles of the several departments of Natural Science; an introduction to which is all that can be attempted in a College course, without substituting certain easy flash studies, included in the inductive Sciences which are feeble developers of mind, for the difficult, deductive Sciences which are mind educators of the highest class.[6]

Since the curriculum of the early Mount Allison Wesleyan College reflects precisely the intent expressed here editorially, we have an answer to the initial challenge: science within the liberal arts at Mount Allison is meant to centre on the deductive natural philosophy of Newton, not the inductive work of natural history.[7] This was not because of the practical utility of Newtonian science, little of which was apparent yet in the 1850s, but because Newtonian science was the better developer of young minds. It was an opportunity to appreciate the truth of divine creation in terms of its first principles as expressed in mathematical terms. The geological, botanical, and zoological information of natural history might have been useful outside the halls of higher learning, but inside these new institutions they were still considered "feeble developers of mind."[8]

Mathematics, especially as required to demonstrate the foundation of Newtonian principles in celestial mechanics and various terrestrial applications, was a hallmark, therefore, of any respectable offering of the liberal arts. Far from being unwelcome novitiates, mathematics and Newtonian science were full members of the liberal arts guild. More than in the philosophy of mind or morals, more than in classical literature, students could obtain in these subjects a direct glimpse of the harmony and beauty of the world through firm deductive truth.

There was nothing new in this attitude. Math and astronomy had traditionally been features of the "quadrivium," which had already been melded into "natural philosophy" by the time Newton secured his mechanical laws of motion at the end of the seventeenth century. Natural philosophy rapidly gained ascendency during the Enlightenment, so that wherever new institutions of higher learning sprang up in North America – whether in the colonies to the south, in the catholic colleges of Quebec and New Brunswick, or in the new Anglican institutions that spread to Canada beginning in the 1780s – they had in common a secure place for math and natural philosophy.

Certainly by the mid-1800s, every institution that had but one professor of science was determined that priority be given to natural philosophy and the mathematical skills that made its appreciation possible. Where there was a second professor of science, as at the University of New Brunswick, natural history or some portions of it might also be taught, but the more common ploy, as at Dalhousie, was that second place be given to chemistry.[9] By the 1860s chemistry had promised some practical benefits to agriculture, the synthesizing of various materials, and, as ever, to medicine. But, after natural philosophy, chemistry also could claim greater theoretical respectability than any of the more inductive Baconian sciences.

In his recent study of Ontario universities, A.B. McKillop points to another product of this remarkably uniform attitude towards the liberal arts curriculum: "In spite of differences of emphasis because of denominational affiliation and ecclesiastical tradition – and they were not unimportant – programs of study nevertheless bore a general similarity of structure and intention. As a result, there existed in the two decades before 1860 within each institution a liberal arts curriculum that admitted no optional subjects."[10] Classical languages, as the tools necessary for exposure to a wide range of classical literature, were invariably a part of this structure. Modern languages and literature may have been available at some institutions – French typically was taught at Mount Allison[11] – but the other anchor of the curriculum was philosophy. In their later years students would delve into mental and moral philosophy. While theology was usually taught separately to those specifically interested in the ministry, a general course in the "evidences of Christianity" was a common capstone required of everyone.

As McKillop notes, there were no optional subjects. The liberal arts education of this era was not characterized by student choice. For the most part the student had to take every subject listed, and in most cases each student would take each subject in each successive year.

Moreover, the range of subjects taught at different institutions was remarkably uniform. There were no separate "courses" as we might understand them, and at least part of the reason for this was scale of operation. There were as yet too few students at any one level, and too few professors to do more than ensure that all required subjects were covered at their appropriate year level. In carrying out these widely shared expectations, professors "aimed to provide their students with the indelible mark of culture."[12]

In Canada variation began to emerge in this common curricular structure after Confederation. In the United States there was a more dramatic development after the Civil War with the establishment of "land-grant" institutions, which had explicit utilitarian intentions. The result was not only in expanded curricula but an institutional structure that was both much larger and more diverse. As has often been argued, the land-grant colleges were in many respects the beginning of the modern university.

Little of this is visible in Maritime institutions. Dalhousie, with the advantage of having Halifax as its base and substantial private funding, stepped decisively into the lead. The pressures for change, however, came less from growth than from changes inherent within the sciences. This required of all the Maritime universities a new set of accommodations.

In Ontario, as McKillop observes, "the sciences were among the liberal arts. A major shift in the academic approach to the sciences began to take place, however, in the years between 1850 and 1880. The result was that reverential science faced evolutionary theories and intellect and emotion stood in uneasy equipoise."[13] I have argued elsewhere that McKillop seems only to see half the picture.[14] The attention Darwin brought to evolutionary theory is well known to have unsettled the easy alliance of Newtonian natural philosophy and natural theology (what McKillop refers to here as "reverential science") during this period, but there are just as substantial changes taking place within the physical sciences themselves.

The utility of Newtonian science became increasingly apparent with experimental and theoretical advances such as electromagnetism, which sparked first telegraph and then telephone, electric lights and the dynamos to energize them. With its loss of non-utilitarian purity, the science of Newton was becoming less a subject simply for training the mind, like Latin, and more the foundation for practical knowledge. Like chemistry before it, this shift in intention called for a style of teaching that moved from demonstration at a distance to experimentation. It required laboratories in which professors could practise science as well as teach it, and in which students could try their own hand.

By 1880, the science professor at Mount Allison was explaining the advantages of chemistry to the farmers of the region; by the end of the decade there were labs, and the chair in natural phisolophy had been replaced by a chair in chemistry and experimental physics. At Dalhousie change had been entrenched in the mid-1870s with the appointment of the first professor of experimental physics. In the same decade the professor of chemistry at Acadia actively involved his students in mineralogical analysis, and the same method was used at King's to attract students who were interested in careers in mining.

Application and career preparation, rather than the "indelible mark of culture," were the new motivations. The 1890s saw the emergence of a wide range of schools for manual training, applied science, and various branches of engineering that challenged the liberal arts tradition of the Maritime institutions – itself an accomodation only a few decades old.

The transformation of the physical sciences had at least as great an impact as the Darwinian revolution in the biological sciences. While this, too, led to substantial changes in how we understand our place in this world and how we pursue science; in key respects the shift in the biological sciences was the opposite of that in the physical sciences. Whereas botany and zoology, and geology too, had traditionally been treated as Baconian sciences whose considerable utility set them apart from the core motives of a liberal arts education,[15] Darwin now focused attention on the theoretical underpinnings of these fields. By the last two decades of the nineteenth century, microscopic work at the cellular level had advanced sufficiently to lead these fields rapidly to their common base in genetics.

The result was rapid growth in the biological sciences within the bigger institutions; even the smaller Maritime universities saw the establishment of chairs in botany, zoology, and eventually biology. The theoretical aspect of the physical sciences that had won them pride of place within the common college curriculum was now fleshed out by experimentation and application within the newly styled universities. The life sciences, or what was once called "natural history", had always been considered useful. But now they were rapidly gaining theoretical respectability and with it, a place in university faculties.

What forms of accommodation did this force upon maritime institutions? At Mount Allison we can mark at least four stages of accomodation, beginning with the introduction of a separate Bachelor of Science degree as early as the 1860s.[16] Mount Allison was not alone in this. UNB introduced its BSc degree by 1870 and Dalhousie soon thereafter. The interesting feature of these early science degrees is that they demanded no more in the way of science than the Bachelor of

Arts. What is more, students could achieve the degree without first passing the usual matriculation and course requirements in Greek and Latin. The BA, which retained as much science as the new degree, remained the preferred degree and after some years the new, less-respected degrees disappeared from their respective calendars. In retrospect, however, they can be seen as an early signal that a curriculum centred on the past was destined to give way to a more "progressive" orientation that looked to improvements in the future.

By the 1880s another stage of accommodation had manifested itself at Mount Allison in the form of the honours degree,[17] already a feature at other Canadian universities. Most students completed a general BA degree, with comparatively little choice, or only slightly more choice in the advanced years than previous generations had enjoyed. But one choice now provided was a more specialized sequence of courses in the advanced years in one selected area. These included physics, math, and chemistry as early options at Mount Allison along with non-science selections. It meant the first years of university education remained much as they had been, with choice towards specialization made available in the latter years.

This was structurally possible since roughly the same number of professors found themselves teaching more students and offering not just the year-level class in a few subjects but "courses" to cover an expanding number of fields. By the 1880s there was also a new generation of professors with more specialized training of their own (a few even had PHDs) struggling to find ways to bring these more specialized expectations into the classroom. Liberal arts remained, no doubt, a common objective, but only as it could be accommodated to the specialization that was sweeping through science.[18]

More specific to the sciences was a third means of accommodation, the special schools of applied science and engineering that arose in the 1890s and into the early years of the new century. These applied schools opened the door to substantial numbers of instructors (again, even in the smaller institutions, as many as there were science professors) and substantially new subject matter. The impact on the liberal arts curriculum was limited, nevertheless, insofar as these were established not as new fields or even new departments but as "schools" that offered their own certificates and were separate from the regular undergraduate programs.

One further accomodation dealt a more direct blow to the status of the liberal arts. Comparatively modest increases in the number of professors and somewhat greater increases in the number of courses finally enabled the sciences to offer their own degree program. This new BA/BSc split was the one we now take for granted. The offer of degree programs in the sciences was dependent upon sufficient resources to mount it, and in the Maritimes Dalhousie and UNB were the first, upgrading their earlier attempts before the turn of the century, while Acadia, St Francis, and Mount Allison followed in the years after the turn of the century.

At some of these institutions the science degree remained similar to the BA during the first two years of the program, offering more exclusive attention to the sciences in the later years. Still, it was plain that the program had dropped any pretence of being a liberal arts program in its own right. It was motivated by the new possibilities opening up for students who had a stronger background in science, and it eventually proved to be the obvious preparation for the newly opening graduate schools. In Canada graduate programs remained modest until after World War I, but as they began to expand, they increased the success of the BSc programs.[18A] Nevertheless, in the first instance the new Maritime BSc retained much of the first half of a liberal arts program and even in the advanced years required a rather broad range of science to complete the degree.

In the United States the same pressures were evident, but to a greater extent. Separate schools of applied science had begun there decades before they emerged in Canada, and graduate programs were well advanced. But the better-known accommodation to these new developments for undergraduate education was the "elective system" that President Eliot had installed at Harvard by the 1880s. This was roughly contemporaneous with, but quite a different tack from, the honours system found in Canadian universities. In many respects, however, the elective system was a response to the same forces of specialization, especially at the much larger institutions.

Eliot said at his inauguration in 1869 that "the endless controversies whether language, philosophy, mathematics or science supplies the best mental training" were no longer of practical concern at Harvard where he expected that every subject would be taught.[19] That being the case, it would simply be left up to the students to choose whatever courses would make up their degrees. As G. Schmidt in his portrayal of this occasion and its impact points out, the elective system was a costly venture.[20] It was at least fifteen years before Eliot had woven it firmly into the fabric of a Harvard education, and by the turn of the century it was still only the larger universities that could afford to offer enough courses consistently to make the system feasible.

Both the proliferation of courses and the freedom to choose as widely or as narrowly as one wished reflected the subdivision of subject matter and consequent specialization typical of the era. An abundance of courses within an elective system could provide admirable depth, but it was quite different from a liberal arts curriculum that had relied upon a few subjects every student had to take in common, providing community leaders with a common set of values and expectations. In the words of Frederick Rudolph, "now the old unity was gone, the avid search for scientific truth was bringing forth great new contributions to knowledge, and specialization was leading to the splintering of subject areas."[21] Maritime universities did not adopt as radical an elective system, but they felt the loss of the old unity in their own way. Honours to a limited extent, and the new BSc degree especially, eroded the older sense of an education all graduates shared in common.

L. Veysey argues that even in the United States Eliot's system was never as widely adopted as its notoriety would suggest.[22] Many universities moved instead to a "group system" in which each student could choose to do more extensive study in one group, i.e., classics, the natural sciences, the new social sciences. This compromise seems a lot closer to the accommodations attempted in Canada and, it might be supposed, one with a very similar impact on what was left of the liberal-arts ideal. It was Veysey, after all, who had declared it the most sweeping transformation of higher education ever seen.

Veysey's description of this transformation included the introduction of a complete set of now-familiar features: numbered courses and credit systems, lecture and seminar teaching styles, course selection, and also administrative hierarchy and departmental organization. By the turn of the century the first four or five of these were in place at Mount Allison and no doubt throughout the Maritimes. But the latter ones arose only from changes in size and scale of operation that came some years later.

When it did come, it affected the core of the university so that by the outset of World War I, where there had been a single professor of science at Mount Allison virtually since the college's inception, the university appointed one professor each in physics, chemistry, and biology, in addition to math and engineering. Once past the disruption of the Great War this pattern of growth continued, with the result that in the 1920s one saw the first truly separate departments and an academic administrator mediating between faculty and the president.

As a function of greater growth, the same pattern was evident a bit earlier at UNB and Dalhousie, and earlier still at McGill and Toronto, but (as in the United States) once institutions reached this point in their development the impact was strikingly similar. I have already noted that the elective system was partly a function of size and consequent diversity, and so to a degree was the shift to subject "majors."

Once again, it was a shift signalled by Harvard, though in this instance more uniformly emulated. Schmidt points to Eliot's successor,

A.L. Lowell, who in his own inaugural address of 1909 declared that "the ideal college ought to produce, not defective specialists, but men intellectually well rounded ... they ought to be trained to hard and accurate thought, and this will not come merely by surveying the elementary principles of many subjects. It requires mastery of something acquired by continuous application."[23] It would seem that Lowell was interested in redressing some of the difficulties introduced by the elective system or any other scheme that promoted specialization at the expense of breadth. Schmidt went on to describe how this was to be accomplished:

> In its most common form, as evolved between 1910 and 1930, this curriculum consisted of the following elements. All courses in the catalogue were grouped under three or four large categories, each composed of a number of departments of instruction that were interrelated ... In his first two years in college the underclassman took a prescribed amount of work in each of these groups ... By the end of his sophomore year the student had chosen a field of major concentration to be pursued for the remainder of this stay in college.[24]

Not only was the pattern described here similar to that at Mount Allison but it was roughly contemporaneous. Structurally it was made possible by the establishment of departmental teaching units, each capable of offering a major of its own. And, at least by Lowell's intent, it might set universities back on the track of producing graduates who were "intellectually well rounded" and also well grounded in some chosen field – both breadth and depth, as we still like to say in our mission statements.

But there was a problem with this final accommodation. In his study of the long history of the idea of liberal education, Bruce Kimball quotes Lowell's conclusion that "the best type of liberal education in our complex modern world aims at producing men who knew a little of everything and something well."[25] As Kimball comments, "This involved rolling back Eliot's electivism ... and reestablishing a prescribed foundation of culture such as a liberally educated person should be expected to know ... developing a critical intellect of strength and plasticity."[26] However, if the result was to prescribe a smattering of courses intended to provide breadth of distribution, and then a set of prescribed courses within the department of each student's choice, Rudolph's "old unity" might indeed be lost. "In effect," according to Kimball, "Lowell's scheme was a concession to the fact that academicians no longer agreed on the content or meaning of liberal education, except that it ought to include a "major" field of study."[27] What Kimball did not discuss was the role of the initial two years, which were the only portion of this twentieth-century accommodation still open to providing what has come to be called "general education."[28]

Rudolph was a little more hopeful in his assessment, at least of the intent behind these changes: "General education proposed to restore some balance, to revitalize the aristocratic ideal of the liberal arts as the passport to learning ... The general education movement from its beginnings at Columbia in 1919 to the celebrated Harvard report on the subject in 1945, was an attempt to capture some of the sense of a continuing intellectual and spiritual heritage that had fallen victim to the elective principle."[29] Universities in Canada, which had not "fallen victim" to electivism to the same extent, were nevertheless concerned about their own modes of accommodation. Honours degrees continued to be the preferred degree, but the rhetoric of the day certainly reflected ongoing concern. P. Jasen summarized the rhetoric of the 1920s and 1930s signifying the continuing "importance of the arts curriculum in making society more humane ... by passing on the cherished 'values' of the Western cultural tradition. Graduates of arts curricula," it was believed, "should possess heightened powers of imagination, reason, moral sensitivity and good taste, and be ready to assume the practical duties of citizenship."[30] While, as Jasen argues, her summary may more accurately reflect the educational rhetoric of the time than the education it produced, it shows the continuing interest in what a twentieth-century version of a liberal arts education could accomplish. The opportunity to accomplish it, however, was from now on restricted to about half the degree.

According to Veysey, emphasis on the subject major expanded inexorably over the next three or four decades. Whereas the major originally comprised twenty to thirty percent of the degree, leaving room for a minor or two, it has grown to roughly twice that proportion, leaving little room for minors at all and still less for the "general" portion of one's education. This squeeze is most evident in Canadian provinces where universities offer a bachelor's degree in three years.

Robin Harris's survey of Canadian universities confirmed that by the 1920s most had reorganized around departments. The larger universities moved directly into requirements for majors. Harris also notes, however, that at many universities the actual size of individual departments remained quite small, so that a full program of majors was often not yet possible. John Reid placed Mount Allison in this latter category.[31] There had been sufficient growth to offer a wider choice within the curriculum, but the first two years of both the BA and BSc remained largely prescribed. Most courses in the final two years were optional, but this presumably meant that students could choose one of several approaches. One was to exercise one's options and complete a fairly general degree; another was to choose somewhat more narrowly and complete something approximating a major, or even a major and minor. Finally, it was always possible to specialize and do an honours degree.

At Mount Allison, with the first two years prescribed, it remained possible to get as traditional a liberal arts education as anywhere in the Maritimes (and probably in English-speaking Canada), if only because the institution had remained too small to do much else. A full range of courses was available in physics, chemistry, and biology. Geology was available in a limited way, covered by one of the engineers. On the arts side, philosophy had spawned psychology. Out of the older political economy had grown history, political studies, and economics. So the usual expansion of subjects was apparent, but there were fewer professors and a shorter list of courses than at larger institutions. This meant that graduates, whatever their major, necessarily had more courses in common than at larger institutions. Except that the arts and sciences as degree programs had become separate, with the result that they retained less and less in common.

In conclusion, a glimpse at challenges from other quarters. Growth, especially after World War II, was sufficient to ease many of the restraints imposed by small size, and that has tended to make the dream of a liberal arts education not easier, but much more of a challenge. Perhaps this was one reason why, in the 1920s, Mount Allison drew back from the opportunity to amalgamate with other institutions in the Maritimes.[32] The opportunity to participate in greater specialization (along with the financial advantages of equipping more specialized programs) was the lure that a federation offered. But the accessibility to Maritime students of these universities, and the type of education each of them offered, would have been lost.

One additional consideration that arose from the commissions and debates of the 1920s and 1930s was the relationship between the university and the men's and women's academies.[33] There were various reasons why this long-standing relationship could not last, but dissolution of the academies had its implications for the preservation of the liberal arts at Mount Allison. The school of applied science had developed a program in household science in the early years of this century, and it had succeeded too well simply to be set aside. Its amalgamation with the university, however, clashed to some extent with a liberal arts ideal. A commercial program presented similar problems.

Two better-known examples of this kind were the music program and fine arts at the women's academy. The practical orientation of these programs also seemed to conflict with the liberal arts ideal. Even the theatrical productions, which were more an extracurricular activity than an academic program, presented a problem.

In each of these cases except drama, the response was to follow the pattern set by science programs of the past. They were established as something like a "school," with more independence than the usual department, or were set up as programs with degrees of their own, or both. To create new departments for these programs would have been a dangerous option, directly challenging the balance that could still be achieved in the 1920s and 1930s at Mount Allison, and its attempt to provide an education in the liberal arts. This accommodation was to set them apart not only to preserve their integrity as programs of some standing but, and especially, to preserve the curriculum at the core.

NOTES

1 Laurence Veysey, "Stability and Experiment in the American Undergraduate Curriculum," in *Content and Context: Essays on College Education*, ed. Carl Kaysen (New York: McGraw-Hill, 1973), 1.

2 P. Axelrod and J.G. Reid, eds., *Youth, University and Canadian Society: Essays in the Social History of Higher Education* (Montreal and Kingston: McGill-Queen's University Press, 1989), xiii.

3 See Appendix Two of Robin Harris's *A History of Higher Education in Canada: 1663–1960* (Toronto: University of Toronto Press, 1976).

4 The numbers cited are drawn from the annual calendars of each university, located in the various university archives.

5 Mount Allison University Archives 8243/5.

6 John G. Reid, *Mount Allison University: A History to 1963. Vol. I, 1843–1914* (Toronto: University of Toronto Press, 1984), 85, emphasis in the original. It is interesting that the reference here to "departments" is not yet to administrative organizations but to fields defined by subject matter.

7 This is a distinction between Newtonianism and Baconianism that I have worked out in more detail in "The Presbyterian Contribution to Higher Education: Teaching Science in Maritime Universities" in *The Contribution of Presbyterianism to Atlantic Canada*, ed. C.Scobie (Montreal and Kingston: McGill-Queen's University Press, forthcoming).

8 The utility of certain fields of science outside in contrast to those fields drawn inside the new institutions of higher learning was first developed in my "Introduction: Establishing Science in the Maritimes," in *Science and Society in the Maritimes Prior to 1914*, ed. P.A. Bogaard (Fredericton, NB: Acadiensis Press and Mount Allison University Centre for Canadian Studies, 1990).

9 Especially indicative is the case of George Lawsen, renowned botanist appointed by Dalhousie University as professor of chemistry. See Suzanne Zeller's "George Lawsen: Victorian Botany, the Origin of Species and the Case of Nova Scotian Heather," in *Science and Society*, ed. P.A. Bogaard, 51–62.

10 A.B. McKillop, *Matters of Mind: The University in Ontario, 1791–1951* (Toronto: University of Toronto Press, 1994), 103. See also B.M. Moody, "Breadth of Vision, Breadth of Mind: The Baptists and Acadia College," in *Canadian Baptists and Christian Higher Education*, ed. G. Rawlyk (Montreal and Kingston: McGill-Queen's University Press, 1988), 11–14, where he comments on the Baptists' lack of interest in controlling the curriculum at Acadia.

11 McKillop, *Matters of Mind*, 107, notes that Ryerson's insistence upon English at Victoria "effectively began to link language and learning to the present rather than to the past."

12 Ibid., 103.

13 Ibid., 111.

14 See my "Presbyterian Contribution."

15 Inventory sciences, as they are called by Suzanne Zeller. She explores the substantive role they had outside universities in her *Inventing Canada: Early Victorian Science and the idea of a Transcontinental Nation* (Toronto: University of Toronto Press, 1987).

16 Again, these are drawn from each university's annual calendars. See also Reid, *Mount Allison University*, vol. 1, 92.

17 Reid, *Mount Allison University*, vol. 1, 178ff.

18 J.G. Reid, "Beyond the Democratic Ideal: The Scottish Example and University Reform in Canada's Maritime Provinces: 1870–1933" in *Youth, University and Canadian Society*, examines the attempt to form a federated University of Halifax, whose proponents thought it could attain a higher level of specialization than smaller, more isolated college-size universities. It did not survive an initial attempt.

18a For a general discussion of the shift from teaching physics to doing research in physics, and the role played by emerging graduate programs in this crucial development, see Yves Gingras, *Physics and the Rise of Scientific Research in Canada* (Montreal and Kingston: McGill-Queen's University Press, 1991).

19 George P. Schmidt, *The Liberal Arts College: A Chapter in American Cultural History* (New Brunswick, New Jersey: Rutgers University Press, 1957), 171; note that Eliot is confirming what we have found in Maritime universities to be the common liberal arts tradition of nineteenth-century colleges.

20 Ibid., 174.

21 Frederick Rudolph, *The American College and University: A History*, 2d edition (Athens, GA: University of Georgia Press, 1990), 399.
22 Veysey, "Stability and Experiment," 36.
23 Schmidt, *The Liberal Arts College*, 209.
24 Ibid., 210.
25 Ibid.
26 Bruce A. Kimball, *Orators and Philosophers: A History of the Idea of Liberal Education* (New York: Columbia University: Teacher's College Press, 1986), 177.
27 Ibid., 193.
28 See R. Hofstadter and W. Smith's "Introduction" to *American Higher Education: A Documentary History*, vol. 2 (Chicago: University of Chicago Press, 1961), 895–6, and the document from Columbia that began this movement, ibid., 904.
29 Rudolph, *The American College and University*, 455–6.
30 Patricia Jasen, "'In Pursuit of Human Values' (or Laugh When You Say That): The Student Critique of the Arts Curriculum in the 1960s," in *Youth, University and Canadian Society*, eds. Axelrod and Reid, 247.
31 J.G. Reid, *Mount Allison University: A History to 1963. Vol. II: 1914–1963*, 36–7.
32 See Reid, *Mount Allison University*, and his "Beyond the Democratic Ideal" for a detailed account of both the 1870s and 1920s attempts at federation.
33 Reid, *Mount Allison University*, vol. 2, 41, 125–6.

CHAPTER SIX

Art at Mount Allison: A History

VIRGIL HAMMOCK

The teaching of art at Mount Allison can be traced back to the opening of the Ladies' Academy in 1854.[1] Since then, art has been an important and continuous part of the curriculum. By 1869 the university had named its first professor of painting and drawing, John Warren Grey. Of Grey's appointment President Allison, the university's namesake, said: "Nor would we forget to express our satisfaction that not only can the young ladies pursue, as usual, their studies in drawing and painting, but that classes are also opened in those branches of Art, as well as in architecture, for such students of the college or male academy as wish to pursue their studies in this direction. A want long felt is at last supplied."[2]

Professor Grey only remained at Mount Allison until 1873. For the next twenty years there was a series of short appointments of women art teachers at the Women's Academy, none of sufficient status to be called professor. Nevertheless, these women carried on the practice of the teaching of art at Mount Allison. The university calendars of the period express Mount Allison's strong belief in the virtue of their unique program.

> The tendency of the study of Fine Arts to cultivate the taste and refine the manners, is fully recognized. Hence adequate provision is made for a thorough and extended course of instruction in Vocal and Instrumental Music and in Drawing and Painting ... The method of Instruction in this Department [Fine Arts] is that employed in the best European schools. Copying, under the eye of a skilful teacher, is regarded as the first means of acquiring correct ideas of the Art; but, from the beginning, the pupil will be taught that nature is her ultimate guide, and as early as possible will be accustomed to make studies and sketches from natural forms. Pupils who become proficient in Drawing and Painting will be entitled to receive a special Testimonial.[3]

The goals of this early program were very different from those of the department today. The young women of the academy certainly were not being trained as professional artists; rather, their art education was seen as part of their overall social deportment. Training in the arts was seen as a mark of culture. In eighteenth- and nineteenth-century Canada much of art was seen as "women's work." In short, in early Canada the burden of culture was often thrust upon the shoulders of educated women.

The year 1893 was important for art at Mount Allison. It was then that John Hammond was appointed professor of painting and drawing, and then too that Mount Allison took control of the Owens Art Gallery. The Owens gallery was founded by John Owens in 1885. It was housed in a converted Methodist church in Saint John, New Brunswick, and Hammond was its first director. By 1893, the gallery was in financial trouble and Mount Allison came to the rescue with a unique offer to move the gallery, its collection, and Hammond to Sackville. Hammond was in place in 1893 and Owens opened its doors in Sackville in 1895. The 1895 building is still the shell on which the current gallery is based. In fact, the original building served as both an art school and a gallery until 1965, when the fine arts department moved to its own building next door. Since then the gallery has been redesigned and is the largest university gallery in eastern Canada.

The original Owens collection, which was put together by Hammond, was an important addition to the teaching program at Mount Allison. In the late nineteenth century, the teaching of art largely involved the copying of paintings and plaster casts. Hammond travelled Europe in the 1880s with the intention of putting together a good study collection. An imaginative collector could have purchased first-rate Impressionist and post-Impressionist art cheaply at the time. Instead, we have a collection of late-nineteenth-century English, Canadian, and French academic painting that has some interest but is rather dull. The fact remains, however, that nearly one hundred years ago Mount Allison had a first-rate art gallery and school in place in Sackville and the university recognized the importance of an education in the visual arts.

John Hammond remained the head of the department from 1893 until 1916. Born in 1843, Hammond was well over seventy years old when he retired from active teaching. The university awarded him an LLD in 1930. He continued to live and work in Sackville until his death in his ninety-sixth year in 1939. Hammond's house was once the home of the president and now houses the university development office (the Black House). His studio, which was next door, is now a student residence (Bermuda House). Regrettably, they have lost all identification with John Hammond or with art at Mount Allison.

Although the teaching of art continued after Hammond's departure, no one was appointed head until 1930, when Elizabeth A. McLeod was given the post for a five-year term. Elizabeth McLeod had been teaching in the department since 1896, when she was still a student. She became a member of the Royal Canadian Academy in 1916. Following her term as head, she continued teaching until her retirement in 1947, having served the university for over fifty years.

It is likely that Elizabeth McLeod was the first woman head of a university fine arts department in Canada, though, as earlier noted, women teachers played a pivotal role in the early period of art education at Mount Allison. With the exception of Hammond and Stanley Royle, who served as head from 1935 to 1945, all of the teaching staff from 1873 until the end of World War II were women. Until the late 1930s, most of the teaching of art centred around the Ladies' College and the curriculum was very different from that of today; nevertheless, art had a very strong presence on this campus because of the dedicated teaching of women like McLeod, Annie Inch, Christian McKeil, and Mrs Edward Hart. In 1954 Mount Allison celebrated the centenary of the opening of the Women's Academy. On this occasion Elizabeth McLeod was given an honourary degree in recognition of her pioneering role in art education, and in symbolic recognition of the contributions of women to education at Mount Allison since the inception of the academy.

In 1935 the British painter Stanley Royle followed McLeod as head of the department. Royle had taught at the Nova Scotia College of Art and Design from 1931 to 1934 and had returned briefly to England before taking up his post in Sackville. He was born in Sheffield in 1888 and educated at the Sheffield School of Art. He was a contemporary of two other graduates of Sheffield, Frederick Varley and Arthur Lismer, both of whom had come to Canada before Royle and went on to become founding members of the Group of Seven.

It was during Royle's term that the Bachelor of Fine Arts (BFA) degree was introduced, the first in Canada. Until 1937 work in the fine and applied arts was done under the direction of the Ladies' College. The Music Conservatory had been taken over by the university some years earlier and was already giving a Bachelor of Music degree. The university now decided that it was the turn of fine arts. The new program was described in the 1937 calendar in the following way:

> The Bachelor of Fine Arts degree has been instituted as in Yale, Princeton, Cornell and other American universities. It will be awarded to those who successfully complete the four years' course in Fine Arts outlined below. In this course the principles of Design, Painting and Commercial Art are taught.

The first two years are the same for all students, but two fields of specialization are offered in the third and fourth years, namely; continuation of work in Fine Arts, or for training for public school teaching of Art. For entrance on this course students must have matriculation as in arts, except that only one foreign language is required.[4]

In 1941 the first three BFA degrees were granted by the university. However, it was a graduate of the second class, 1942, that was to give early credibility to the program. Alex Colville, who was living in Amherst, entered the program in 1938. Royle's professionalism as an artist impressed the young Colville and inspired him to continue as a teacher as well as an artist. Immediately following his graduation, Colville was commissioned as a war artist, but after the war, he returned to Mount Allison as a teacher in the department. He remained a member of staff from 1946 until 1963, when he resigned to become a full-time artist.

Colville was an important influence on the first two generations of Mount Allison art students after World War II, who were to include Tom Forrestall, Chris and Mary Pratt, and D.P. Brown. There were other important teachers during the same period. The post-war department was very small but very professional. Another decommissioned war artist, Lawren P. (Phillip) Harris, the son of Group of Seven founder Lawren S. Harris, was named head the same year, 1946, that Colville was appointed. For a time they taught virtually all of the "fine" art courses.

"Applied" art courses had been taught in the department since its early days and continued to be taught until 1961. At that time the university dropped all courses based on the crafts. This change from a fine and applied art department to a fine art program may have been a mistake. The artificial split between the fine and applied arts is one of the major reasons contemporary art is so alienated from the rest our society.

Fine arts studio programs in university settings have always been an uneasy fit. They tend to emphasize practice rather than theory or scholarship. Crafts, or the applied arts, are even more problematic because they lack the cachet of the traditional fine arts such as painting and sculpture, which have no function other than the aesthetic. However, the practical function of a quality craft object obviously does not preclude an aesthetic quality equally worthy of artistic effort. A beautiful ceramic teapot, besides being beautiful, can also hold tea and function well as a pot, while a ceramic sculpture's sole function is that of aesthetic contemplation. However, this is not an essential difference. Furthermore, craft items must, of necessity, be well made. Fine art, on the other hand, can get by with less craftsmanship by claiming to possess artistic "meaning." The neglect of the applied arts is often motivated by a kind of snobbery. Many fine artists, particularly those who teach in universities, may see themselves as part of the humanist tradition, academics first, to be counted as thinkers rather than doers, certainly not mere artisans or craftspersons. They may attempt to secure their place as academics by excluding or eliminating the teaching of crafts. This was certainly the case at Mount Allison.

It was not considered appropriate by the university to have students making jewellery or pots as part of the university curriculum. The separation of form and function was seen to be necessary if art was to be taken seriously by the rest of the Mount Allison community. Art, artifice, can, and often does, isolate itself from everyday concerns. The chief function of a beautifully made craft object, a piece of furniture, a chair for instance, is as a place to sit regardless of its beauty; if it does not function well as a place to sit, it is a failure as a chair. Fine artists are not by and large concerned with making everyday functional objects more beautiful.

The Bauhaus movement, which flourished in Germany between the two world wars, thought differently, but in the end, with very few exceptions, their utopian ideas failed. The Bauhaus wanted to train artists to serve the needs of society through design. It was their intention to reintegrate artists with society – a new arts and crafts movement. Their idea was to end division between the fine arts-and-crafts. It would all be art and serve different functions, aesthetic or otherwise, equally. It was a socialization of the arts. Indeed, the Bauhaus had very leftist leanings and was closed very quickly once the Nazis came to power. Its faculty, forced to flee, attempted to take their idealism to new locations in Europe and North America, but events overtook them and their idealism was lost in the process.

Fine arts education in North America took a very different route. Applied art was to be taught in art colleges and academies, but classical studio arts such as painting and drawing gained a foothold early in this century within the liberal arts curriculum within the universities, most notably in the Ivy League at Yale. In order for that to happen, art had to shed itself of any function outside the aesthetic. Much of the visual arts of this century, and certainly the vast majority of the second half of the century, are divorced from the concerns of common people for whom their products remain a mystery. Even crafts are problematic because the manufacture of quality goods by hand is a foreign concept to most people in our society; but at least in the case of crafts, the public can identify with the functions of the craft objects and understand the people who made them.

Whatever the cause of the alienation of contemporary art and artists, it continues to be fostered by the way that art is taught in North American universities. A curriculum that insists on the separation of form from function and sets the fine artist apart from the practical and applied reinforces the notion that art and artists are an élite, misunderstood by an insensitive public. Education in the applied arts is far less likely to encourage such élitism. It teaches students to make objects of quality that will captivate a broad audience. Ideally, students in the fine arts should have some formal education in the applied arts, which was possible at Mount Allison before 1961. This would give them both a sense of craft and, more importantly, a sense of humility.

In 1949, Colville and Harris were joined by Edward (Ted) Pulford. Pulford graduated from the Mount Allison program that same year. Like his colleagues, Pulford was a veteran, but unlike them he had not been a war artist; however, Pulford had already decided before the war that he wanted to become an artist. When he was decommissioned he came to Mount Allison because it was the only university in the country offering professional training in fine arts. Once in the faculty, Pulford became a remarkable teacher, a fact that has been attested to by many of our graduates. Both Colville and Harris were trying to balance professional careers along with their teaching. Pulford, however, put his whole life into teaching, although he was a great watercolour painter. He remained on the faculty until 1980, and only after he retired did he find more time for his own art.

Before Helen Dow was hired in 1961, art history was taught by the studio instructors. Dow, who went on to write the first major book on Alex Colville, remained on staff until 1964. She was soon followed, in 1966, by Mervyn Crooker, who is still a mainstay in the department. Over the years Crooker has taught a wide variety of art history courses both to our students and to the general university population. Other art history courses have been taught since 1969 by the directors of Owens Art Gallery and more recently by the department of classics and by myself. The department now offers, in addition to the BFA, an honours degree in art history, joint honours in art history with a number of other departments, and both a major and minor in art history. Most recently, the department has offered a major and minor in fine arts to students in other degree programs in the university. This can be a combination of art history and studio courses.

Lawren Harris introduced intaglio print making to the program in 1963 with the hiring of David Silverberg. Sculpture followed in 1969 with Colin Campbell and in 1973 with Marcel Braitstein. Lawren Harris retired in 1975 and my tenure as professor of fine arts and head of the department began. Since then, the scope of the department's course offerings has enlarged to reflect the changing nature of contemporary art. We now offer concentrations in painting, sculpture, print making, photography, and mixed media. The department remains conservative in that basic skills are emphasized. Drawing, for example, is a required course in each of the first three years of our four year program. Our BFA students take a common foundation year, which is followed by an additional three years of studio courses in various studio areas. Generally students end up majoring in one or two areas; however, the trend is for students to combine two or more areas into what is loosely called mixed media, for instance, photo-sculpture, photo-based print making and video or performance-based art.

The department firmly believes that studio courses are academic courses. Studio courses are discipline based with a teachable body of knowledge like any other discipline in the university. In addition, however, to studio courses, students in our department are required to take eight non-studio academic courses. Of these, four must be in art history. The remainder are chosen from the university calendar with the advice of the student's faculty advisor. Students also take theory-based seminars in their third and fourth years.

In a small university in a rural setting such as Mount Allison, isolation from the larger art world is a handicap. For this reason, our visiting artist program and regular field trips to major art centres are especially important. The department was the pilot project for the Canada Council Visiting Artists Programme when it was introduced over twenty years ago. The program allows us to bring a number of artists to the campus each year to give workshops and lectures both to our students and to the general artistic community. For the past fifteen or sixteen years we have taken our third and fourth year students on an annual field trip to a major art centre such as New York, Boston, or Montreal. We have tried to make sure that all of our graduates have a chance to visit New York simply because of its importance as an international art centre.

The Department of Fine Arts has become more integrated with the rest of the university than it once was. It was a professional school whose students took their electives from other departments within the university but that offered little in return. The only service, although an important one, that was provided by the department to the rest of the university was art history courses, which were open to any student in the university. Non fine arts students were not allowed to take studio courses even if they wanted to do so on a non-credit basis. Our building was physically isolated and few non fine arts students ever ventured into it. Our students were regarded by other students and even some faculty as being different – with talent, but basically not academic in their interests. In fact, however, fine arts students have always had to be admitted to the BA program before they were considered for the BFA program and are, as a group, high academic achievers in their courses both within and outside the department.

Over the past decade there has been a dramatic increase in the traffic in both directions between fine arts and the rest of the university. The university has recognized that studio courses are academic courses, and it now allows students in any degree program to take them as a major, a minor, or as electives. This has been a major breakthrough towards the integration of fine arts into a liberal education. It benefits all students as those in the fine arts come to realize that other students can be "creative" too, while non fine art students come to realize that art making is as much a discipline as the traditional academic disciplines.

The arts, in particular music and visual arts, have had a long presence at Mount Allison, far longer than most other "academic" departments on the campus. They go back to the university's very beginnings. They have had a civilizing effect on generations of Mount Allison students, but much of this effect was marginal to the students' formal education. The main impact of having a school of fine arts in a small liberal arts institution has been in providing the fine arts students with a solid base in the humanities. Other students certainly benefit from the presence of the art gallery and the events associated with it. They benefit from concerts and other events of the Department of Music. The increasing integration of fine arts courses with the general undergraduate curriculum means that they can gain experience in doing art as well as academic understanding.

Art is central to the understanding of one's own or other cultures and thus has an essential place in a liberal education. Canadian art is simply art made by Canadians, but it defines us as a people in a way that, say, Canadian chemistry cannot. Of course, art is international as well, but part of what we are as a nation is defined by our arts. Their presence on university campuses, especially a liberal arts campus, should serve not only to train future artists but to remind everyone of how central the arts are to the education of the whole person.

NOTES

1 The immediate source of material on the early history of the Department of Fine Arts is Virgil Hammock, *Art at Mount Allison ... a History* (Sackville, NB: Owens Art Gallery, 1977). This essay was written for an Owens Art Galley catalogue.

2 Ibid., n.p.
3 The Mount Allison Wesleyan Female Academy Catalogue and General Circular (1972–73), pp. 36–7.
4 *Calendar of Mount Allison University 1937–38* (Truro, NS: News Publishing Company, 1938), 62.

CHAPTER SEVEN

Drama, the Campus, and the Curriculum at Mount Allison: "This green plot shall be our stage ..."

MARK BLAGRAVE

Theatre history is fairly new as a discipline in Canada, and the study of our own country's historical past is even newer. In the twenty years or so since the formation of such groups as the Association for Canadian Theatre History, however, the discipline has been subject to a compressed version of the evolution and devolution experienced by other, much older, historiographically-based disciplines. Twenty years ago, the prevailing belief was that the highest priority should be placed on feats of quantitative scholarship – the collection of raw data, the making of calendars of performance, the "facts." More recently, in tune with general trends in thinking about historiography, the shift has been towards studies of the basic impossibilities of reconstructing the historical record with anything like objectivity or reliability.[1] Many theatre historians, faced with a perception that all history is merely one more form of fictional text, have even come to prefer overtly anecdotal and obviously biased accounts since these, at least, make little attempt to hide their agendas.

The present study reflects several of the tensions felt in the discipline at large. It does not profess to be exhaustive in its collection of the "facts" from existing archival material, reasoning that the archival record itself has been subject to unstated but nonetheless exclusive principles of selection (and to plain accident) over the years of its accrual. It does not attempt to present its material in a chronological narrative, in recognition of the various fallacies and biases that may be engaged by such an ordering. Nor does it try to deal with the record from the time of the first dramatic presentation at Mount Allison until the present day. It does, however, stop short of arguing that the study of the past, because so fraught with difficulties, is a meaningless pursuit. Rather, this study attempts to identify and evaluate a number of "measurables" and to recognize some of the "variables" that affect them, in an effort to illuminate some persistent issues over a period of about seventy-five years. The portrait that emerges may be read as a kind of rehearsal of key questions that continue to be asked whenever the role of drama studies within liberal arts institutions is debated.

In selecting the indicators to use in constructing the character of drama at Mount Allison from 1920 until now, I have been alive to the fact that each carries with it a host of questions as to its relevance or its reliability or both. The most obviously measurable data are enrolment figures. These may indicate a program's sensitivity to student and societal need, but they may also fail to take account of the interdisciplinary nature of a program; or they may merely reflect a lack of space in other courses or programs. A second possible means of measurement is the reconstruction of course content from calendar descriptions. To rely on such information, however, is to assume, not always correctly, that these descriptions match what is actually delivered to the students in any given year. A third indicator, library support, is difficult to determine and interpret, relying as it often does on budget priorities and individual initiatives in collection building – not to mention the nature of the discipline being investigated and the level of publication within it. Just as problematic is the listing of numbers of faculty members involved in a program and of their credentials, since this fails to come to terms with the individual talent or with questions of political or personal dynamics. A fifth possible means of measurement, determining the relationship of dramatic activities to other activities outside of the lecture hall, may be distorted in its reconstruction by the biases of editors who prefer to print news of defeats in sport over triumphs in the arts. Despite their manifest problems, each of these criteria will be invoked in this paper, along with far less problematic indicators such as the numbers of dramatic productions and their public profile, the flavour of the repertoire performed, and the placement of students following graduation.

These indicators cannot construct the character of drama at Mount Allison, however, without recognizing several of the variables involved over time: changing pedagogical philosophies in the discipline and about the curriculum at large, the sporadic appearance of individual talent, changes in levels of student autonomy, and changes in spaces and facilities.

Early in the century, a pattern of interdisciplinary cooperation in dramatic activities and studies was set. Between 1920 and the mid-1930s, theatre in the Mount Allison community was, as it had been for many years before, chiefly the responsibility of the oratory department of the Ladies' College. Although their approach might sound like (and was, to an extent) the sort of self-serving finishing-school frill that was railed against by the Massey Foundation Commission on Methodist Schools in Canada in the 1920s, the teachers of oratory in the Ladies' College easily made the transition to work with the students of the university, as they directed play after play for the sister institution.[2] When, in 1936, the Department of Oratory vanished as the Ladies' College was reorganized into the Mount Allison School for Girls with three departments – academic, music, and art – "dramatics" fell under the aegis of the academic section rather than being joined to one of the other "art" departments. It was taken on, in fact, by the teacher of mathematics.[3] As is clear from the calendar of the School for Girls in the late 1930s, however, the teaching of dramatics continued to have a strong practical focus in the production of plays by the students.[4] Academic rigour and sound practical experience were seen to be mutually supportive.

The replacement of the Ladies' College by the School for Girls marked the beginning of a general move towards establishing clear lines between the university proper and its related institutions. In the field of drama, however, the lines remained blurred, as the practice of the college plays' being managed by a member of the school's staff persisted. While the faculty of the university proper showed some interest in taking over "the college play" during the war, Margaret Masten of the School for Girls resumed responsibility for the major productions of 1945 and 1946 and continued even after the closure of the school in 1947.[5]

Not until 1950 did the English department take over theatre on the campus on what appeared to be a permanent basis, following the appointment of C.F. MacRae in 1949. MacRae made a third in the Department of English, allowing it to broaden its curriculum and branch out into more studies in dramatic literature, as well as in Canadian and American literature, for which he also took responsibility.[6]

Michael Sidnell, who overlapped briefly with MacRae in the early 1960s, took advantage of the existence in the university of two other disciplines that had once been part of the Ladies' College when he asked music professor Carleton Elliot to provide a score and an orchestra for *King Lear* and asked fine artist David Silverberg to design the set for the same production.[7] By the early 1970s, faculty members in the French department had also become involved in practical theatre as a complement to their teaching of dramatic literature.[8] It was not unnatural, then, that in 1975 an interdisciplinary area of concentration in drama should be proposed and accepted by the university senate. This was designed as an interdisciplinary program that would build on existing departmental strengths and at the same time institutionalize the practical aspects of an education in drama that had long been a part of the Mount Allison tradition.

Ironically, the further forward one moves in time, the harder it is to establish enrolment figures for courses of study in drama at Mount Allison. We know that enrolments in the oratory department of the Ladies' College rose steeply from forty-seven in 1928–29 to 165 in 1929–30, corresponding to an increase in overall enrolments in the Ladies' College of one hundred students.[9] We also know that, in 1931, enrolments in the Department of Oratory stood at 165, as compared with those in the literary department at 161; household science at 147; the conservatory at 167; and fine arts at 147.[10] It was, in other words, an equal sharer with these other enterprises. However, it is not possible to trace accurately the numbers of those who were interested in drama specifically once "dramatics" became subsumed under the larger Department of Academics at the School for Girls.

Similarly, at the university, where dramatic literature formed part of a broader curriculum in literature at large, it is impossible to separate the statistics into those who had a specific interest in drama and those who saw it only as part of a broader program. The best that can be done is to state the obvious: that given the population size of Mount Allison, those who studied English with Professors Trueman or MacRae, or, later, with Professors Sidnell or Campbell, also worked with these same professors in the Mount Allison Players Society; and it is unlikely that they never mixed in their conversation one kind of business with another.

Until the late 1960s and on into the 1970s, there were in Canada no university programs in theatre or drama on which a curriculum could be modelled. Even after 1975, when the area of concentration in drama was initiated based on the graduate model at the University of Toronto, the statistics on student enrolments are blurred by the interdisciplinary nature of the program itself. It is quite common for a student to complete the core requirements for the program but to graduate with a concentration in one of the literature disciplines or, indeed, in a science discipline.

The interdisciplinary nature of drama studies also means that levels of library holdings are not reliable as an accurate measure of the importance of the enterprise to the university at large. Moreover, certain aspects of study in drama are not supported by library holdings in the same way as, say, the study of novels might be. Initiatives in collection building, however, may indicate a level of interest. In the early years, for example, Dr Archibald worked to build up the Mary Mellish collection. In 1933, the librarian's year-end report notes

Archibald's gift of the multiple-volume set *Materials for the Study of Old English Drama*, valued at seven hundred dollars and believed to be the only complete set in Canada.[11] In 1936, the Mary Mellish collection was given a set of phonographic recordings of Shakespeare's plays, spoken by the young John Gielgud.[12] Later initiatives included a major Social Sciences and Humanities Research Council of Canada grant for acquisitions in the late 1980s and the temporary establishment by Richard Knowles of a Playwrights Union of Canada reading room/repository in the Canadian Studies Centre.

The fact that library resources can figure at all in a discussion of drama at Mount Allison may suggest something about its position in relation to other outside-the-lecture-hall activities. While it is often described as an "extracurricular" activity, the sobriquet has never meant quite what it means when applied, for instance, to football, or to student government, or even to debating. Rather, from the days of the Ladies' College forward, it has enjoyed a "paracurricular" position.

Although there are long periods, particularly in the history of The *[Alumni] Record*, during which sporting events receive several pages' coverage on a regular basis while drama and other events and activities receive none, one of the key competitive events on campus from 1939 until the 1960s was the Interclass Drama Festival.[13] The *Argosy* of 3 December 1955 describes this as "perhaps [the] most keenly contested" of all interclass competitions.[14] Yearly, in the fall, each of the four classes mounted a production of a one-act play; and each year an adjudicator awarded a cup. The fact that the rivalry was set up as among freshmen, sophomores, juniors, and seniors and not, for instance, along house lines or according to friendship ties may suggest an academic flavour to the affair, although similar arrangements were not unknown in sports. The serious nature of the material chosen for performance, however, certainly bolsters the sense of paracurricular pursuit. The fare of the Interclass Festival was not a variety-show assemblage of skits but rather some of the most challenging contemporary material imaginable: Synge, Yeats, Lady Gregory, O'Neill, and the like figured highly.[15]

Equally serious thought was given to choosing adjudicators with good credentials for the festival. Over the years they included Mount Allison professors Trueman, Gundy, Payzant, and Sidnell, as well as drama specialists Sipprell from Acadia and Shaw from the University of New Brunswick, and Donald Wetmore, a major figure in the development of amateur theatre in Nova Scotia. Alumni of the calibre of Ron Irving and Bill Langstroth were also invited back as judges.[16]

The carefully vetted credentials of adjudicators for the festivals were consistent with the level of faculty expertise involved in the annual (sometimes twice-yearly) major production from the 1920s to the 1970s.

Ida Leslie and Florence Stewart of the Ladies' College, who steered these productions in the 1920s, both were graduates of Emerson College with the degree of BLI.[17] Marion Purdy, an alumna of the Ladies' College's own School of Expression, organized the Little Theatre Group on campus in 1933, and by 1936 she had also become head of Expression.[18] During her tenure at the Ladies' College, she continued to improve her credentials by taking a special course in public speaking at Columbia in the summer of 1934. When she resigned from the college in 1936, most likely as a result of the reorganization of departments, she returned to Columbia to pursue her studies in speech.[19] Purdy's replacement in "dramatics" in the new School for Girls was Miss Evangeline Lewis, whose Master of Arts (MA) degree from Edinburgh was probably more directly pertinent to her teaching of mathematics.[20] She did, however, teach drama at the summer school in Saint John in 1938; and when she left Mount Allison in 1939 it was to further her studies in drama, not in mathematics.[21] During the war years, the gap left by Miss Lewis's departure was in part filled by the continuation of Professor Harold Hamer's Gilbert and Sullivan productions with the Choral Society, and by Professor Wilgar's production of *Romeo and Juliet* in 1943.[22] Professors Gundy and Trueman also acted as advisors to the Players Society in these years.

Following the war, and after a brief period where the School for Girls once again supplied the directing expertise to the university in the person of Margaret Masten, a succession of professors of English became interested in drama on the campus, continuing the tradition of having a solidly trained academic directly involved in theatrical pursuits. Some, like C.F. MacRae and, twenty years after him, Arthur Motyer, came with expertise in the area; others, like Michael Sidnell in the 1960s and Richard Knowles in the 1970s and 1980s, developed much of their expertise here and then went elsewhere as specialists in drama (in these two cases, to the universities of Toronto and Guelph). Some, like Peter Mitcham, held a doctorate in English or another literature; others, a master's. Until very recently, none held graduate degrees specifically in drama because such courses only became available in Canada in the early 1970s. As a consequence, the university has retained its interdisciplinary approach to drama studies instead of moving to establish a separate department of drama or theatre.

Perhaps, in sketching the portrait of drama at Mount Allison, the most satisfying quantitative work can be done with the repertoire that was favoured by those leaders whose names I have mentioned. In the final analysis, the choices of types of play, the particular favourites that get repeated, and the patterns that emerge over time may be the most reliable indicators of the ideals (often not explicitly articulated) that have driven drama on the campus since 1920.

In light of the move in 1973–74 from one, and sometimes two, large productions per year to significantly larger numbers, it seems best to present the data pertaining to repertoire in two chronological phases, 1920–73 and 1974–93.

Records of performance suggest that Shakespeare was afforded seven major university productions at Mount Allison between 1920 and 1973.[23] The earliest of these, in 1920 and 1921, were *A Midsummer Night's Dream* and *As You Like It*, both directed by Ida Leslie of the Ladies' College. The latter was also produced in 1950, directed by C.F. MacRae. These two comedies were joined by Arthur Motyer's *Twelfth Night* in 1971. On the tragic side, the bard was represented by a production of *Romeo and Juliet* in 1943, under Professor Wilgar (with Arthur Motyer as Romeo), by Michael Sidnell's production of *King Lear* in 1964, and by J. Douglas Campbell's *Macbeth* in 1969. Shakespeare's close contemporaries enjoyed only two productions in the same period: Richard Green's production of *The Revenger's Tragedy* in 1966, and student Ron Ormston's rendition of *'Tis Pity She's a Whore* in 1972. Molière's *Le Bourgeois Gentilhomme* was produced by Alex Fancy in 1972. The Restoration dramatists, for reasons that are probably not difficult to find in a Methodist college, were unrepresented between 1920 and 1973, although Michael Sidnell did manage to produce the older and bawdier Aristophanic comedy *Lysistrata* in 1962. Of eighteenth-century comedies there was only one production: Goldsmith's *She Stoops to Conquer* in 1947, directed by Miss Masten. More popular comic dramatists were Shaw, with two major productions, and Noel Coward with three. Rattigan, Eliot, Fry, and Pinter each enjoyed a production as their respective stars rose in the firmament, as did Durrenmatt, Beckett, Sartre, Anouilh, and the rediscovered Jarry. What these productions have in common, for all their variety, is the fact that the plays they were based on were widely thought to have literary significance and were either already part of the canon or destined to become so. Each could legitimately find itself on a course syllabus in one or more of the literature departments. Admittedly, they were on occasion tempered by lighter "commercial" fare such as *Peg o' My Heart* (1930), *Smilin' Through* (1928), *Harvey* (1951), and *Hotel Universe* (1955), but such productions were either marked exceptions or balanced in the same year with more serious works. In addition, between 1932 and 1954, at least ten Gilbert and

Sullivan operettas were performed under the direction of Professor Harold Hamer and, later, Dr Geoffrey Payzant.

The twenty years between 1973–74 and the present have seen more than twice the number of major productions at Mount Allison than the fifty-three years preceding them. Typically, five major productions and as many as six smaller ones have been produced annually. The repertoire has remained true to the predominantly non-commercial flavour set as far back as the 1920s and solidified in the 1940s and 1950s. In a 1990 report to the Dean, Arthur Motyer wrote:

> In the years since 1975, Windsor Theatre, the essential lab for the whole programme, has produced about two hundred plays of all styles and periods, in English and French ... Dramatists produced have included Aristophanes, Beckett, Shakespeare, Beaumont and Fletcher, Molière, Goldsmith, Wedekind, Ibsen, Chekhov, Tremblay, Anouilh, Stoppard, Brecht, Ionesco, Pinter, and dozens more from all the major periods in English and French, including musicals and design work initiated by students as special projects in their own music and fine arts programmes; and a number of Canadian plays, either already established or newly created.[24]

The richness of the Windsor Theatre offerings over the past nearly twenty years stems largely from the efforts of Professors Arthur Motyer and Alex Fancy, themselves graduates of Mount Allison and both involved in the area of concentration in drama from its outset. They are but two of many alumni who have built on their experience as undergraduates to pursue a life related to the theatre. Motyer was president of the Players Society in 1944, succeeding another Canadian theatre luminary, Nathan Cohen, who was president in 1942. Ron Irving of Theatre Prince Edward Island was also a Players Society president (1952–53). Allison Bishop, who directed a production of Rattigan's *The Deep Blue Sea* in 1957, has gone on to a very successful career in Nova Scotia's cultural department. Typical of the breadth of the society's constituency, however, were two other Players Society presidents: David Critchley, who went on to a distinguished career in the public service both in Canada and in his native Bermuda, and Tom Simms, who went on to a highly successful career in the private sector.

In 1990, when a list was devised of the occupations of graduates who had been involved in the Windsor Theatre over the fifteen-year period since 1975, it was found that at least thirty-eight had gone on to theatre-related careers that ranged from the teaching of drama in a university to professional acting and design, to opera, to stagecraft.[25] While they were students, these people, and many others who did not go on to pursue lives in the theatre, obviously had much to do with the shaping of drama at Mount Allison. As with any undertaking in any university, but perhaps to a greater degree than many, the fortunes of a drama program are highly sensitive to the talents, interests, and overall profile of an ever-changing student body; and this is one of the primary "variable" features that must be examined.

I have already mentioned some of the graduates of the Ladies' College's Department of Oratory whose manifest qualities as students led them to become qualified teachers at various institutions; likewise some of the students in the 1940s who distinguished themselves in drama at Mount Allison before proceeding to further study and influence. All of them flourished under a system that was markedly dominated by faculty authority. As might be expected, it was not until the 1950s and 1960s, two decades coinciding with general increases in student autonomy, that one found students taking much of the initiative, without direct faculty support. While C.F. MacRae was directing the popular success *The Man Who Came to Dinner* in 1953, for instance, a fourth year fine arts student called Lorin Mair was directing a production of Anouilh's rather more biting *Antigone*; and in 1956 another student, Len St Hill, directed Giraudoux's *The Madwoman of Chaillot*, which was accorded the honour of being played at closing that year – an honour usually reserved for Gilbert and Sullivan productions or for efforts directed by members of the faculty. This was followed in February 1957 by Allison Bishop's production of *The Deep Blue Sea*, mentioned earlier, while C.F. Macrae prepared Shaw's *Candida* for April of that year. In 1972, while Alex Fancy directed *Le Bourgeois Gentilhomme* in the Windsor Theatre, student Ron Ormston produced *'Tis Pity She's a Whore* in Convocation Hall.[26]

The restructuring of the Windsor Theatre and the establishment of the drama program in 1975 have led to a renewed coherence among faculty efforts, student efforts, the classroom, and the stage that has both fostered and allowed for the reward of student initiative in the theatre. In 1992–93 it became possible for senior students, in possession of several prerequisite courses and under close supervision, to direct a play and produce supporting documentation in fulfilment of one term course in drama – providing formal recognition of the enormity of the initiatives taken and the efforts made by student directors. In other words, a mechanism has been found to ensure the coordination of student initiative with an intellectual rigour consistent with formal coursework in drama.

Many disciplines in the university are sensitive to the availability of special facilities and to the general level of development of a physical plant. Among arts disciplines, this is true for drama in much the same way as it is for music and the fine arts; and this is a second major factor to be addressed. In the 1920s, the practice was often to "take the college play downtown" to the Musical Hall (also called the Imperial) theatre in the Wood Block. Ida Leslie's productions, and many before them, had enjoyed the relative splendour of the facilities there.[27]

By the 1930s, when Gilbert and Sullivan productions became the standard fare for "closing" festivities each spring, Fawcett Hall, with its conventional proscenium set-up, appears to have become the exclusive venue for live university theatre in Sackville.[28] In 1958 it was still considered a sufficiently viable theatre space to host the New Brunswick Drama Festival, and until the mid-1960s it continued to house the Mount Allison Players' productions.[29]

When the old Fawcett Hall was replaced in 1966 by the current Convocation Hall, the *Mount Allison Record* crowed hopefully that it would "fill the needs of student and University players."[30] The hope, however, was unfounded, as major productions flagged in 1967–68. It is perhaps telling that Spring Convocation festivities in 1968 included an alumni-sponsored production of *The Odd Couple* by Halifax's Neptune Players in Convocation Hall, in place of the traditional Players Society revival or Gilbert and Sullivan production. In all, only five major campus theatrical productions have joined the more recent Garnet and Gold musical comedies in braving Convocation Hall: *Macbeth* (1969), *The Flies* (1970), *Twelfth Night* (1971), *'Tis Pity She's a Whore* (1972) and *The Lion in Winter* (1976).

As early as 1962, when Fawcett Hall was still standing, there were indications that students might like a more flexible and experimental space in which to work. November of that year saw Tweedie Hall temporarily transformed into a "theatre-in-the-round" for an evening of short plays that could take advantage of such a configuration.[31] (In more recent years, Tweedie Hall has been a staple rehearsal space and has been pressed into service occasionally as an "overflow" performance space.) After the building of Convocation Hall, the need for alternative arrangements became even more pressing. In the early 1970s, in an attempt to address the poor actor-audience dynamic of the space, Arthur Motyer designed and had built a thrust stage to fit onto the Convocation Hall stage. J. Douglas Campbell experimented with the area adjacent to the Lily Pond for three summer productions of Shakespeare: *Love's Labour's Lost* (1968), *Henry IV* (1969) and *Much Ado about Nothing* (1970).[32] The Chapel saw a production of the medieval morality play *Everyman* in 1974.

In 1971, with the refurbishment of the old library as the University Centre, the Windsor Theatre that was created on the building's second floor appeared to be the solution to Mount Allison's need for a flexible, modern theatre space. Its unobstructed floor space and relatively high ceiling clearance suited it to black-box studio production. Minimal renovations to the space in 1975 made for excellent sightlines for the audience on movable raked seating and provided much-needed storage space. Hand in hand with the improved theatrical facility went an enormous increase in the number of productions, as previously described. In fact, it seemed that the drama program would quickly outgrow the Windsor Theatre as its sole venue. In 1981 and 1982 productions were mounted in Hesler Hall, which permitted for more innovative staging and allowed advanced stages of work to proceed on two major productions at once. As early as 1984, plans for a new drama centre were being formulated. Toronto architect Brian Arnott was commissioned to do a study on refurbishing the old Music Hall in the Wood Block as a theatre for Mount Allison (the building's current owner, since buying it from the university, is reviving a plan for its renovation as a community theatre); and in the late 1980s plans were made for a new flexible theatre space to be part of a multipurpose building to be erected on the campus. Although the project was approved by the Maritime Provinces Higher Education Commission and matching funds were earmarked by the Province, this new building project was dropped because of the university's difficulties in maintaining its current physical plant.

Having sketched the history of drama at Mount Allison between 1920 and the present, it remains to try to identify Mount Allison's answer to the challenges of integrating drama studies within a liberal-arts context. Among these challenges, the most commonly perceived include defining the relationship of drama studies to value-oriented studies in the literary disciplines; integrating the practical making of theatre with a critical understanding of how and why it might be made; and "de-streaming" practical and theoretical approaches to the subject.[33]

The formalization in 1975 of the interdisciplinary nature of drama studies at Mount Allison in the area of concentration coincided with a larger pattern of change to liberal arts curricula across the continent. The shift in emphasis from mastering content in certain classical disciplines to breadth of acquaintance with a number of methodologies, usually through distribution requirements, created the ideal milieu for the "new" program in drama. Its essentials, however, had been rehearsed for many years.

The size of Mount Allison and its sense of community no doubt always exerted an influence on the kinds of plays produced here. I have characterized the repertoire as "non-commercial"; the epithet is both economic and aesthetic. What might be referred to as the "hot-house" atmosphere of the small liberal arts college, coupled with the necessarily interwoven paths of large numbers of the student body and (to be blunt) the relative absence of other diversions, has afforded the opportunity to do serious work in the theatre, to experiment with, and give life to, works that would not necessarily find their way into the commercial repertoire.

From the outset of the period studied here, it seems clear that the making of theatre at Mount Allison has been connected in some way to work within the main body of the more traditional curriculum. The presence of Miss Leslie and Miss Purdy as credentialed teachers in the Department of Oratory and, at the same time, as directors of the college plays provides early evidence of this, as does Miss Lewis's situation in the Department of Academics, where she nonetheless placed emphasis on practical play production. When, with the closure of the School for Girls, the university was forced to fend for itself in theatre, the active involvement of English professors Gundy and Trueman as advisors to the Players Society, and of Wilgar, MacRae, Sidnell, and others as directors, suggests a necessary, if not formal, cross-pollination, given the tiny size of the department and therefore the inevitability of students of English studying under these men. A limited student body and a small pool of professors operating within a small and isolated campus forged links between the classroom and the theatre that were to inform the structure of the area of concentration in drama. The program, moreover, recognizes what may be the most significant feature of the Mount Allison experience as it has related to theatre and drama in the liberal arts context: the ability to cross, even the necessity of crossing, intra-institutional borders. In the 1920s, just as students at the Ladies' College frequently took their courses at the more senior Mount Allison institution, so the instructors in oratory and expression loaned their talents to the university for the annual play. When borders between the Ladies' College, restyled the School for Girls, and the university became more clearly marked in the 1930s, the drama specialists continued to cross those borders. In the 1940s and 1950s, when it would not have been difficult for the English department to stake out a "monopoly" in drama (as English departments elsewhere did and continue to do), the backgrounds and future occupations of the students involved in the Players Society suggest that this was not so. Efforts in the 1960s to involve members of faculty in music and the fine arts in the presentation of theatre (in the absence of a department of theatre design or theatre music), and the growing involvement in the 1970s of the Department of French (and, later, of other literature departments) in the Windsor Theatre, all pointed the way to the kind of interdisciplinary program that developed. It has been in some ways an exercise in successful adaptation, a fruitful working out in practical terms of the implications of the kind of arbitrary decision made by Peter Quince and his Attic players in *A Midsummer Night's Dream*, that "this green plot shall be our stage."

NOTES

1 See, for example, Hayden White, *The Content of the Form* (Baltimore: Johns Hopkins University Press, 1987) and *Tropics of Discourse* (Baltimore: Johns Hopkins University Press, 1978).
2 See John Reid, *Mount Allison University: A History to 1963, Volume II: 1914–1963* (Toronto: University of Toronto Press, 1984), 40–1, on the Massey Commission.
3 See *Mount Allison Record* 20, no. 1 (Oct.-Dec. 1936): 1, which announces the appointment of Miss Evangeline Lewis (MA, Edinburgh) to teach dramatics and mathematics in the School for Girls; a photo appears on p.10.
4 "School for Girls Calendar," 1938, p. 21, cited in Reid, *Mount Allison University*, vol. 2, 129.
5 See *Mount Allison Record* 26, no. 2 (May 1943): 41 for an account of Professor Wilgar's production of *Romeo and Juliet*, that year's "college play," repeated as part of closing exercises. Margaret Masten's involvement is chronicled in Rhianna Edwards, Mount Allison Players Society Accession 8656 Inventory and Notes (Mount Allison University, Ralph Pickard Bell Library Archives).
6 See Reid, *Mount Allison University*, vol. 2, 251, 260, 274, 347 for materials on MacRae's career at Mount Allison.
7 The production is written up in the *Mount Allison Record* 47, no. 1 (Winter 1964): 11.
8 See Edwards, Mount Allison Players Society.
9 These statistics are printed in the *Mount Allison Record* 15, nos. 3–4 (Jan. 1932): 75.
10 From ibid., vol. 14, no. 6 (Feb. 1931): 105.
11 See ibid., vol. 16, nos. 5–6 (Feb.-March 1933): 89, "Librarian's Report."
12 See ibid., vol. 20, no. 1 (Oct.-Dec. 1936): 12.
13 See "On Stage at Mount Allison, 1875–1985," *Campus Notebook* 5, no. 13 (4 April 1986): 1.
14 See Reid, *Mount Allison University*, vol. 2, 274.
15 The flavour of the interclass festival's fare may be reconstructed from the following examples, for which I am indebted to Rhianna Edwards: in 1943 Jean Scarth (senior class) directed Synge's *Riders to the Sea*,

while the freshmen produced Lady Gregory's *Spreading the News*; Rupert Brooke's *Lithuania* was directed by David Critchley in 1946 and by Ron Irving in 1952; Yeats's *Purgatory* and *The Death of Cuchulain* were produced in 1963–64; and in 1948–49 O'Neill's *The Emperor Jones* was entered by sophomores in the Interclass Festival and sent on to regional and national competitions (see also *Mount Allison Record* 21, no. 3 (Fall 1949): 12–13, where Dr J.C. MacFarlane of the Canadian Manufacturer's Association is quoted to the effect that this latter production is an example of what Mount Allison might contribute to restoring "the lost curricula.")

16 This listing is based on Edwards, Mount Allison Players Society.

17 Descriptions of Miss Leslie's productions may be found in the *Mount Allison Record* 4, no. 6 (April 1920): 46; ibid., vol. 5, no. 5 (May 1921): 38 and ibid., vol. 11, no. 8 (May 1928): 82. Accounts of Miss Stewart are found in ibid., vol. 14, no. 1 (Sept 1930): 4, and vol. 14, nos. 9–10 (June 1931): 151. Ibid., vol. 26, no. 2 (May 1943): 63, published an obituary for Ida Leslie, who was head of oratory from 1917 to 1930.

18 For Purdy's activities see ibid., vol. 13, no. 9 (May 1930): 139; ibid., vol. 17, nos. 1–3 (Oct.-Dec. 1933): 3; ibid., vol. 19, no. 2 (Jan.-March 1936): 72; and ibid., vol. 18, no. 1 (Oct.-Dec. 1934): 25.

19 Ibid., vol. 19, no. 2 (Jan.-March 1936): 77, announces that Purdy had resigned to continue studies in speech at Columbia.

20 See ibid., vol. 20, no. 1 (Oct.-Dec. 1936): 1.

21 See ibid., vol. 22, no. 1 (October 1938): 8; and ibid., vol. 22, nos. 6–7 (April-May 1939): 138.

22 Wilgar's *Romeo and Juliet* has been cited previously. Hamer's wartime Gilbert and Sullivan productions included: *Iolanthe* in Fawcett Hall with Choral Society (ibid., 129; p. 136 reports that *Iolanthe* was broadcast through a new association with CKCW in Moncton; a central studio was located in the Conservatory, with remote lines to all areas of the campus); *The Gondoliers* in Fawcett Hall (ibid., vol. 25, no. 3 [May 1942]: 67; and *The Pirates of Penzance* in Fawcett Hall (ibid., vol. 17, no. 2 [May 1944]: 40).

23 The record of repertoire used for this portrait is derived from Edwards, Mount Allison Players Society, and from the *Mount Allison Record* between 1920 and 1973.

24 "Report of the Dean's Advisory Committee to Review the Drama Programme" (1990), 8–9. A calendar of performance, 1975–90, is included as Appendix D.

25 Ibid., Appendix C.

26 See *Mount Allison Record* 36, no. 1 (Spring 1953): 15, 31; ibid. (Spring 1956): back cover; see also Edwards, Mount Allison Players Society.

27 See *Mount Allison Record* 3, no. 7 (April 1919): 51, regarding the by then long-lived custom of putting on "the college play" in the theatre in town. Specific instances include a production of *Miss Fearless and Co.* by students of the Department of Oratory (Ladies' College) at the Opera House (ibid., vol. 3, nos. 8–9 [May-June 1919]: 57) and the presentation of *A Midsummer Night's Dream* as part of closing exercises in 1920 at The Imperial (ibid., vol. 4, no. 6 [April 1920]: 42).
28 The thirties saw productions of HMS *Pinafore* presented in Fawcett Hall as part of closing by the Choral Society under Hamer (ibid., vol. 15, nos. 8–9 [May-June 1932]: 141–2); *Pirates of Penzance* by the hundred-member Ladies' College Choral Society (ibid., vol. 17, nos. 1–3 [Oct.-Dec. 1933]: 3); *Mikado* (ibid., vol. 16, nos. 3–4 [Dec.-Jan. 1933]: 67 and ibid., vol. 16, nos. 7–9 [April-June 1933]: 124–5); and HMS *Pinafore* (ibid., vol. 19, no. 3 [April-May 1936]: 102). Productions of Gilbert and Sullivan in Fawcett Hall continued into the fifties with such productions as *Ruddigore* under the direction of Geoffrey Payzant (see *Mount Allison Record* 36, no. 4 [Winter 1953]: 87 and ibid., vol. 37, no. 1 [Spring 1954]: 20–1).
29 *Mount Allison Record* 41, no. 2 (Summer 1958): 77.
30 Ibid., vol. 49, no. 4 (December 1966): 5.
31 This is noted in Edwards, Mount Allison Players Society.
32 See ibid.
33 For a discussion of such issues, see R.P. Knowles, "Otherwise Engaged: Towards a Materialist Pedagogy," *Theatre History in Canada*, 12, no. 2 (Fall 1991): 193–9; and ibid., "Times Change Values, Don't They? Drama, Theatre, and the Myth of the Liberal Education," *Drama Contact* 16 (Fall 1992): 11–13; as well as Laurin Mann, "Teaching Acting: Four College Programmes," *Canadian Theatre Review* 78 (Spring 1994): 32–7.

CHAPTER EIGHT

Religion at the Small University: A Comparison of Three Maritime Universities

MARK PARENT

The twin themes of change and continuity characterize the religious life of Mount Allison University from its inception to the present day. While much has changed, much has remained the same. It is important for scholars and interested participants who wish to discuss the role of religion in contemporary Canadian universities to take note of both the continuities and the changes.

In order to highlight the similarities and differences between past and present, I will compare the roles of religion at Mount Allison, St Francis Xavier University (a Roman Catholic institution), and Acadia University (a Maritime Baptist institution). While observations will be advanced concerning the history of each university in its entirety, I have chosen to concentrate on the post-World War II era for two reasons. First, the post-World War II history of these institutions has been studied less than the pre-war period. Second, the most dramatic changes in the religious texture of the life of the three universities occurred during the post-war period. Significant events that influenced their religious profiles took place prior to 1945, but their effect was blunted by the strong religious ethos of both university and society.[1]

Since World War II, the religious life of the universities under study has changed so dramatically that the word "secularization" has been advanced time and again to describe what has been happening during this period. Thus, at Acadia, changes in the board of governors in 1966 resulted in what has officially been called the "secularization" of the university. At St Francis Xavier, the first lay president, David Lawless, sought to reassure university supporters in his 1992 presidential report that his appointment would not further erode the Roman Catholic character of the institution. Instead, Lawless vowed to "protect" the religious heritage of St Francis Xavier, pointing out that laicization did not necessarily imply secularization.[2]

The term secularization is, however, of limited value in trying to discover and understand the changes in the role of religion at the three universities. In first instance, the charge of secularization depends upon some perceived "golden age." This was the attitude taken in the 1950s by a Mount Allison student, Stephen Poirier. Preaching in Perry F. Rockwood's church in Truro, Nova Scotia, Poirier attacked Mount Allison for having become modernistic when compared with its supposedly solid Christian past.[3]

A similar attitude is evinced in a letter from the Reverend Fred Gordon, editor of *The Maritime Baptist*, to the executive secretary of the United Baptist Convention of the Atlantic Provinces, Rev. Harry Renfree. Written during the critical decade of the 1960s when the first non-Baptist was chosen to serve as principal, Gordon's letter was part of a larger correspondence concerning Baptist "control" of Acadia University. In this particular letter, Gordon expressed his strong concern that changes in the size of the student body as well as "apathy" on the part of the new university president, Dr Jim Beveridge, would inevitably lead to the serious diminution of the Christian character of Acadia University. Adopting a rather plaintive tone, Gordon wrote: "In my humble opinion time is not on our side, and ... if we hope to keep Acadia as a 'truly' Christian university, with a 'truly' Christian mission, then somewhere, somehow, steps will have to be taken *immediately* to keep Acadia's enrolment at its present figure"[4] (my emphasis).

Statements about the golden past are also stressed by Peggy MacIsaac in the local Antigonish paper concerning recent controversies at St Francis Xavier. Writing in the 12 February 1992 edition of *The Casket*, MacIsaac warns, "There's a crucial debate going on at St Francis Xavier, the outcome of which will determine whether the university remains Catholic or becomes secularized." MacIsaac then describes the strong Roman Catholic character that prevailed from the founding of the university up until, according to MacIsaac, the 1980s.[5]

The golden-past syndrome, however, fails to do justice to the flow of history. For example, it can well be argued that at their inception Mount Allison and Acadia were secular institutions; likewise St Francis Xavier, to a lesser degree. Such an approach depends upon using the political, ideological, and ecclesiastical situation of the Middle Ages as the yardstick of secularity rather than the immediate past. Thus, the "secular" character of the three universities is clearly revealed in the "non-sectarian" claims that were such a prominent feature at their foundings. While Acadia and Mount Allison were to be firmly Protestant (and Evangelical Protestant at that), and St Francis Xavier was to be Roman Catholic, the founders of each institution nonetheless embraced the concept of non-sectarianism in order to justify the establishment of their respective schools.[6]

What historians have overlooked is that this emphasis upon tolerance towards other faiths and the individualization (and subsequent privatization) of one's own religious beliefs is one of the defining features of modern "secular" civilization.[8] Read in this light, the religiosity expressed in Charles Allison's verbal offer of an endowment to a joint meeting of Methodist missionaries in Halifax on 12 July 1839 takes on a very different hue.

Charles Frederick Allison was diffident and rather shy as he put forward his offer but was quite confident that his generosity was inspired by religious convictions. As he stated, "The Lord hath put it into my heart to give this sum towards building a Wesleyan Academy ... I know the impression is from the Lord, for I am naturally fond of money."[8] As Peter Penner notes in his history of the Sackville Methodist (later United) Church, Allison's concept of and desire for Methodist education "grew out of his conversion to Methodism [from a nominal Anglicanism], out of a sense [as Allison himself phrased it] ... 'of accountability to that Gracious Being who [*sic*] I will ever recognize as the source of all good that is done in the earth.'"[9]

In recounting the history of the evolution of religion at Mount Allison, however, it is important to dwell not only on the form of piety that prompted Allison's "liberal offer" but on its inner nature. The intense focus of Methodism upon the responsibility of the individual believer to make his or her decision for Christ was one that could be said to have already proceeded far along the historic road of secularism. Whether one dates the rise of Western secularism and secularization from the onset of the Reformation (as Max Weber does) or from the emphasis on religious tolerance that arose out of the religious wars of the sixteenth and seventeenth centuries, one key factor in the process was the ideological revolution initiated by the French philosopher René Descartes. Although Descartes himself remained a committed Christian, the dethronement of the person of God by the human self – given voice in Descartes's celebrated comment "I think, therefore I am" – helped unravel the medieval philosophical and theological synthesis that had reigned for some one thousand years over Western Europe. More to the point, it was an important part of a great cluster of events and perspectives that gave birth to our modern era, which is characterized, in large part, by the elevation of the human self and the priority of the autonomous ego in decisions of religious adherence and faith.

With its intense focus upon the conversion and commitment of the individual "believer," Methodism (and the Baptist movement as well) harnessed the energy of this philosophical revolution. Freed from the constraints of the historical Church, which provided a counterbalance to the individual self in both Roman Catholicism and Anglicanism, Evangelical Protestantism was ideally suited to the temper of its time, as well as to the new world of the Americas. This priority of the self, along with the growing economic might and respectability of the Baptists and the Methodists of the Maritime provinces, contributed in important ways to the development of Acadia and Mount Allison alike.

To reiterate, the birth of Acadia, Mount Allison, and St Francis Xavier could be said to have taken place in the midst of "modern secular" beliefs in the priority of the individual self that undergirds much of modernity. One could very easily claim that, viewed from the context of medieval society, these three universities were at their inception radically secular institutions.

As noted at the outset, however, in describing the changing role of religion in the universities under study, a more productive avenue of investigation is to examine the changes and the continuities in each, paying particular attention to the post-World War II period.

CONTINUITIES

One key similarity between past and present at Acadia, Mount Allison, and St Francis Xavier is the denominational connection that perseveres to this day. It is formalized in different ways in each of the universities, St Francis Xavier having (as might be expected) the strongest denominational ties. Nonetheless, all three institutions have members of their founding denominations on their governing boards through appointment by those denominations. At St Francis Xavier, moreover, the bishop of the diocese is by virtue of office the chancellor of the university and by precedent the chairperson of the board.[10]

Thus, while institutional control of Acadia, Mount Allison, and St Francis Xavier passed out of the hands of the Baptist, United, and Roman Catholic churches in the 1960s, each university is still tied to its founding denomination. Legacies, archival material, and reputation also identify each university with its founding denomination. A short visit to the archives of either Acadia or St Francis Xavier is sufficient to impress upon the visitor the denominational background of these two institutions. Recent structural changes to the board of regents of Mount Allison have dramatically reduced representation on the board by members of the United Church, which has warned that it might drop its designation of Mount Allison as a United Church–related institution. Nonetheless, at present the denominational tie persists on the official board level.

One other similarity among the three institutions that has a direct bearing on their religious origins is the composition of the community in which each school is situated. Not only are they all located in small, maritime towns but each is placed in an area where the founding denominational community, although less dominant than in the past, still wields influence. In fact, St Francis Xavier and Acadia are located where they are largely because of the concentration of Roman Catholics in the Antigonish area and Baptists in the Wolfville area.

The anomalous location of Mount Allison in the only English-speaking province where the Baptists rather than the United Church have always had numerical dominance is explained not only by the relatively strong Methodist presence in Sackville during Charles Allison's time but also by the fact that, in many important ways, Mount Allison has looked to Nova Scotia rather than to New Brunswick for leadership. If this is an overstatement of the case, it is clear that the founders of Mount Allison fought against suggestions that a Methodist school be located in the growing city of Saint John rather than the small town of Sackville with the argument that the new school would exist to serve the Maritime provinces as a whole and not just the Methodists of New Brunswick.[11]

Besides being located in pockets that historically have been dominated by the founding denominations, the religiosity of the entire Maritime provinces also plays a part in maintaining the continuing religious texture of each institution. As Lethbridge sociologist Reginald Bibby and Queen's historian George Rawlyk have each pointed out, Canada's "Bible Belt" is not to be found in the West but rather in the East.[12] The complex and dynamic interplay between this religiosity and the ongoing life of the three universities is beyond the scope of this paper, but it is an important factor that is as present today as it was in the past. The student parades of the 1950s to the Sackville United Church and the Wolfville Baptist Church no longer form part of the tradition at Mount Allison and Acadia universities, yet the two churches continue to have close connections with their respective schools. At St Francis Xavier, the Roman Catholic cathedral of St Ninians is included in university functions not simply for reasons of space.

The close connections between the founding denominations and the universities are exemplified most clearly by the chapel buildings that are such dominant features of the university landscapes. Mount Allison's chapel is the most centrally located of the three. As late as 1989, Donald Wells (then president of the university) claimed that the centrality of the chapel served to symbolize an ongoing "partnership of faith and higher learning."[13] The Manning chapel at Acadia, built in

1963 (two years earlier than Mount Allison's), while not as central, is nonetheless a dominant and attractive architectural feature of the university, as is the much larger university chapel at St Francis Xavier built in 1948.

Just as important as the chapel buildings is the continuity of chaplaincy service that has characterized each institution. Acadia hired a full-time chaplain, Charles Wellington Rose, in 1930, but this early attempt to establish a full-time university chaplaincy fell through because of financial pressures arising out of the Great Depression.[14] It was not until the 1950s that another chaplain was hired. Acadia led the way with Rev. Charles Taylor, followed by Mount Allison, where Rev. D.I. Macintosh was hired in 1957. Even without full-time chaplains, the work of chaplaincy was always carried out at Acadia, Mount Allison, and St Francis Xavier.

Chaplaincy work at St Francis Xavier was provided by the priests who taught in the university, many of whom also served as dons in the various university residences. While the majority of the priests undoubtedly performed their pastoral duties towards the university students with compassion and dedication, their combined workload as teachers and dons proved very heavy. Clerical dissatisfaction with this arrangement coincided with student calls to serve as their own dons. In 1951 an experiment was instituted at one of the student residences whereby the students rather than the priests meted out much of the discipline.[15] As this process of extending lay control continued, the office of the chaplain (until recently known as the director of Religious Affairs) took on a more prominent role within the university. In 1954, for example, with the appointment of Rev. Gregory MacKinnon as Religious Affairs director at St Francis Xavier (he later became president of the university), theological courses came to be taught once again by university staff rather than volunteer parish priests.[16]

At Acadia the work of chaplaincy prior to the hiring of Rev. Charles Taylor (subsequently a professor of clinical pastoral education at the Acadia Divinity College) was usually handled by professors in the Department of Theology. Acadia was always meant to be a training centre for Baptist ministers in the Atlantic Provinces, and, unlike St Francis Xavier, which began with the same motivation, it has continued the tradition.[17] This has meant that for much of its life Acadia has had a ready supply of part-time chaplains. The revival of the office of chaplain in the 1950s was due not to the absence of chaplaincy services but, in large part, to a growing student interest in religion, which necessitated a more formalized chaplaincy service.[18]

The situation at Mount Allison was similar to that of Acadia and St Francis Xavier except for the impact that church union had upon the division of training in the Maritime institutions of the new United Church of Canada. As a result of the union of the Methodist, many Presbyterian, and most Congregational churches in 10 June 1925, the bulk of theological training at Mount Allison was transferred to the Pine Hill Divinity School in Halifax, Nova Scotia. However, the pre-theological stream continued at Mount Allison and its professors provided chaplaincy services in addition to their teaching load. Until the hiring of the university chaplain in 1957, the president of Mount Allison performed chaplaincy duties as well, especially those connected with public worship.

Thus, while each of the three universities has seen fit since the Second World War to hire chaplains dedicated solely to chaplaincy, each institution has always sought to provide pastoral care and to further religious devotion. Moreover, although the present chaplain at Acadia was hired as chaplain to all denominations (and indeed to all major faith groups), Rev. Roger Prentice is a Baptist minister affiliated with the United Baptist Convention of the Atlantic Provinces. At St Francis Xavier, the two chaplains that are presently employed by the university are Roman Catholics.[19] In fact, it is only Mount Allison that has departed from its denominational allegiance, the last three chaplains having been Baptist-affiliated clergy.[20]

This is not to say that chaplaincy services at Acadia, Mount Allison, and St Francis Xavier have remained the same since the universities were founded. Apart from the establishment of full-time chaplaincies, significant change has been evident in the greater ecumenism that has prevailed since World War II. Indeed, from their formation in the 1950s, the chaplaincies at Mount Allison and Acadia have revealed an ecumenical spirit. At St Francis Xavier, it was not until after Vatican II that the ecumenical vision caught hold, but catch hold it did. Today it has the most developed ecumenical chaplaincy of the three universities, providing office space, secretarial support, and "official" university sanction for Anglican, United, and Pentecostal clergy.

Another interesting change that has occurred particularly at Mount Allison and Acadia has been a move towards interfaith dialogue and support for religious pluralism. This was pioneered at Mount Allison in the early 1960s under the leadership of the then chaplain, Rev. Dr Eldon Hay. Dispensing with the traditional university mission, Hay instituted an Inter-Faith Weekend. Limited in its scope to the inclusion of a Roman Catholic priest and a Jewish rabbi, along with several Roman Catholic and Jewish subleaders, this pluralistic approach nonetheless revealed an important broadening out of chaplaincy services at Mount Allison.[21]

Following Eldon Hay's move into full-time teaching in the Department of Religious Studies at Mount Allison, the interfaith emphasis was augmented by his successors with programs devoted to social-justice issues and the cultivation of human relationships. With the hiring of the university's eighth chaplain, Rev. Dr Seiichi Ariga, the interfaith emphasis begun by Eldon Hay was clearly enunciated. In an introductory letter written in September 1983, Ariga noted: "My role on campus as University Chaplain is a combination of church minister, school teacher, and a big brother of yours. If you are Christian, let us worship and work together. If you are not Christian, but of a certain faith, let us deepen our spirituality through inter-faith dialogue."[22]

An interfaith emphasis has been one of the key features of the chaplaincy at Acadia University in recent years, as well. Indeed, the current chaplain at Acadia, the Reverend Roger Prentice, was hired with the direct mandate of providing chaplaincy services to all the major faith groups.[23] The chapel at Acadia remains as a centre of specifically Christian identity, but Prentice seeks at public university functions to be as inclusive as possible.

Again, St Francis Xavier differs from the two Protestant institutions. While ecumenical cooperation is, as mentioned, firmly entrenched, interfaith cooperation is as yet in its infancy. In part this may be due to a confusion of terms. For example, in response to a published letter from a professor affiliated with the Coady Institute, David Lawless defended his actions in pushing for a renewal of the Roman Catholic character of St Francis Xavier. He then went on to insist that ecumenicity and interfaith relations were an important feature of St Francis Xavier, but his use of descriptive labels betrays a confusion of thought. Lawless writes: "Personally, I hold ecumenism highly and, although we have made considerable progress since Vatican II, believe all of us, especially Christians, have a big agenda before us ... Especially during this Week of Christian Unity we should all pray for understanding and tolerance among the churches. St Francis Xavier should dare to take the lead in being a place that encourages dialogue among those of all faiths."[24]

Clearly from Lawless's comments, "interfaith" dialogue is confined almost exclusively to "intra-Christian" dialogue and has not yet progressed to include members of non-Christian faith groups. This serves as an example of the differences in the religious texture of St Francis Xavier and the other two universities under study. St Francis Xavier's more overt relationship to its founding religious community subtly influences the religious texture of the university.

Along with the organizational linkages between the three institutions and their founding religious bodies, as well as the ongoing work of chaplaincy, a further similarity between past and present is the continuing emphasis upon a liberal arts education that has typified all three universities. Controversies over student size and degree programs have all had as one of their focuses the defence of the concept of a liberal arts program concentrating mainly on undergraduate students. The connection between this emphasis and the religious shape of each institution is a close and consistent one, as the definition of what constitutes a liberal arts education has always been a holistic one with strong emphasis upon the "character formation" of the attending students.

Changing social issues and forms of university discipline should not blind the observer to this important facet of the educational philosophies of Mount Allison, Acadia, and St Francis Xavier. While each of the three universities has abandoned to a large degree the concept of the university as "parent away from home," the task of training and fostering personal growth has never been abandoned. Mario Creet's insistence that "around the turn of this century higher education in Canada began to change rapidly and radically from God-centred preparation for life to job-oriented mastery of factual knowledge"[25] holds true for Acadia, Mount Allison, and St Francis Xavier. Yet it would not be accurate to claim that this new emphasis on factual knowledge totally displaced the former emphasis. The three universities under study have placed a high priority on "preparation for life" and continue to do so to the present.

This is not to claim that the rise of specialization within the academic disciplines has not had an important effect upon these universities. Major changes have altered their religious and ethical shape, but the move away from a purely Christian ethic has not meant the loss of any concern for ethical development. For example, in David Lawless's July 1992 summation of the strategic plan that is to guide St Francis Xavier into the next century, he notes: "Through the development of the whole person, we will continue to provide society with future leaders. The development of the whole person requires us to attend to the quality of social, spiritual, cultural, and recreational life of our students and not solely to the teaching and learning process. *We expect responsible behaviour from our students and, within the limits of our resources, we will provide an environment in which they will develop maturity*"[26] (my emphasis).

Similar statements appear in the Acadia document on long-term planning as reported in the 1991–92 presidential report. In that document the fourth goal articulated the desire "to provide for the personal development of the student in an academic, athletic, cultural, social and spiritual context, recognizing the special needs that may exist among such groups as mature students, international students and part-time students."[27]

While presidential statements may differ from the reality of student life, it would be erroneous to claim that character formation is not a stated intention of these three Maritime universities, as Creet seems to claim in regard to the larger Canadian situation.

CHANGES

While continuity continues to mark the religious life of Mount Allison, Acadia, and St Francis Xavier, significant changes also deserve mention. One change that occurred very early in the history of these schools was the supplanting of theological education for ordained ministry by an emphasis upon a broad-based education for future professionals.

Theological training was reintroduced at Acadia in the 1960s, and it remains a distinctive feature of this particular university. However, the influence of Acadia Divinity College upon the religious texture of Acadia is difficult to quantify. Many of the students at the divinity college are older and hold part-time jobs that mitigate against any sustained involvement in the university proper. Moreover, the semi-independent status of the college and the fact that it has its own chapel tend to minimize its impact upon the wider university population. It is worth noting, however, that Acadia Divinity College student Daniel Kirkegaard took part in a publicized debate on abortion held at Acadia in 1988.[28] While Kirkegaard's involvement in the wider life of the university was likely the exception to the rule, the presence of a theological seminary on the campus sets Acadia off from the other two universities.

How the religious life at Mount Allison and St Francis Xavier would have been influenced by a continuation of the original vision of theological education for professional ministry is impossible to determine. With a large dose of hyperbole but perhaps a measure of truth, Arthur Ebbutt, founding professor of the Department of Religious Studies at Mount Allison, commented on the diminution of theological training at Mount Allison due to church union. Reacting against the proposed Excellence Report, which would dramatically affect the Department of Religious Studies, Ebbutt pleaded:

> By no manner of thinking could I conceive that a Church college would do away with a Department of Religion altogether. On a deeper thinking into the whole question of a Christian philosophy of education, I now feel that a Department of Religion must have a central place among the disciplines, although academically it may play a subordinate role as we shall see. *Once before Mount Allison gave away its soul, its Department of Theology to*

Halifax at the time of Union. Surely it will not commit the same error twice.[29] (My emphasis)

Another difference between past and present is the growth of the three institutions. While comparatively small in the context of other Canadian universities, Mount Allison, Acadia, and St Francis Xavier are much larger today in comparison with pre-World War II years. For example, in 1932 the total enrolment at Mount Allison numbered 390 students, while in 1960 that figure had almost quadrupled to 1,144 students.[30] At Acadia, there were 492 students enroled at Acadia in 1943 and 1,233 in 1962.[31] The impact that large enrolments have had upon these schools is important in any consideration of their religious texture. At Acadia and St Francis Xavier, the growth in the student body and the concomitant growth in faculty were perceived as a threat to the Christian character of the institution.

Various reasons can be advanced for this attitude. As the number of students and affiliated alumni grew at Acadia, there was a corresponding pressure to change the board of governors. Regulations that confined membership to active Baptists disenfranchised a large and growing number of non-Baptist alumni. While the major changes did not take place until 1966, alumni disenchantment with the Baptist stranglehold on the board resulted in structural changes in 1957. Viewed from today's perspective the changes were small indeed. Viewed from the perspective of many Baptists at the time, the changes were significant. Alumni nominees were increased to fourteen, of whom one-half did not have to be Baptists. They did, however, have to be "members in good standing of Protestant churches."[32]

At St Francis Xavier, the growth of students and faculty resulted in changing patterns of religious life through the faculty rather than the student body. While claims that sixty percent of St Francis Xavier students are Roman Catholic[33] are impossible to substantiate, it is clear that the percentage of Roman Catholics who practise their faith in its institutional dimensions is higher at St Francis Xavier than the percentage of United Church students at Mount Allison or Baptists at Acadia. In part, this may be because St Francis Xavier places stronger emphasis than the other universities upon its connection with the church to which it is affiliated.[34]

With the vast majority of its student body adhering to the faith of the university founders, it has mainly been in the diversity of faculty that the ramifications of numerical growth have been felt at St Francis Xavier. Prior to World War II, prospective faculty members were mostly well known to the university's Roman Catholic-dominated administration, which could weed out non-Roman Catholic faculty as well as Roman Catholic adherents who did not practise their faith. However, with the growth following the war, and then again in the 1960s, the necessity of hiring a large number of new professors, many of whom were lay and personally unknown to the university administrators, resulted in the hiring of non-Roman Catholics. In 1941, for example, only 18.5 percent of the faculty at St Francis Xavier were lay people. In 1971 that figure had risen to 66 percent.[35] An emphasis upon academic proficiency rather than denominational background, coupled with the need for large numbers of new professors, had a decided impact upon the faculty of St Francis Xavier.

In fact, this shift in emphasis from Christian affiliation to academic expertise has been very marked in all three schools. Both Watson Kirkconnell, president of Acadia from 1948 to 1964, and L.H. Cragg, president of Mount Allison from 1963 to 1975, sought to hire "Christian" faculty whenever possible, but this was not an easy task in the growth decade of the 1960s. Watson Kirkconnell noted in a personal letter to Nova Scotia MLAs: "In my sixteen years as President, I preferred to hire a practising Protestant if a competent one were available, so as to have as many men as possible who were congenial by faith and temperament to the traditions of the institution. Unfortunately, with the lowest pay salary schedule in Canada and faced by a dire scarcity of trained instructors for all departments everywhere, I sometimes had to recruit men who had been brought up in other traditions."[36]

The development of legislation that protects against discrimination due to religious persuasion has exacerbated this trend towards religious pluralism. Today's administrators, even if they so desired, would be unable to ensure that faculty came from a Christian tradition, much less a specific denominational background. This growing pluralism of religious belief at the three universities has not been without its tensions. At St Francis Xavier, the new president, David Lawless, has attempted to underscore the Roman Catholic "character" of the school through comments in the strategic plan for the university as well as through the invitation of a guest speaker who addressed the issue of what it meant to be a Roman Catholic university. Lawless's actions have provoked a vigorous response by St Francis Xavier faculty. They would prefer the university to be described as having not a Catholic character, but a Catholic "heritage."[37] While it may be argued that this is a concession to secularism, it is also a recognition of the religious pluralism that now characterizes the faculty of St Francis Xavier.[38]

At all three universities, the most important change between postwar eras has been the increased proportion of government and business funding. This shift in funding has had the effect of minimizing the need for and importance of denominational monies and, thus, denominational control of the universities. For instance, while I was assured by a former president of St Francis Xavier that the Nova Scotia government never pressured St Francis Xavier to reduce its religious affiliation as a prerequisite for government money (indeed, according to Father MacDonell, quite the opposite was true),[39] it must be difficult nonetheless to be denominationally chauvinistic when the vast majority of funding is provided by non-church sources.

This increase in the relative significance of business over denominational funding began before World War I. At Acadia University, it was the business money of the Rockefellers that ensured the success of the "First Forward Movement" at the beginning of the twentieth century and, to an even greater degree, the "Second Forward Movement" held in 1903, when Rockefeller money accounted for one-half of the financial goal of $200,000.[40]

While business gifts and charitable foundations began quickly to surpass the amounts contributed by the founding denominations even prior to World War II, government funding in the post-war era played an even greater role in loosening ties to the founding religious communities at each of the three institutions. Immediately after the war, the three universities began to pressure government for increased funding. In a brief on university education submitted to the provincial government in February 1951 by representatives of New Brunswick universities, the point was forcefully made that "a changing economy has produced new conditions. The necessarily increasing demands of the cost of the welfare state no longer make it possible for large gifts and bequests to be made to higher education by individuals as formerly and we have to turn to the new recipient of such monies, namely the source of increased taxation, the organized governments of our country."[41]

The success of such pleas resulted in large infusions of government money, starting in the 1960s.[42] More than the earlier business funding, this dramatically altered the religious shape of each of the institutions under study. There are several reasons for this. The symbiotic relationship between business and the Christian communities in North America is a well-established fact.[43] Thus, while business funding served to lessen dependence upon denominational support, it did so under the rubric of an allegiance to Christianity. In fact, many of the business leaders who provided funding, such as the Rockefellers, were well-known Christian laymen and women. Arriving on the funding scene later, though, when Canadian society was beginning to change and diversify, governments were conscious of the need to serve *all* Canadian society. While the effects of this attitude were blunted at Mount

Allison, Acadia, and St Francis Xavier due to the confessional origin of most Maritime universities and the greater allegiance to Christianity in the East, the net effect of government money was further to erode denominational importance. In the 1960s, a former president of that university, Watson Kirkconnell, commented that "a denominational tiger may continue, as in my day, to breath down the president's neck, but its teeth have been pulled."[44]

One of the most interesting changes at the three universities concerns student religious societies. No more than passing mention can be made here to these societies but further study would be extremely beneficial in helping historians to understand student perspectives on religion. Suffice it to note that the Student Christian Movement (SCM), which was such an important part of the religious life of Acadia and Mount Allison immediately following World War I, has all but disappeared. Its place has been taken by a more conservative Christian group oriented towards personal spiritual growth and evangelistic outreach rather than the social, economic, and political concerns that were paramount with the SCM. While numbers are notoriously difficult to unearth, the Inter-Varsity Christian Fellowship (IVCF) groups at Acadia and Mount Allison clearly outnumber the remnants of the SCM. An IVCF group exists at St Francis Xavier as well, its roots extending back to the mid-1970s.[45]

Numbers, however, are extremely small when compared with the past. At present, for instance, only about twenty to thirty students attend the IVCF meetings at Mount Allison on a regular basis. Moreover, Campus Crusade and the Navigators, two other conservative Christian groups that are popular on the campuses of some Canadian universities, are almost non-existent at Mount Allison, Acadia, and St Francis Xavier.

Nonetheless, the growth of the IVCF, small as it may be, is of significance when viewed against the backdrop of a move away from Christian affiliation in Canadian society, and given the lack of university administrative support for, and sometimes even active opposition to, the establishment of IVCF groups at the universities under study. While at St Francis Xavier such student groups as the Knights of Blessed Sacrament and the Holy Name Society have disappeared, and while the SCM has become a pale shadow of its former self at Mount Allison and Acadia, groups such as IVCF have continued to emerge. Just as important has been the establishment of support groups for Bahai, Buddhist, Muslim, and Jewish students at these universities. The diversification of student religious societies provides further evidence that, while Mount Allison, Acadia, and St Francis Xavier have changed in their religious orientation, religion is still a notable feature at all three.[46]

The establishment of departments of religion marks another interesting and significant change in the religious life of these universities.[47] Mount Allison led the way with its Department of Religious Studies, established in 1960 by Rev. Dr Arthur Ebbutt, while Acadia followed suit in 1970 with the hiring of Dr Jim Perkin to head up the new academic department at the school. St Francis Xavier has also followed the same path, seemingly more by accident than design, as two of the priests who were sent away for training in the teaching of religion – including the current head of the Department of Theology, Burton MacDonald – returned to St Francis Xavier and then left the priesthood. The change at St Francis Xavier, however, is much more recent and in all likelihood should be dated to the 1980s.[48]

The establishment of departments of religion grew from very similar roots in all three institutions, as confessional approaches to the teaching of religion gave way to non-confessional "academic" approaches. Thus, in each of the universities previous instruction in religion paved the way and formed the basis for these new departments. Nonetheless, it was probably new continent-wide movements sparked by changes in the United States that led to this change. Since Mount Allison was the forerunner, it is useful to describe the history of the department in greater depth in order to understand this important aspect of religion at the three universities under study.

As earlier noted, a department of religion was established at Mount Allison in 1960 – a watershed year in the movement towards the non-confessional study of religion in the United States[49] – by Arthur Ebbutt, formerly professor of Greek and Hebrew before he became dean of Arts. At first it was a one-person department, but in 1962 Eldon Hay was hired on a shared arrangement with the chaplaincy. Ebbutt was insistent that the chaplaincy play second fiddle to the teaching that Hay was to undertake. This insistence, along with the heavy demands of two jobs, reinforced Eldon Hay's own personal interests and led to his resignation from the chaplaincy in 1964 and his employment as a full-time teacher in the new department. Ebbutt exulted over Hay's move, believing that the more "liberal" theological approach that he offered coupled with Hay's neo-orthodoxy would provide a good theological balance.[50]

This balance was not matched by a balance in areas of instruction. Hay was expected to cover theology, religious (mainly church) history, and comparative religion, and it was little wonder that with 160 full-time students and such a wide variety of disciplines, the plea for a third staff member was issued by Ebbutt in his 1965–66 report. However, thanks to a severe drop in student enrolment in the department the following year (from 160 to ninety-seven full-time students),

Ebbutt's request was shelved. In his 1967–68 annual report, Ebbutt attributed the drop in registration to a decline in candidates for the United Church ministry.[51]

The 1967–68 academic year saw a rise in enrolment back to 1965–66 levels and Ebbutt renewed his proposal for a third staff member, this time tying it to the possibility of creating a major in Religious Studies. Ebbutt envisioned himself continuing with the biblical and linguistic courses while Hay confined himself to the theological stream. The third teacher would have expertise and training in history and comparative religion. However, to Ebbutt's displeasure, Eldon Hay found himself increasingly drawn to the teaching of comparative religion, thus necessitating a search for a candidate in Christian theology. A 1969–70 sabbatical leave allowed Hay to begin specializing in comparative religion. While he and Ebbutt carried on a disagreement concerning teaching methods,[52] the search for a third staff member resulted in the hiring of Colin Grant in 1971.

Ebbutt's leadership at Mount Allison came to an end in 1972 when Charles Scobie was hired to be head of the three person Department of Religious Studies, a name it had acquired in 1968. Scobie, a former professor at McGill University, won his first victory when the university approved the proposal for a major in Religious Studies. This move to upgrade the department was accompanied by briefs to the New Brunswick Department of Education asking that more than two subjects out of twenty be applied to the Bachelor of Education degree.

In part as a result of these initiatives, new enrolment highs were reached in 1973–74 as 213 full-time students opted to take religious study courses. However, a round of sabbatical leaves and part-time replacements meant that enrolment figures dropped again for the next six years, and the 1973–74 levels were not reached again until 1980–81. In 1979–81 Mount Allison assumed significant leadership in the academic study of religion in Atlantic universities. The first Conference of Religious Study Departments and Theological Schools in the East was held at Mount Allison in May 1980.[53] By then the principle of a non-confessional study of religion was well established at Mount Allison and Acadia universities and taking root at St Francis Xavier as well. As Scobie put it in Mount Allison's 1980–81 departmental handbook:

> The study of religion deals with the deepest and most basic questions of human existence: the meaning and purpose of life, relations with a divine presence and power, inter-personal relations, and ultimate human destiny ... Such a programme does not exist to advocate one faith rather than another, and least of all to proselytize on behalf of one denomination. But it is designed to

encourage students to study a most important aspect of human existence, and it may help them to focus and clarify their thinking on these matters.[54]

While this principle of non-confessionalism was firmly established on the ideological level, the reality may have been slightly different. Course listings in 1982 reveal how strong the Christian orientation remained at Mount Allison. Of the twelve courses listed (excluding the opportunity individual students were given to take directed study courses), eight dealt specifically with Christianity, one with religious sociology, two with issues of religious philosophy, and only one with comparative religion.[55] Of course, the small size of the department as well as the numerical dominance of the Christian faith within Canadian society has been a factor in the selection of courses at Mount Allison. Moreover, teaching about Christianity is far different than the confessional approach to Christianity, as Scobie's statement in the 1980–81 departmental handbook made clear.

Charlie Scobie's assumption of the office of dean of Arts in 1981 placed pressure on a small department. From a high of 219 students in 1981–82, enrolment dropped to a low of 135 students in 1982–83. However, the department continued to earn recognition in the university and was moved to new quarters in Hart Hall in 1984, where the department staff members and secretary could be located on the same floor. It was also in 1984 that Mount Allison agreed to pay the dues and become a corporate member of the Canadian Corporation for Studies in Religion. When the first honours student, Jackie Throop, graduated two years later, the department gained further academic momentum.

The Ebbutt Trust Lecturers are another important facet of the department's programs and a boost to its reputation. Inaugurated in the 1982–83 academic year in honour of Arthur Ebbutt, the Ebbutt Memorial Trust has funded sabbatical replacements as well as speakers of note, such as Douglas Hall of McGill University, the British scholar G.B. Caird, and Eileen Schuller of McMaster University, who address large multidisciplinary audiences at Mount Allison.

In spite of these important achievements and the long history of religious study at Mount Allison, the Department of Religious Studies could not avoid the financial constraints that began in the late 1980s. Pleas for funds increasingly formed part of the department reports and dissatisfaction was voiced in the 1989–90 report that no monies could be found to replace Charlie Scobie, who had taken a well-deserved sabbatical. Dissatisfaction over funding shortages was soon overshadowed by concern over administrative proposals to amalgamate the departments of Classics, Religious Studies, and Philosophy, an idea that was viewed as having negative implications for the religious texture of Mount Allison. Oddly enough, the proposal came the year before the department reached its highest enrolment level, with 244 full-time students in the 1992–93 academic year.

At present, the Department of Religious Studies at Mount Allison continues with three full-time professors and two part-time teachers. Whether it will last into the next decade is difficult to ascertain, but continued high enrolments and the respect the full-time professors hold in the university community auger well for its future.

Such is not the case at Acadia, where economic cutbacks and the loss of Jim Perkin to university administration and ultimately to the presidency resulted in a reduction from three to two staff. Coupled with Roger Forsman's move into the teaching of philosophy, this has meant that the Department of Comparative Religion at Acadia has had to rely on a one-and-one-third level of teaching staff. A recent outside evaluation called for the restitution of the three-person system. Unfortunately, administration officials argued that if a full staff complement could not be obtained in the present economic climate, the only option was to close the department. At present, courses in comparative religion can still be taken at Acadia, but there is no official department and an honours program in religious studies is no longer a possibility. On the other hand, the Department of Theology at St Francis Xavier is expanding and hopes to have five full-time staff in the near future.

CONCLUSION

The theme of change and continuity raised in this paper is likely to mark the future of religious studies at the universities discussed here. Economically, the boom times that helped fuel chaplaincies and departments of religion are over. Educationally, calls for more technical education that will be of "greater profit" in the workplace affect the academic study of religion at Mount Allison and Acadia. The continuing erosion of church attendance and the reduced institutional power of both the Roman Catholic and Protestant communions in Canada cannot help but be reflected on the university campuses.

To many observers, these changes signal a decline in the role of religion at the universities. However, this view ignores such achievements as the establishment in recent decades of departments of religion and chaplaincy offices, as well as the growth of student groups catering to persons of non-Christian faiths. Pluralism of religion is well established at all three institutions. Moreover, the explicitly Christian ethic that once characterized the attitudes of staff, administration, and students at the three institutions is giving way to a multifaceted ethical system whose outlines are not yet clear.

However, I believe that the quest for meaning and purpose as well as the transcendental search for life beyond life necessitate some sort of religious expression. At a faculty meeting held to decide on a vote of censure concerning the leadership of Mount Allison president Ian Newbold, senior professor Arthur Motyer pleaded for "academic leadership, where *moral and spiritual courage ... match intellectual resolve*"[56] (my emphasis). The call for such leadership will persist.

I prefer to believe that there will be not decline, but a new growth of religion at the three universities in question. As the hubris that has too often accompanied modern academia gives way to a new humility, the gods of both past and future become attractive options for many students. This may be optimistic thinking on my part. One thing is certain: there will be continuity with the past, but there will be new ventures as well, as changes and continuities persist in characterizing and shaping the texture of religion at all three universities.

NOTES

1 At Acadia during the period following World War I a protracted controversy over dancing took place. The Baptist community at that time (and still, to a large extent, today) frowned upon dancing, particularly at a Baptist institution. In the end the administration took the position that the university could not be expected to correct "moral" deficiencies that had been overlooked in the home. The ramifications of such a decision were important. According to Acadian historian Dr Barry Moody, the controversy over dancing was the beginning of the dissolution of the close historical connection between the Baptist community and Acadia university. (Dr Barry Moody, interview with author, Kentville, Nova Scotia, 29 September 1993.) At St Francis Xavier the establishment of the Coady Institute during the interwar period also had important ramifications for the religious life of that institution, while at Mount Allison significant theological shifts took place before World War II. However, the full impact of these changes was not felt until after the war.

2 *Campus News* (Antigonish, NS: St Francis Xavier University, 19 November 1990): 1.

3 Stephen Poirier, *Changed from Romanism to the Light of the Gospel: With an Exposure of Modernism at Mount Allison.* Sermon delivered at People's Church, Truro, Nova Scotia, 20 March 1949 (Sackville, NB, Mount Allison University Archives). While Poirier may well have been correct in his attack on the theological shifts that took place at Mount

Allison from its inception, his comment is included as an example of those who establish some sort of benchmark from which all religious change is measured.

4 Rev. Fred Gordon to Rev. H.A. Renfree, 20 November 1964 (Wolfville, NS, Acadia University Archives).

5 Peggy MacIsaac, "Wednesday's World," *The Casket* (12 February 1992): 3.

6 It may well be that the non-sectarian statements were motivated by political desires to attract government support and undermine opposition by established schools. Moreover, non-sectarian did not mean non-Christian. However, in spite of such provisos, statements such as the following contained in the minutes of the board of governors of Acadia University in 1873 were a marked departure from the past: "The principles on which we are organized as a college prevent us from making sectarian differences prominent in our work, and we are pleased to observe that young men of different religious persuasions find their associations here as students harmonious and advantageous" (Norman Peveril, highlights of minutes from United Baptist Convention of the Atlantic Provinces concerning convention relationship with Acadia University, contained in letter from Harry Renfree to Member of the Higher Education Committee of Convention, 26 January 1965, Archives, Acadia University, Wolfville, Nova Scotia). Similar statements are found, for example, in the 1856–57 annual report for St Francis Xavier. Thus: "The College is open to all Denominations. No offence is ever given to Parents or pupils on account of their religious persuasions" (Antigonish, NS, St Francis Xavier University Archives).

7 See Wolfhart Pannenberg, *Christianity in a Secularised World* (New York: Crossroad, 1989).

8 Quoted in John G. Reid, *Mount Allison University: A History to 1963. Vol. I: 1843–1914* (Toronto: University of Toronto Press, 1984), 17.

9 Peter Penner, *The Chignecto 'Connexion': The History of Sackville Methodist/United Church, 1772–1990* (Sackville, NB: Sackville United Church, 1990), 32. Along with this "modernistic, secular" emphasis upon the autonomous self, one other important feature in the genesis of all three schools was the Baconian-Newtonian world view. Thus, the post-World War II conflict between science and faith was not a feature in the early years of these universities precisely because of accommodations to modernity that were present at their genesis.

10 St Francis Xavier University, *Act of Incorporation 1981*, 8.

11 See Reid, *Mount Allison University*, vol. I.

12 See Reginald Bibby, *Fragmented Gods: The Poverty and Potential of Religion in Canada* (Toronto: Irwin, 1987), 87f; *MacLean's*, 12 April 1993.

13 Donald Wells, "Preface," in J.G. Reid, *The History of Mount Allison University: 1939–1989* (Sackville, NB: Anchorage Press, 1989), vi-vii.
14 J.R.C. Perkin, "Chaplaincy at Acadia: Retrospect and Prospect." Report to the Governors of Acadia University, 3 February 1992, 4.
15 *Xaverian Weekly*, 15 January 1971, 1.
16 R.B. MacDonald, "Theology, Religion, Theology at St FX," 12 December 1992 (Antigonish, NS, St Francis University Archives).
17 For a time theological education lapsed due to efforts to centralize the training of Baptist ministers at Senator McMaster's university in Ontario, but the cost of travel, among other factors, put an end to this arrangement and prior arrangements were revived. See Ronald Stewart Longley, *Acadia University, 1838–1938* (Wolfville, NS: Kentville Publishing, 1939).
18 Charles Taylor, interview with author, Wolfville, NS, 1 October 1993.
19 The senior chaplain is Rev. Brian MacGillivray, a Roman Catholic priest, assisted by Jovita MacPherson, a Roman Catholic Religious Sister.
20 Rev. Hugh Kirkegaard, Rev. Dean Carter, Rev. J. Perkin.
21 "Report of the Chaplain 1965–1965" (Chaplain's File, Chaplain's Office, Mount Allison University, Sackville, NB).
22 Seiichi Ariga, Letter to Students, September 1983 (Chaplain's File, Chaplain's Office, Mount Allison University, Sackville, NB).
23 Roger Prentice, Interview with author, Wolfville, NS, 29 September 1993.
24 *Xaverian Weekly*, 5 February 1992, 7.
25 Mario Creet, "H.M. Tory and the Secularization of Canadian Universities," *Queen's Quarterly*, no. 4 (Winter 1981): 718.
26 David Lawless, "The Strategic Plan for St Francis Xavier University: President's Summary" (Antigonish, NS, St Francis Xavier University, July 1992), 1.
27 "Presidential Report, 1991/92," (Wolfville, NS, Acadia University).
28 *Athenaeum* (student newspaper), 3 November 1988, 2.
29 A.J. Ebbutt, "A Look at the Report on Excellence" (Sackville, NB, Mount Allison University Archives), 77.
30 John G. Reid, *Mount Allison University: A History to 1963. Vol. II: 1914–63* (Toronto: University of Toronto Press, 1984), 442.
31 Watson Kirkconnell, *The Fifth Quarter-Century: Acadia University, 1938–1963* (Wolfville, NS: Governors of Acadia University, 1968), 2–3.
32 Ibid., 25.
33 Florence Brophy, "Chaplaincy Services at St Francis Xavier University: A Survey of Student Usage and Attitudes" (March 1993, Chaplain's Office, St Francis Xavier University).
34 For example, the president's report for Mount Allison University noted in 1983 that the number of Roman Catholic students at the school exceeded the number of United Church students. Clearly, religion has

not been used by the administration of Mount Allison to attract secondary students to the university.

35 For this information I am indebted to Jim Cameron, St Francis Xavier University historian.

36 See Watson Kirkconnell, *A Slice of Canada: Memoirs* (Toronto: University of Toronto Press, 1967), 169.

37 "Faculty Response to the Strategic Plan Put Forward by the Strategic Planning Committee of the Board of Governors" (Antigonish, NS, Faculty Committee, St Francis Xavier University, 5 February 1992).

38 For a different perspective on the rise of religious pluralism in North American universities see George M. Marsden and Bradley J. Longfield, eds., *The Secularization of the Academy* (New York: Oxford University Press, 1992).

39 Father Malcolm MacDonell, interview with author, Antigonish, NS, 9 September 1993.

40 Longley, *Acadia University*, 105–7.

41 "A Brief on University Education in the Province Submitted to the New Brunswick Cabinet, February 28, 1951" (Mount Allison University Archives, Sackville, NB).

42 Paul Axelrod, "Higher Education, Utilitarianism and the Acquisitive Society: Canada, 1930–1980," in *Modern Canada, 1930–1980s: Readings in Canadian Social History*, eds. Gregory Kealey and Michael Cross (Toronto: McLelland and Stewart, 1984), 198f.

43 For interesting personal observations on the close relationship between North American Christianity and North American business interests see R. Niebuhr, *Leaves from the Notebook of a Tamed Cynic* (New York: Da Capo Press, 1976).

44 Kirkconnell, *A Slice of Canada*, 171. While Kirkconnell himself was an extremely religious man and did not want to see the Christian foundations of Acadia weakened by the crippling of the Baptist "denominational tiger," the effect of government funding served nonetheless to distance Acadia from Baptist control.

45 *Xaverian Weekly*, 6 November 1981, 8.

46 Bebbington makes a similar point concerning the religious texture of British universities: "The other factor tending to sacralize rather than secularise the universities has been the existence of substantial voluntary religious organizations. Many have declined in recent years, but they are still far from negligible" (Bebbington, "The Secularization of British Universities," in *The Secularization of the Academy*, eds. George M. Marsden and Bradley J. Longfield, 272).

47 "The two most profound structural changes in theology in the last three decades have been the formation of university departments of religious studies and the ecumenical clustering of theological colleges in major

university centres." N. Keith Clifford, "Universities, Churches and Theological Colleges in English-speaking Canada: Some Current Sources of Tension," *Studies in Religion* 19, no. 1 (1990): 1.

48 Burton MacDonald, interview with the author, Antigonish, NS, 9 September 1993. It should be noted, though, that the ecumenical vision of Vatican II quickly affected the teaching of religion at St Francis Xavier, as two Protestant professors were hired in 1967–68 to teach in the university's department of theology.

For further material on the history of the Department of Religion of Mount Allison University see A.J. Ebbutt, "History of the Department of Religious Studies" (Sackville, NB, Department of Religious Studies, Mount Allison University, 1971). "Academic Planning Submission – Department of Religious Studies January 1991" (Sackville, NB, Department of Religious Studies, Mount Allison University). For material on St Francis Xavier University see R.B. MacDonald, "Theology/ Religion/ Theology at St Francis Xavier" (Antigonish, NS, St Francis Xavier University Archives, 12 December 1992). For material on Acadia University see "A Proposal Regarding the Academic Study of Religion at Acadia University 1987," and "Report of the Programme Review Committee for the Department of Comparative Religion December 1992" (Wolfville, NS, Department of Religious Studies, Acadia University).

49 See Stephen D. Crites, *The Religion Major: A Report, The American Academy of Religion Task Force for the American Association of Colleges* (American Academy of Religions, 1990).

50 Mount Allison University, Department of Religious Studies, Annual Report, 1965–66 (Sackville, NB, Department of Religious Studies, Mount Allison University).

51 Ibid., 1966–67.

52 Ibid., 1970–71.

53 Ibid., 1979–80.

54 Department Handbook, Department of Religious Studies, Mount Allison University, 1980–81.

55 Mount Allison University, Department of Religious Studies, "1982 Course Submission" (Sackville, NB, Department of Religious Studies, Mount Allison University).

56 Arthur Motyer to Mount Allison Faculty Council, 9 March 1993, Sackville, NB.

PART FOUR

Contemporary Issues in Liberal Education

CHAPTER NINE

The Financial Problems Facing Canadian Universities: Some Unpleasant Economic Principles

J. FRANK STRAIN

INTRODUCTION

The liberal arts university is organized around a curriculum designed to help a student develop "character," discover and build upon intellectual heritage, and nurture an inquiring mind (see vanderLeest and Storm and Storm in this volume). But a liberal arts education involves more than a particular curriculum. A student's intellect and moral character mature as a direct consequence of presenting ideas that draw feedback from faculty. Moreover, formal and informal guidance from faculty is required if the student is to build on the thinking of other intellectuals. Thus, human contact between professor and student is an essential part of a liberal arts education.

This paper focuses on the financial consequences of this special relationship between student and faculty in a liberal arts university. The objective is to broaden debate over the future of the liberal arts in a society characterized by rapid technological change and capitalist social institutions.

Debate over the future of the liberal arts has focused on curriculum. Supporters of the liberal arts argue that a technological and capitalist society, with its strong materialist bias, is a threat to the liberal arts curriculum. The almost single minded focus on curricular change designed to ensure that graduates have concrete skills demanded in the labour market is an especially important concern. Professionalization and technical training have steadily eroded the liberal arts curriculum, especially its emphasis on non-materialist values, and the defenders of the liberal arts rightly fear further erosion in the future.

Unfortunately, the focus on curriculum has obscured another important threat to the liberal arts posed by a technologically advanced capitalist society. It is often assumed that technological progress will assure a thriving and increasingly accessible liberal arts education system by generating material wealth and hence the means to support education. However, technological progress will only have this effect if some important indirect consequences of technical progress are understood and addressed. Indeed, the thesis of this paper is that technological progress in a capitalist society threatens the financial viability of the liberal arts university by increasing the cost of acquiring a liberal arts education.

The arguments in support of this thesis are advanced using a simple but powerful economic model that formalizes connections between technological change, capitalist institutions, and a liberal arts education involving close personal relationships between students and faculty. The presentation is aimed at a non-specialist audience, but many of the arguments will undoubtedly be of interest to academics specializing in university finance. Because the intended audience will not be familiar with dynamic economic modelling, the tools used in the paper are restricted to those found in a standard freshman economics course. Important points are reinforced using very simple simulations.

THE MODEL

The dynamic economic model used as a basis for the arguments advanced in this paper was originally developed by Baumol, extended in Baumol, Blackman, and Wolff and in Osberg, Wolff, and Baumol, and presented in a widely used first-year principles of economics text.[1] This economic model can be thought of as an artificial and mechanical world constructed by an economist to capture certain gross features of the world in which we live.[2] Because the mechanical and artificial world exists only in the economist's mind or on a computer, it is possible to conduct *controlled* thought experiments (or computer-simulation exercises) that will reveal how the artificial economy evolves given any set of initial conditions. If it is a good model, the simulation experiments should generate outcomes that resemble those of the real world.

The artificial world Baumol constructed is populated by "*Homo economicus*," the identical interacting robots economists typically study. The robots are capable of producing two goods – let us call these automobiles and liberal arts education – and the two goods differ in one fundamental respect: ongoing technological change in automobile production continually reduces the amount of labour time required to produce an automobile, while in liberal arts education the faculty time required to educate a student remains constant through time.

In the artificial world of this model the cost of liberal arts education grows faster than the cost of producing an automobile. Three features of Baumol's artificial world account for this. First, wages and salaries in the two sectors tend to go up and down together. Why? Because the population of identical *Homo economicus* in this economy will change jobs when one sector in the economy offers higher wages than the other. This forces firms in the sector losing workers to increase wages to stay in business. Second, wages in the automobile sector in the model grow at the same rate as output per worker in that sector. This too is a result of an underlying assumption that the economy is organized on competitive capitalist principles. The increase in productivity in auto production results in a reduction in the cost of producing an automobile. Assuming that wages and prices initially remain at levels that existed prior to the productivity increase, the reduction in cost will increase the profitability of the automobile sector. This in turn generates an expansion in activity in the automobile sector and an increase in the demand for labour. The only way automobile-producing firms can secure more robot workers is to offer higher wages, and it is profitable to pay higher wages as long as the percentage increase in wages is less than the percentage increase in productivity. Thus, wages rise as a result of productivity growth. Moreover, the profit-maximizing auto-producing firms will compete for labour (and bid up wages) to the point where hiring additional labour is unprofitable; hence the wage increase (in percentage) will be just equal to the percentage productivity increase. Finally, the assumption that productivity growth varies across sectors – perhaps due to limits on class size and choice of teaching technique imposed by the traditional approach to liberal arts education – is critical. If the number of cars produced per worker grows at the same rate as auto workers' wages, the cost per car will not change. But if student/faculty ratios remain unchanged in the face of growing faculty salaries, the cost of university education per student must grow over time. In the absence of offsetting growth in revenues or reductions in cost, this secular tendency that emerges in the model must manifest itself in financial crisis in the university.

The axioms that generate financial problems for universities in the artificial world of Baumol's model are not patently unrealistic. In the "real world" the population is not as responsive to wage differentials as the *Homo economicus* robots of the model. However, it is still reasonable to expect that any sector of the Canadian economy experiencing a relative decline in its wage rate will tend to lose its labour force. University faculty can find jobs elsewhere. Young people can decide not to pursue careers as university faculty. Thus, in the long run, auto workers and university faculty in the "real" economy will see their wages rise at roughly the same rate.

The relationship between productivity growth and real wage growth assumed in the Baumol model should not be controversial either. Economists have found that competition for potential workers in real economies has resulted in a close correlation between real wage growth and productivity growth.

Thus, the assumption that productivity growth varies across sectors is critical (and potentially controversial). This assumption is discussed in more detail below. But if the assumption is accepted, the evolution of costs observed in the artificial world of the Baumol model should, in the long run, also be observed in "real" economies.

The significance of unbalanced productivity growth for university costs can be illustrated in a simple simulation experiment. In this exercise we make a number of assumptions: (1) the cost of producing a car is initially four thousand dollars and the cost of educating a single student is two thousand dollars; (2) all wages and prices are growing at a rate of five percent per period due to autonomous inflationary pressures; (3) that output per worker in the automobile industry is growing at a constant rate of five percent per year; (4) that this generates a five percent increase in real wages for both the automobile sector and university professors; and (5) that there is no growth in the student/faculty ratio. Chart 1 illustrates the evolution of costs over a span of forty time periods. Initially university education costs half as much as an automobile. At the end of the simulated history university education costs over three times as much as an automobile. Moreover, the relative cost of university education will continue to grow if the simulation is extended to cover additional time periods.

It is important to re-emphasize that the growth in the relative cost of university education in the simulation is a result of assumptions about basic structural characteristics of the economy. The growth in relative cost has nothing whatsoever to do with the way universities are run. No managerial initiatives can solve the cost problem. It should also be clear that many features of the current financial crisis in Canadian universities are not captured in this model and that the model is intended to illuminate only one aspect of the current crisis.

The simple model can be used to discuss, in very general terms, the two solutions to the financial difficulties of liberal arts institutions. First, the institutions can curtail costs. In the artificial world of the model there are only two ways of doing this: either change the assumption about productivity growth and allow for the continuous introduction of productivity-enhancing technical change in the liberal arts, or change the assumption about behaviour and assume that permanently

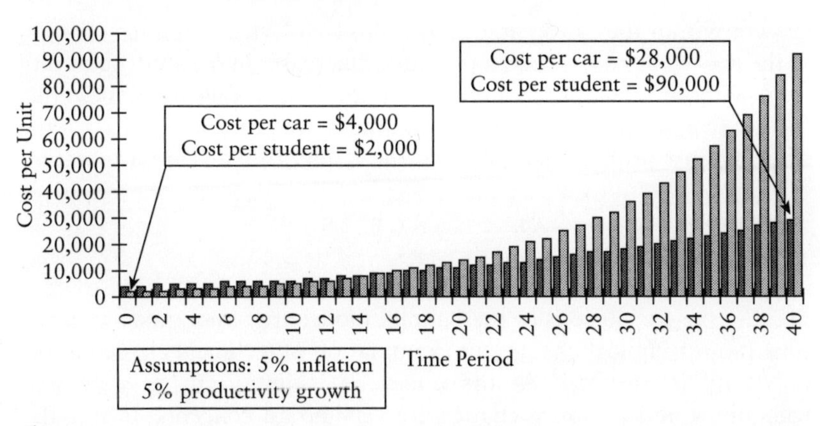

Chart 1
The Evolution of Unit Costs

freezing faculty salaries would not affect the numbers of people willing to enter university teaching. Alternatively, the financial difficulties can be solved by simply increasing the flow of funds to universities to cover the increase in costs. Significantly, the simple model gives some indication of how rapidly revenues will have to rise. Specifically, university revenues will have to grow at the same rate as productivity growth in the automobile sector to ensure that a constant number of students receive university education. Notice, as well, that the very existence of the slow-productivity-growth university sector results in a rate of growth of real output in society as a whole that is less than the rate of productivity growth in the automobile sector. Consequently, to educate a constant number of students in each period, a growing share of per capita income, or Gross Domestic Product (GDP), will have to be spent on university education. If student numbers increase over time, university revenue will have to grow still faster.

In sum, if the insights of the simple Baumol model are deemed applicable to the real-world problems of liberal arts institutions, three fundamental conclusions follow. (1) Productivity growth in the rest of the economy and severely limited productivity-increasing possibilities in the liberal arts combine to push up the relative cost of a liberal arts education in the long run.[3] Ironically, the better the performance of the economy as a whole (the higher its productivity and wage growth), the worse the potential problems of liberal arts institutions. (2) The solution to this problem favoured by the university community – revenue growth – requires that a growing proportion of society's output flow to the university sector. Thus, opposition to this solution should not be surprising. (3) The solution favoured by governments, parents, and students – cost reductions – requires continuous productivity growth within the universities. Since this involves continuous changes in the way education occurs (continuous increases in the student/faculty ratio without affecting quality), society may be asking the impossible.

The remainder of this paper examines the two solutions to the growing cost problem identified in the Baumol model in more detail.

TECHNICAL CHANGE IN THE UNIVERSITIES

Because the conclusions of the Baumol model are based on an assumption about technical change, an examination of technical change in the university is essential. At the outset, it is important to note that technology and technical change are very broad concepts. In popular discussion these terms are frequently used to refer to machines, computers, and other physical objects, but in economics they are used differently. Economists use the term technology to describe the process by which any set of inputs is transformed into outputs. In education, inputs – "uneducated" students, books, journal articles, monographs, teachers, laboratories, classrooms, etc. – are used to produce output, the "educated" student. Thus, "technology" describes the entire process of educating a student, and "technical change" refers to any change in the education process.

In the literature on technology two separate types of changes are identified: changes in the production process (changes the way students become "educated") and changes in the final product (changes in type of education received). Productivity growth occurs if a change in the process achieves the same education with fewer inputs, or if changes in the product result in more valuable output from the original inputs. It should be obvious that university education is an extremely complex product and the production of university educated students an extremely complex process. As a consequence, it is virtually impossible to develop a *measure* of productivity that would support definitive conclusions about the relative rate of productivity advance in university education.[4] Nonetheless, a number of considerations suggest that the rate of productivity advanced in the university sector is not as rapid as elsewhere and that the insights of the Baumol model are relevant.

First, education is a very personal experience. The student masters material, develops analytical ability, and cultivates creative talents largely through personal effort. Productivity advance would require continuous reductions in the amount of time students need to master a given amount of material and attain a given level of analytic and creative ability. There is no concrete evidence to suggest that this type of productivity advance has occurred. Second, as Roy Radner has noted, certain "relations among human inputs and outputs have remained at the heart of the educational process since at least the time of Socrates and may even have changed little from his day to ours."[5] In other words, education also involves a relationship between teacher and student that is difficult to change. A description of the educational production process offered by economist Sherwin Rosen provides a possible explanation for why changes in technique have been so difficult to achieve in university education.

> Effective teaching requires teacher-student interchange and [this] becomes increasingly difficult as class size increases. In addition large scale production degrades the signal content of teaching. A teacher produces a uniform message and that message becomes garbled as class size and diversity increase. Teaching a large class compels one to broadcast to the median student, lending a certain mediocrity to the end product, which is a phenomenon that will be well known to television viewers. Judging from what one sees on television, it just does not seem possible to transmit most difficult and abstract ideas on a mass scale through the airwaves, and that state of affairs is unlikely to change in the foreseeable future.[6]

Third, even if there are "product" changes – if students are learning more over time, or if the value of what they are learning over time is increasing – the length of time required to acquire an education and the student/faculty ratio are still the critical determinants of unit costs. Moreover, as long as the student/faculty ratio does not continually increase, the universities will face the problem of rising relative unit costs.

It is worthwhile noting that slow productivity growth is not just a problem in teaching. Many other areas within the university involve relations between human inputs and outputs that are impossible to change without damaging the quality of service (counselling and student advising are two areas within administration and student services where the possibility of productivity growth is seriously constrained). Consequently, these costs too are likely to grow faster than costs in other sectors of the economy.

Thus, despite the absence of definitive evidence supporting the assumption of unbalanced productivity growth, there are sound reasons for believing that this assumption is reasonable and that the basic insights of the Baumol model are relevant.

But why has productivity growth been slower in the university sector? Arguments advanced above about the personal nature of education and the special relationships between human inputs in the production process implicitly suggest that there are "natural" limits on productivity-enhancing measures in the education process. Indeed, if there are "natural" limits, increasing productivity (continually increasing the student/faculty ratio or reducing the time students devote to education) will reduce the quality of education attained. Hence there is no way to reduce costs without reducing quality in the long run. Society cannot possibly get more for less.

This said, it is important to recognize that the limits to productivity advance may not be "natural." It is possible that the absence of productivity advance in education is due to the very nature of university institutions. Modern theories of productivity growth suggest that productivity growth within an industry is directly related to the investment firms within an industry make in research and development. Perhaps universities are not investing enough in R&D or have failed to employ relevant knowledge to change the education process and enhance the productivity of their own operations.

One can think of many developments over the past one hundred years that have the potential to increase productivity in the university sector. There are many new learning techniques and strategies that allow students to master material in less time. Speed-reading techniques, for example, enable readers to cover more material without loss of comprehension. The efficiency of the conventional university lecture has been questioned while a variety of alternative techniques have been discussed in the education literature. It is not even clear that the use of mass media is as ineffective as Rosen suggests, especially if employed in innovative ways. For some reason these advances in knowledge have not been reflected in university education. Thus, there may be a problem with the adoption of new knowledge in the universities.

The failure to adopt productivity-increasing technical change in the university is particularly evident if one compares the university and competitive amateur sport. The times achieved in track and swimming events have declined dramatically in this century despite the fact that successive generations have believed that the "natural limits" of human ability had been reached. New training techniques, computer searches for "optimal running style," and better equipment (shoes and tracks, for example) have helped athletes achieve new heights despite apparent "natural" constraints. In contrast, universities have not applied new knowledge in a way that would allow students to push back the "natural" limits.

It is also known that private-sector firms in Japan and the United States devote over 2.5 percent of revenue to in-house R&D.[7] In contrast, universities have no "formal" research policy aimed at improving productivity of their own operations. The absence of an "explicit" policy is an interesting puzzle, given that universities are at the centre of research and development for society as a whole.[8]

Thus, there is indirect evidence to suggest that universities are not investing enough in R&D into their own operations and that there may be a problem with the adoption of new knowledge. Recent work in economics suggests that creation and adoption of new knowledge in an industry is influenced by a variety of factors including industrial structure, rivalry, and demand conditions. Firms will only be innovative if they are forced to be by competitors or customers. Hence the absence of pressure and institutional rigidities *may* account for the absence of productivity growth in universities rather than some "natural" constraints on productivity advance in education.

These considerations seem to suggest that institutional change can produce an environment in which the growth of relative costs of university education can be contained. However, no researcher has explicitly tackled the problem of technical change within the university (this is another example of the problem), and it is impossible to say anything with any confidence. Indeed, without further research, it is not clear how much of a contribution institutional change could make, if any.

In the remainder of this paper it is assumed that productivity growth in the university sector will continue to be lower than in other sectors. This assumption is based on a belief that there will be no dramatic change in the institutional environment in which universities operate, so that they will continue to operate as they have in the past.

Before considering the second escape from the predicament posed by the Baumol model, it is important to make two final points about technical change. First, the growth in relative cost can only be controlled through "continual" productivity change (continual increases in the student/faculty ratio and continual reductions in the length of time a student needs to acquire a specific level of education). Once and for all, increases in productivity will not permanently contain cost growth. Second, productivity-enhancing measures that could be implemented immediately such as increasing class size, increasing the number of courses taught by individual faculty members, or eliminating sabbatical leaves are once and for all measures, not continual technical changes, and they would likely result in a deterioration in the quality of university education and certainly in a reduction in university research. Attempts to hold down faculty salary growth would also certainly affect the quality of the faculty and thus of the education it provides and research it produces. Consequently, society faces a difficult choice: either an increasing proportion of society's resources must be devoted to university education, or the quality of education and research must fall.

INCREASING REVENUES

Decreasing costs or increasing revenues are the only two ways to assure that the liberal arts remain financially viable. In the previous section it was argued that it will be very difficult to decrease costs without affecting the quality of education. Although dramatic institutional change was mentioned as a possible method of reducing costs, it was also noted that little was known about the institutional options or their consequences. Cutting revenue will not necessarily induce the appropriate changes. Indeed, casual reflection (speculation) suggests that the resulting changes can be counterproductive. In the following sections attention is focused on two of the most important revenue sources: transfers from government and student fees. A brief discussion of deficit finance is also included.

Government Funding of Universities

Liberal-arts institutions finance their activities from a number of revenue sources: direct payments from students, private donations and bequests, commercial enterprises, and transfers from government. In Canada, the transfers from governments are most important.

The system of government grants to universities in Canada is extremely complex. Under the Canadian constitution provincial governments have direct responsibility for education. Consequently, transfers to universities come from the provinces. The complexity arises in part because each province uses its own criteria to disperse funds to the universities.[9] However, the federal government also has an indirect but important role in financing university operations. Hence the complexity of the transfer system stems to some extent from the complexity of Canadian federal-provincial fiscal arrangements.

Only one feature of the transfer system will be considered here. The dynamic unbalanced-productivity-growth model suggests that the cost of educating a student will grow faster than the cost of producing most other products. As a consequence, it also suggests that the revenue universities receive per student must grow at the same rate as costs and faster than average income in the society. Thus, the rate at which government transfers to universities grow is of critical importance. In this paper attention is focused on "the rate of growth of transfers" and not on the formula that determines "the level of transfers."

One simple way to emphasize the importance of rates of growth is to examine how fast transfers to universities would have to grow to keep the government's share of the cost per student constant over time. Recall that in the unbalanced-productivity-growth model the cost of educating a student is growing faster than total income, or Gross Domestic Product. Thus, if population is growing and a constant proportion of the population is educated each period, the share of society's resources being transferred to universities must grow over time. In other words, the tax rate governments must implicitly impose on society's output to finance their share of the cost of university education must also grow over time.

This can be graphically illustrated in another simple simulation. Assume that (1) governments finance half the cost of university education; (2) the cost per student is initially two thousand dollars; (3) there are currently 100,000 university students enrolled at university (the government transfer to universities must initially be $100,000,000); (4) the value of society's initial net output (Gross Domestic Product) is $1,000,000,000; and (5) the cost of university education is growing three percent faster than society's GDP, which is growing at a rate of five percent. The last assumption imperfectly captures one of the most important consequences of unbalanced growth in the simple Baumol model.[10]

The evolution of the transfer as a share of total output from governments to universities produced by the simple simulation is illustrated in Chart 2. At the outset the transfer was equal to ten percent of GDP; by the end of the twenty-fifth year (time period) the transfer was almost twenty percent of GDP. In other words, the tax rate implicitly imposed on society's output to finance university education must double.

The critical feature of the simulation is that the transfer to universities must grow faster than the rate of growth in GDP. In contrast, the actual transfer per student from governments in Canada to the Canadian universities has, in recent years, grown at a rate that is less than the rate of growth in GDP.

In part, the slow growth of transfers to universities is determined by the growth in federal-provincial transfers. Under the Established Program Financing (EPF) legislation of 1977, transfers from the federal government to provincial governments in Canada to support university education were designed to grow at approximately the same rate as GDP.[11] Consequently, if our simulation model were rerun using the federal-transfer growth rate imposed by the 1977 legislation, the federal government's share of the per-student cost of university education would fall over time and the transfer from own-source provincial

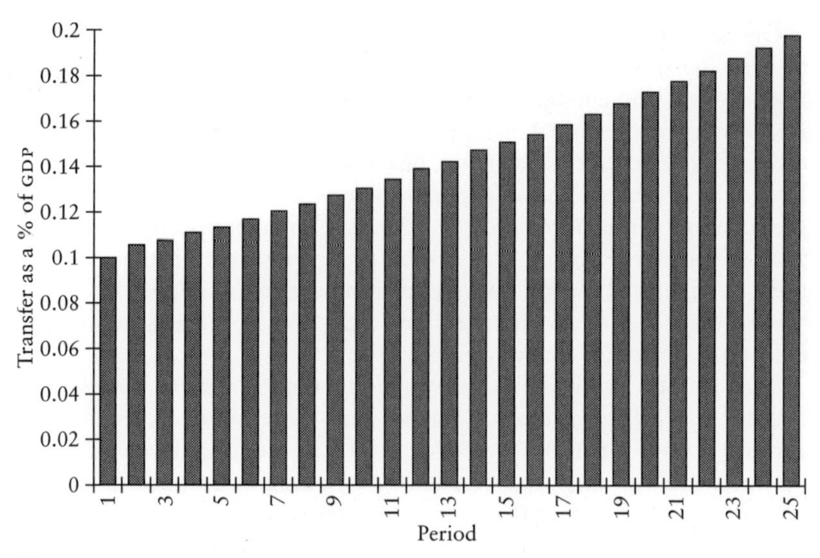

Chart 2
Simulated Growth in Government Transfers

revenue would have to grow even more rapidly than the cost per student to maintain the total government share of the cost of educating a student at a constant level.

Of course, the 1977 legislation was amended by successive federal governments to reduce the rate of transfer growth to a figure below that of GDP. Indeed, the escalator was eliminated by the Conservative government. As a consequence, the provincial governments were given more financial responsibility and this forced them to contemplate significant tax increases to cover higher costs arising from unbalanced productivity growth and the declining federal government share.

The direct transfer to universities from provincial governments is determined as part of overall budgetary policy. Although all provinces use some type of formula (which incorporates student numbers and subject mix), the rate of growth in the provincial transfers to universities is not tied directly to increases in the cost of education. Provincial governments, faced with declining federal transfers and pressures to control spending, have been reluctant to increase taxes as rapidly as necessary to preserve the government share of costs. Indeed, a number of provinces have chosen to freeze (and in some cases, reduce) transfers. As a result, the universities are facing severe financial difficulties.

The implications of the policy of freezing government transfers to universities in the artificial world of the Baumol model can be seen by rerunning the simple simulation experiment above. Recall that the

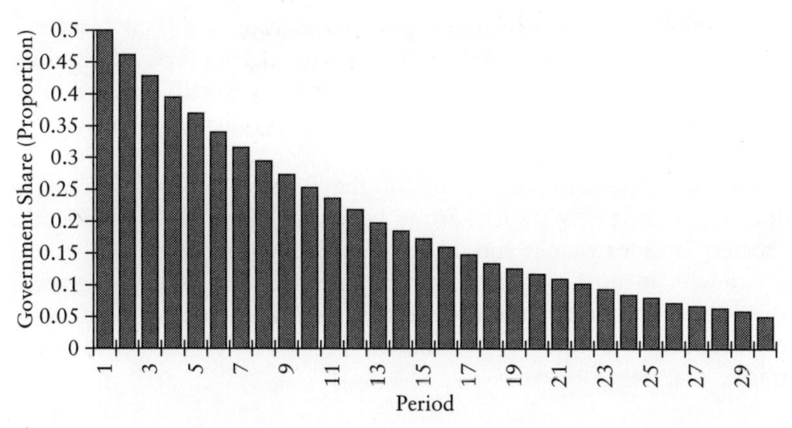

Chart 3
Change in Government Share

simulation was based on the following assumptions: (1) that the cost per student is initially two thousand dollars and grows at eight percent per year (it maybe illuminating to assume that five percent of this is due to pure inflation and three percent to real productivity growth in other sectors of the economy); and (2) that the government transfer initially covers one-half of the cost. Unlike the earlier simulation, which was based on the assumption that the share of cost assumed by government remains constant, this simulation is based on the assumption that the transfer remains constant at one thousand dollars per student. Chart 3 illustrates the consequences of this assumption for the share of cost per student assumed by government.

The impact of current government policy in the artificial Baumol world is dramatic. In just ten years the share of per-student costs covered by government is cut in half, over twenty-five years the government share falls from fifty percent to less than ten percent. If the real world resembles the Baumol world at all – and it seems reasonable to think it does – continuation of current policy for even a short period of time will revolutionize the way universities in Canada are financed. Unless the universities can secure dramatic increases in revenue from other sources, current policy is potentially disastrous.

In passing, it should also be noted that the decline in EPF transfers, when combined with caps on the growth of equalization payments, are especially damaging in Atlantic Canada where the provincial governments face a relatively meagre tax base. The limited tax base in Atlantic Canada forces provincial governments there to impose tax rates on citizens that are higher than tax rates imposed elsewhere to cover the same share of per-student costs as other provincial governments.

Levying high taxes on a relatively poor population is difficult and it is reasonable to expect that reductions in federal transfers, when combined with a secular tendency for the cost of university education to rise, will result in particularly severe financial problems for universities in Atlantic Canada.

In sum, in the artificial world of the Baumol model the cost of educating a university student grows faster than income. Consequently, if society decides that it should cover a fixed proportion of the cost per student, it must employ a transfer formula that takes the growth in cost into account. If the transfers do not take the growth in costs into account, the role of government in university finance declines rapidly.

Student Fees

Student fees are also an important source of revenue for Canadian universities. In the long run, fees have to grow at the same rate as university costs – which in the Baumol model grow faster than consumer prices generally – if the share of total costs covered by fees is to remain constant over time. Given the reduction in the rate of growth in transfers from government, the Baumol model suggests that fees will have to grow at a very rapid rate since they must cover not only a fixed share of the higher costs but also the reduction in the share of costs covered by government.

The combined impact of escalating cost per student and a freeze on government transfers in the simple simulation experiment of the previous section is illustrated in Chart 4. Again we assume that costs are originally two thousand dollars per student and grow at eight percent per year, and that government transfers are frozen at one thousand dollars per student.

Chart 4 shows that tuition fees increase at the same rate as costs (eight percent) in period one. Assuming an inflation rate of five percent (as above), students will undoubtedly find this high. But when the freeze on transfers from government at period-one levels is introduced, tuition fees must escalate much more rapidly than costs. Indeed, in the first year tuition fees must rise by sixteen percent. Eventually, as government declines in importance, the rate of growth in tuition fees declines (in the long run it will eventually equal the rate of growth in costs).

Many recent studies of the financial problems currently facing Canadian universities advocate substantial fee increases, and current government policy on transfer payments must reflect at least implicit acceptance of this recommendation. In part, the policy stance is motivated by a widespread belief that the benefits from university education

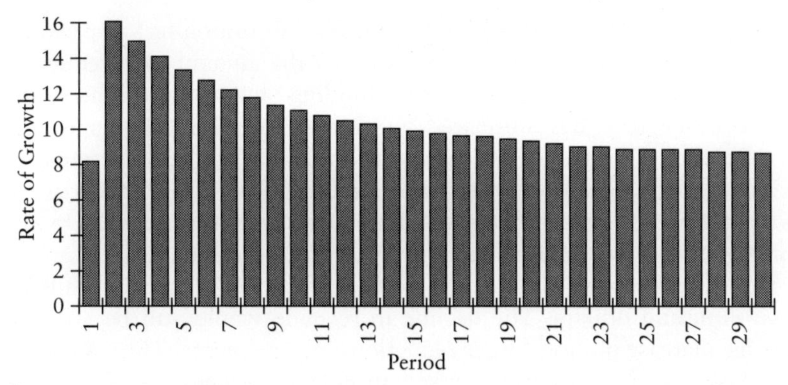

Chart 4
Rate of Growth in Tuition Fees

largely accrue to the students who are being educated; the underlying ethical premise suggests that the government should not be forcing the average citizen to pay a substantial share of the cost of educating this élite group in society. Higher tuition fees, it is argued, will simultaneously improve the allocation of resources in the society by forcing students to weigh costs and benefits when deciding whether or not to attend university and improve the distribution of income by reducing the transfer of income from taxpayers generally to students who have relatively high lifetime incomes. In part, advocates of higher student fees are motivated by pragmatic considerations. Governments cannot and are not going to pay more. Consequently students must pay if the quality of university education is to be maintained.

Identifying the private and public benefits of higher education is extraordinarily difficult and a critical examination of the benefit argument for higher tuition fees is well beyond the scope of this paper. Instead, I will concentrate on the pragmatic rationale for higher fees and some of the consequences of raising fees.

Anyone who has taken a first year course in economics will undoubtedly recall a lecture that explained why price increases do not necessarily increase revenues, let alone increase surplus available to an organization. When the price of any product is increased, some customers decide to stop purchasing the product and to do other things with their money. The demand curve has a negative slope,[12] thus revenue is lost. Total revenue only increases if the additional revenue generated from the customers who continue purchasing the product exceeds the revenue lost because some customers stop purchasing the product.

The economic principle is often formalized by examining certain properties of total revenues. Total revenues in time period t are defined by $TR_t = f_t{}^*s_t + o_t{}^*s_t + O_t$ where f_t is the level of tuition fees in period t, s_t is the number of students enrolled, o_t is the amount of revenue per student from other sources that base funding on student numbers, and O_t is other revenues unrelated to student numbers. Imagine that $f_t = \$1{,}000$, $o_t = \$1{,}000$, $s_t = 1{,}000$, and $O_t = 0$. Total revenue must be $2,000,000. If fees are then increased by $100, revenues rise to $2,100,000 *assuming that student numbers are unchanged.* On the other hand, if we assume that fifty potential students decided not to enrol in response to the price increase, total revenue actually falls by five thousand dollars. The decline in revenue would still be larger if the fee increase induces larger reductions in enrolments. Thus, a tuition increase does not necessarily result in higher revenues.

But how responsive are students to price increases? A large number of studies of student price response in higher education suggest that demand is relatively inelastic. If we assume, using the findings of a review of over thirty studies of student price responsiveness by Leslie and Brinkman, that enrolments decline by 1.8 percent in response to the one-hundred-dollar fee increase, we can predict that the one-hundred-dollar fee increase in the example above will cause revenues to increase by $62,200.[13] This seems to suggest that fee increases are a reasonable pragmatic response to the financial crises since they will generate additional revenue.

On closer examination, however, the apparent success of the policy of increasing fees begins to disappear. One problem generated by fee increases can be identified by formally incorporating price responsiveness into the artificial world of the Baumol model. In an earlier simulation of the evolution of the artificial Baumol world, it was assumed that 100,000 students were enrolled in university. How do enrolments change if fees in this world must rise to cover the growth in cost due to unbalanced productivity growth and the reduction in the government share that occurs with a freeze on transfers? This question is answered in Chart 5, which reports enrolments that emerge when it is assumed that enrolments fall by 1.8 percent for every one-hundred-dollar increase in fees.

It is clear from Chart 5 that increasing fees can have a dramatic impact on enrolments even when it is assumed that students are not that responsive to price. While fee increases may cover the increase in cost (but see below for a discussion of why even this might not be true), they also affect the level of education in the labour force, which might have serious implications for the economy in the future.

The apparent success of the price increase may also disappear even if we assume that the increase is only motivated by the growing relative-cost problem emphasized in the Baumol model. For example,

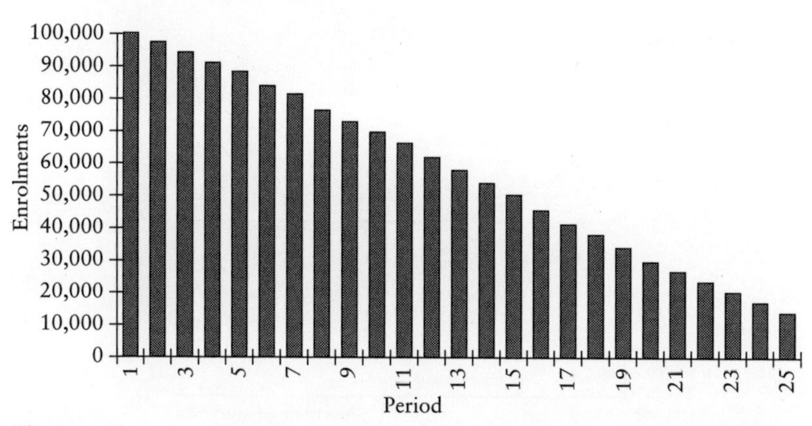

Chart 5
Simulated Changes in Enrolments

suppose the total cost of educating ten thousand students at a single university grows from $20,000,000 to $22,000,000 (i.e., the cost per student grows by two hundred dollars), that governments contribute an additional one hundred dollars per student, and that universities increase fees by one hundred dollars to cover the remainder of the increase in cost per student. Since enrolments decline in response to the price increases, the success of the policy in covering the cost increase will critically depend on the change in per-student cost associated with the decline in enrolment. Note that total costs may not fall at all since faculty and administrative layoffs are unlikely, especially in the short run. If total costs do not change in response to the change in enrolment, the total change in cost per student will be approximately $240 (assuming enrolment declines by 1.8 percent). Thus, the university will face a deficit of approximately $400,000. Only if the average cost of educating a student remains constant as enrolment changes will the fee increase eliminate the immediate financial problem arising from the growth in the relative cost of university education.

In the long run one expects that some cost savings arise with lower enrolments, but the size of this cost reduction will depend on the relationship between per-student costs and total student enrolments. Economists capture the relationship between per-student costs and total enrolments with what is known as the long-run average-cost curve. This tool shows the relationship between per-student costs and enrolment assuming universities have adjusted their operations in a way that assures students are educated at minimum cost.

Two examples of possible long-run cost curves are illustrated in Figure 1. LRAC1 assumes that per student costs do not change in

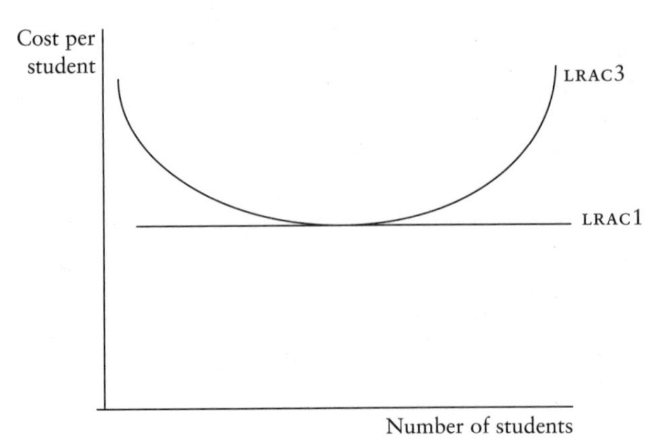

Figure 1
Economies of Scale

response to changes in enrolment. In this case, if enrolment falls by 1.8 percent costs fall by 1.8 percent. The other possibility, illustrated by LRAC3, captures a situation where unit costs initially decline as enrolment increases, reach a minimum at a specific level of enrolment, and then rise when enrolment is increased further.

Unfortunately, little is definitively known about the cost structure facing universities. A recent study of the university-cost function for Australia by Thorsby suggests that LRAC3 applies and that minimum unit costs are achieved at a student enrolment of approximately 13,000 full-time equivalent students.[14] But another study of English universities by Johnes found that subject mix explained most of the variation in unit costs and that scale did not have a significant impact.[15]

If Johnes's results apply in Canada, fee increases can be used to cope with the secular tendency for the cost of university education to rise. But if the Thorsby results are applicable, the impact of price increases will vary across universities. Universities with enrolments that exceed the level of minimum unit costs will experience a decline in unit costs when enrolments fall, other things being equal. Thus, these large universities will be able to rely on price increases to solve their financial problems in the long run. On the other hand, small universities (universities with enrolments below the level associated with minimum unit cost) will find that unit costs rise as enrolments decline; hence fee increases will not solve financial problems emerging with the growth in the relative cost of university education.

The variation in the impact of price increases when economies of scale are present also has implications for the long-run evolution of the university sector. Small universities will experience relative reductions in enrolments, large universities will experience relative increases in enrolments. There are two possible reasons for this. Since continuing price increases lower costs in large universities relative to small universities, large universities can either charge relatively lower prices or use the revenue gain to improve quality. In either case, students should respond by favouring large universities.

This section has identified a number of considerations that must be taken into consideration when assessing a move to higher tuition fees. First, higher tuition fees will reduce enrolments. (This is not true for each university since demand for space by qualified applicants currently can and does exceed supply in some institutions.) The effect on enrolments raises issues not only of accessibility but also of future economic growth in society as a whole. Second, reductions in enrolments may not reduce costs proportionately. Moreover, the impact of lower enrolments on costs will depend on the size of the university if there are scale economies. Third, if governments choose to freeze transfers per student, the rate of increase in fees one observes in the artificial world of the Baumol model is incredible.

The Income Elasticity of Demand

The discussion of the impact of fee increases on enrolment and costs assumed that the price of university education was the only factor influencing the long-run evolution of demand for university education. This is a very restrictive assumption since a wide variety of factors are likely to come into play including incomes, demographic developments, and the prices of related products.

In the simple model of unbalanced productivity growth discussed above, productivity growth results in higher incomes; hence one should expect that demand for university education will grow as a result. The growth in demand due to rising incomes may offset the decline in demand due to the price increases that accompany the growth in the relative cost of university education. Indeed, if the growth in demand more than offsets the reduction in demand due to price increases, small universities gain relative to large universities. In this case, the growth in enrolments over time allow small universities to exploit scale economies, while large universities find costs rising due to diseconomies of scale.

As a consequence, the income elasticity of demand, defined as the percentage increase in enrolment arising from a one percent increase in income, is a critical factor in the evolution of the university sector and the potential for price increases to solve financial problems.

A number of studies have attempted to estimate the income elasticity of demand. Unfortunately for Canadian universities, especially the small universities, the resulting estimates tend to suggest that demand is relatively income inelastic. This finding may come as a surprise but there are good reasons for it, as the following excerpt from a study by Galper and Dunn makes clear:

> The demand for undergraduate enrolments within an income class is saturated when all recent high school graduates are enroled who have the desire to do so and such an income class will show an income elasticity of demand for enrolments of zero. As average real incomes in the United States rise, a higher percentage of the population will have reached the saturation point. Income elasticities can be expected to be high only for those income groups with low current incomes and enrolments. If a large and growing proportion of the population is at (or close to) the saturation level of demand, which may well be the case, then the income elasticity for the United States as a whole will be relatively low and would decline through time.[16]

What is more, the studies examining the income elasticity of demand have generated results that have especially discouraging implications for universities serving relatively poor populations. The poor are much more responsive to changes in price than the more affluent. Consequently, reductions in demand due to price increases will be larger in universities serving relatively poor populations.

Short-Term Deficits in the Long-Run Model

Many within the university community, especially faculty, advocate short-term deficits as a means of accommodating the current crises. This stance is based on a belief that the current financial problems are temporary. (One argument is that the financial problems are caused by an aging faculty and that a flurry of retirements over the next few years will eliminate the problem.) The model used to discuss the financial problems of the universities in this paper suggests, in contrast, that basic structural features of productivity growth are an important cause of the current financial problems and that these will continue to be a source of problems in the future. Consequently, short-term deficits are not considered desirable.

In freshman economics courses, instructors generally discuss a number of considerations that rational decision makers should weigh when choosing whether or not to borrow to finance a private organization's operations. In general, if the funds borrowed are used to generate revenue in the future sufficient to cover payments, borrowing is considered rational. Indeed, if future revenues are more than needed to cover payments, not borrowing is irrational.

On the other hand, borrowing to cover a gap between costs and revenues arising because of unbalanced productivity growth is irrational.

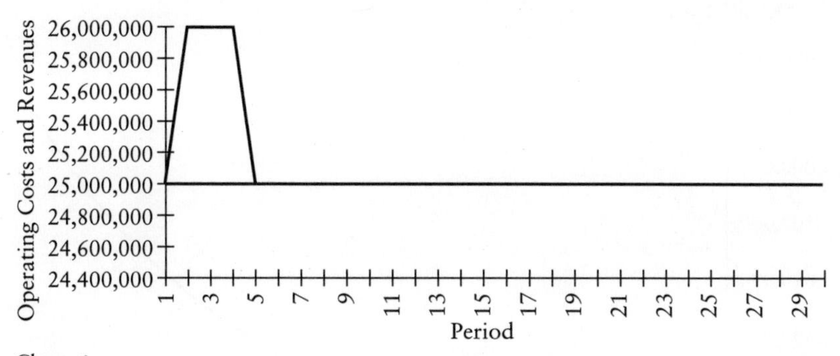

Chart 6
Simulation Assumptions

As governments are only too aware, accumulated debt increases costs because of the annual flow of interest payments. The miracle of compound interest quickly becomes a nightmare for any organization that finances activities that do not generate a future return to cover interest payments.

Another very simple simulation dramatically illustrates the nightmare. The simulation is based on the following assumptions: (1) that university operating costs (exclusive of interest payments) are initially $25,000,000, increase to $26,000,000 for a period of three years, and then return to $25,000,000 and remain at this level for the rest of the simulation through time; (2) that revenues are initially $25,000,000 and remain at this level throughout the simulation; and (3) that the university borrows to cover any deficit. The first two assumptions are illustrated in Chart 6.

The university runs a deficit for three years, but the borrowed funds are not used in a way that generates future revenue to offset the interest costs. Since we assume that the university borrows to cover any deficit, interest payments are covered by additional borrowing. The consequences of this borrowing for the deficit are illustrated in Chart 7, which is based on a ten percent interest rate. Clearly, the policy of borrowing to cover current operating deficits is unsustainable and total expenditures must be reduced to the level of revenues. Short-term borrowing simply delays the adjustment. Indeed, it makes it more difficult since borrowing increases future costs. The evolution of debt is illustrated in Chart 8.

The lesson from the simulation experiment is simple: do not borrow unless the borrowed funds are used in a way that will generate enough future income to cover interest payments. Thus, borrowing is not a solution to the financial problems introduced by the escalating costs predicted in the Baumol model. Indeed, borrowing will only exacerbate problems in the long run.

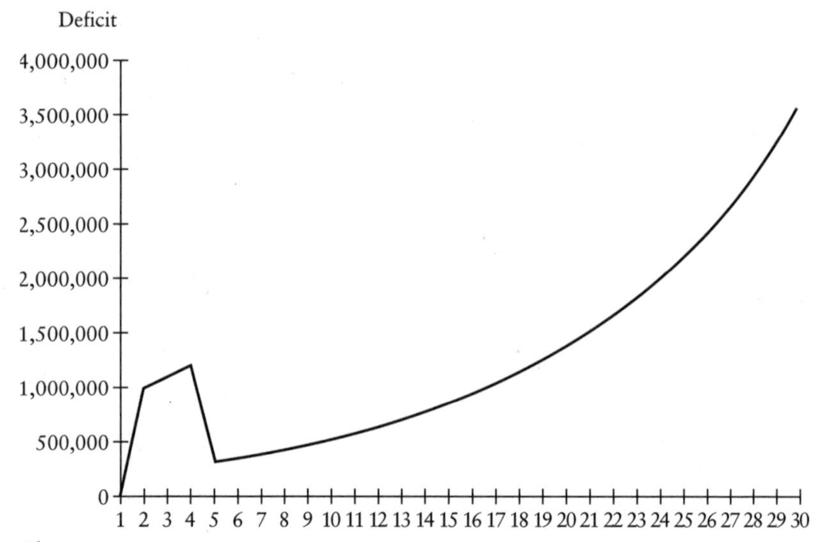

Chart 7
Deficit Simulation

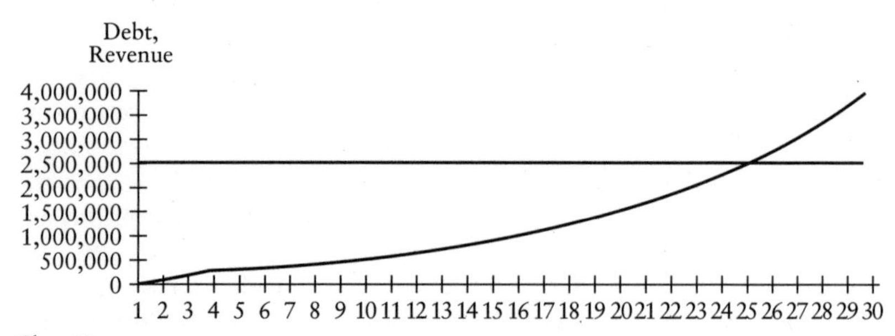

Chart 8
Simulated Debt vs. Revenue

Private-Sector Financing of University Education

Gifts, donations, and bequests from alumni, friends, private foundations, and corporations are the only significant source of funds that have not been examined in this paper. As government funding declined, universities devoted more and more attention to this potential revenue source. In the long run gifts, donations, and bequests will have to grow much faster than incomes generally if this revenue source is to rescue Canadian universities from the secular tendency for unit costs to rise. It is impossible to predict whether this growth will emerge.

CONCLUSIONS

This paper began by suggesting that liberal arts institutions currently face a serious predicament. On one hand, the cost of educating a student is growing faster than the revenues society is providing the universities. On the other, society is demanding more from universities because it realizes that continued prosperity will depend on the education of the labour force and the stock of scientific, technical, and market knowledge available.

The purpose of the paper was to show how a simple model of economic growth can be used to illuminate this predicament and to critically analyze potential solutions. The most important point was that productivity growth in the rest of the economy can result in rapid growth in the relative cost of a liberal arts education if productivity growth in the university sector is slow. In other words, universities can experience financial problems as a result of the rest of the economy becoming "richer." In the simple model there are only two ways universities can avoid financial problems: by securing sufficient additional revenue to cover the higher costs, or by continually adopting new educational methods to increase productivity. Both approaches were discussed in the paper.

In the discussion of cost reduction it was noted that, despite being at the centre of research and development for society as a whole, universities have not been very innovative in the delivery of education. This may be because the methods currently in use are the only ones possible. But it may also be a consequence of the institutional environment in which universities operate. Although at present no one knows whether it is possible to cut costs without reducing quality, it may be possible to do so. More research on education techniques and the possibilities of resource-saving innovations are clearly needed.

If we assume that there are "natural" limits on potential productivity advances in education – and this seems the most reasonable assumption given the current state of knowledge – the universities will not be able to contain cost growth without reducing quality. As a consequence, if revenues from society do not rise, the quality of education will fall. No amount of administrative reform or temporary solutions can prevent this.

Canadian universities currently secure revenue from a number of sources. If it is not possible to increase the productivity of the universities, the total revenue universities receive from all sources will have to grow at a faster rate than total output (GDP) to preserve current levels of operation. Thus, if the relative significance of different revenue sources is to remain constant through time, all revenues will have to grow at a rate that exceeds the rate of growth in GDP.

This implies that government transfers, student fees, and private donations will all have to increase at a rate faster than GDP. Given current government policies, it is unlikely that transfers will grow at the rate required to cover the growing cost. Consequently, universities are being forced to look elsewhere for funds, especially to students. But this will have implications for enrolments, the characteristics of the university system, and the skills of the future labour force.

Most ironically, the financial problems and difficult choices identified in the model used in this paper are a result of society becoming richer (more productive). The people populating the artificial world captured in the Baumol model can afford to pay the price required to keep the university sector healthy if they want to. Canadian society is in the same position.

NOTES

1 See W.J. Baumol, "Macroeconomics of Unbalanced Growth: An Anatomy of Urban Crises," *American Economic Review* 57, no. 3 (1967): 415–26; W.J. Baumol, S.A. Batey-Blackman, and E.N. Wolff, "Unbalanced Growth Revisited: Asymptotic Stagnancy and New Evidence," *American Economic Review* 75, no.4 (1985): 806–17; W.J. Baumol, W.B. Blinder, and W. Scrath, *Economics: Principles and Policies* (Toronto: Academic Press, 1986); and L. Osberg, E.N. Wolff, and W.J. Baumol, *The Information Economy: The Implications of Unbalanced Growth* (Halifax: The Institute for Research on Public Policy, 1989).

2 This description of economic-growth theory is found in R.E. Lucas, Jr, "On the Mechanics of Economic Development," *Journal of Monetary Economics* 22 (Jan. 1988): 3–24.

3 Of course, the forces identified in the Baumol model do not necessarily result in growth in the relative cost of educating a student at university since a variety factors can combine to limit the faculty wage bill per student educated in the short run. For example, the age distribution of faculty might result in significant levels of retirement among older, highly paid faculty reducing the growth in the wage bill; increasing the use of part-time staff could also result in reductions in the wage bill; temporary wage freezes will have the same effect. But in the long run, it is virtually impossible to hold down salary growth.

4 The problem of measuring productivity advance is not restricted to university education. For example, in the automobile sector, where products are relatively standardized and it is possible to describe the physical production process, one is still faced with continual change in the final products, the product mix, and the quality of inputs. However, in

university education it is not even possible to describe the production process or the final output.

5 R. Radner, "Faculty Student Ratios in US Higher Education," in *Education as an Industry*, eds. J.T. Froomkin, D.T. Jamison, and R. Radner, National Bureau of Economic Research (Cambridge: Ballinger Publishing, 1976), 140–63.

6 Sherwin Rosen, "Some Economics of Teaching," *Journal of Labour Economics* 5, no. 4 (1987): 572.

7 See E. Mansfield, "Industrial R&D in Japan and the United States: A Comparative Study," *American Economic Review Papers and Proceedings* 78, no. 2 (1988): 223–8. The contrast between the experience of the university and health-care sectors is also striking. See B.A. Weisbrod, "The Health Care Quadrilemma: An Essay on Technological Change, Insurance, Quality of Care, and Cost Containment," *Journal of Economic Literature* 29, no. 2 (1991): 523–52, for a discussion of the nature of technical change in the health-care sector and some interesting passing comments on technical change in education.

8 It should be noted that considerable resources have been devoted to product innovation in the university sector. Curriculum is continually evolving. The puzzle is not why there has not been technical change – since there has been – but rather why technical change has occurred in the direction it has, i.e., focusing almost exclusively on product quality and not on cost-process innovations.

9 In the Maritime provinces of Nova Scotia, New Brunswick, and Prince Edward Island an intergovernmental commission, the Maritime Provinces Higher Education Commission, develops funding recommendations for the three provinces using standardized criteria. However, these recommendations are not always followed by individual provinces.

10 The simulation used ignores an index-number problem that emerges when one attempts accurately to measure output (GDP) growth in a two-sector model with unbalanced productivity growth. The simulation was kept as simple as possible to emphasize an important principle.

11 The transfer was actually designed to grow at a rate equal to a three year moving average of national GNP growth.

12 The first year economics textbook explanation for a downward-sloping demand curve is actually inadequate in this case. University education is demanded, in part, because it increases future income. Although an increase in price will result in a reduction in demand, other things held unchanged, it is probably inappropriate to invoke the *ceteris paribus* assumption in this case. A reduction in enrolment will reduce future supplies of university-educated workers, which in turn will increase the relative incomes these workers enjoy. Because university incomes rise, university education is more attractive and enrolments rise. The net

impact of a price rise can only be assessed theoretically in a general-equilibrium framework. But, as noted below, empirical studies do suggest that the demand curve is downward sloping.

13 See L. Leslie and P.T. Brinkman, "Student Price Response in Higher Education: The Student Demand Studies," *Journal of Higher Education* 5 (March/April 1987): 200–2.

14 C.D. Thorsby, "Cost Functions for Australian Universities," *Australian Economic Papers* 25, (Dec. 1986): 853–62.

15 J. Johnes, "Unit Costs: Some Explanations for Differences Between UK Universities," *Applied Economics* 22, no. 7 (1990): 853–62.

16 H. Galper and R.M. Dunn Jr, "A Short Run Demand Function for Higher Education in the United States," *Journal of Political Economy* 77 (Sept. 1969): 975.

CHAPTER TEN

Unbalanced Productivity Growth and the Financial History of Mount Allison University

J. FRANK STRAIN

A theoretical model of economic growth with sectoral differences in productivity advance was outlined in chapter 9 to show why universities providing a traditional liberal arts education can face continuing financial difficulties. In this paper, a modified version of the model is applied in a detailed case study of the experience of a single Canadian liberal arts university: Mount Allison University in Sackville, New Brunswick.

The theoretical model advanced in chapter 9 predicts growing financial difficulties for universities providing a liberal arts education. The argument is extremely simple. First, wages and salaries throughout the economy tend to go up and down together. Otherwise, an activity whose wage rate falls seriously behind will be unable to attract workers. Thus, in the long run, auto workers and university faculty must face the same rate of wage growth. But second, productivity growth varies across sectors, in part due to limits on class size and choice of teaching technique imposed by the traditional approach to liberal arts education. If the number of cars produced per worker grows at the same rate as auto workers' wages, the cost per car will not change. But if student/faculty ratios remain unchanged in the face of growing faculty salaries, the cost of university education per student must grow over time. In the absence of offsetting growth in government transfers, endowment income, or tuition fees, this secular tendency must manifest itself in financial crisis in the university.

As noted in the previous chapter, the theoretical model was initially developed by Baumol and extended in Baumol, Blackman, and Wolff and in Osberg, Wolf, and Baumol, and it has been applied in an empirical examination of public-sector growth by Spann.[1] The methodological approach adopted by Spann involved choosing reasonable empirical estimates for the important parameters of the model and comparing the predictions generated by the model with actual outcomes. He found that the predictions were broadly consistent with the facts. Spann's methodology can also be applied to examine the history of the Canadian university sector. Indeed, it can be shown that the predictions of an unbalanced-productivity-growth model that incorporates reasonable parameter estimates are also broadly consistent with the facts in the Canadian university sector.[2]

Nonetheless, this paper adopts a different methodological framework when applying the unbalanced- productivity-growth model in an examination of the financial history of a single university. Some of the features of the methodological approach adopted here are discussed in the following section. Section 3 focuses on one small liberal arts university – Mount Allison – and how it managed to cope with the secular tendency towards fiscal crisis implied by the unbalanced-productivity-growth model. It will be shown that a variety of mechanisms have been employed to counter this tendency including higher tuition fees, attracting funds from both public and private sectors, keeping salary increases below the rate of increase elsewhere in the economy, larger class sizes, administrative efficiency, and internal transfers of resources to teaching from other parts of the university. It will also be shown that, while all these measures have been used over Mount Allison's history, the university still faces financial problems. Conclusions are offered in the final section of the paper.

APPLYING THE BAUMOL MODEL IN AN EXAMINATION OF A SINGLE UNIVERSITY

The methodological approach adopted here does not involve a "test" of the unbalanced-productivity-growth model using data from Mount Allison. Instead, I begin by assuming that the unbalanced-productivity-growth assumptions invoked in the Baumol model are true and that the conclusions with respect to the evolution of unit costs are a logical outcome of the unbalanced-productivity-growth assumptions.

The approach is based loosely on a framework applied by Karl Marx in *Das Kapital*, where Marx develops a theory of value that he uses to identify the tendency for the rate of profit to fall under capitalism. This tendency is in turn used as the analytical basis for much of Marx's critique of capitalism.

Marx's methodological approach is novel. The tendency for the rate of profit to fall is identified at a high level of abstraction. It does not necessarily manifest itself in a fall in the actual rate of profit. Since other factors also influence the rate of profit, these other factors can counter the tendency for the rate of profit to fall. Labour-saving technological change, free trade, and new social institutions can increase the intensity with which workers must work or lower the cost of the workers' consumption goods to offset the tendency of the rate of profit to fall. But in Marx's analytical method these countervailing tendencies only emerge as one moves from the highly abstract to the concrete. The great virtue of beginning with the tendency of the rate of profit to fall was that it provided an organizing framework for Marx's penetrating examination of the concrete experiences of capitalist economies.

The Baumol model suggests that unit costs in the university sector have a tendency to rise relative to other sectors of the economy. Like the tendency for the rate of profit to fall, the tendency for unit costs to rise provides an analytical basis for concrete historical studies. The tendency for unit costs to rise may or may not manifest itself in rising unit costs and financial difficulties since countervailing developments are possible. The advantage of the Baumol model is that it puts a fundamental structural problem front and centre and emphasizes the continual tension that exists between the fundamental tendency of unit costs to rise and countervailing measures that potentially offset this tendency. This is how the Baumol model is used to guide our analysis of a single university in the following sections of the paper.

One feature of the Baumol model receives particular attention in this case study. The model generates a very special "blame the faculty" view of financial crises. Faculty are responsible because they "force" universities to pay salaries equal to the value of the faculty members' labour time elsewhere in the economy, and because faculty are unable to increase their revenue productivity without seriously reducing the quality of the service they are providing. Thus, special attention is given here to faculty salaries and faculty revenue productivity.

Before turning to the case study itself, it is first necessary to adapt the Baumol model slightly. The basic model is based on a number of simplifying assumptions that may have to be altered. For example, it is unlikely that the demand for the space at a single university is price inelastic. If a single university increases tuition relative to others in the system, enrolments are likely to be affected. Although it is inaccurate to assume that universities are price takers given existing variation in tuition fees across Canada, it is not an unreasonable simplifying assumption (variation in price is relatively small). Moreover, tuition fees are not set in a competitive market where they cover unit costs of production. Rather, tuition fees are best thought of as administered prices set through a highly political bargaining process involving the universities, interest groups (including students), and politicians.

On the supply side the basic model was based on a simple single input/single output production function with no economies of scale. A better description of production possibilities would allow for the joint input/joint output technology that actually exists in the university sector. Unfortunately, empirical work with this type of production function has not progressed very far and therefore will not be employed in this paper. Economies of scale are also ignored. The neglect of economies of scale is not justified by a belief that they have no potential impact – they do, since a decline in unit costs due to expanded scale can offset some or all of the rise in unit costs that occurs as faculty salaries rise without offsetting declines in the faculty/student ratio. Instead, the neglect of scale economies is based on the ambiguity of the results of recent empirical cost studies.[3] These studies fail to conclude that there are empirically identifiable scale economies in the provision of university education.

The modified version of the Baumol model adopted for use in the historical study in this paper is based on a simple version of a single university's budget constraint. This can be written: $P_tN_t + r_tE_t + G_t + M_t + D_t = S_tF_t + O_t$, where P_t = average tuition per course in period t; N_t = total student enrolment (number of students * average course load of a student) in period t; r_t = average rate of return on endowments in period t; E_t = total endowment in period t; G_t = government grants in period t; M_t = donations and other contributions to operating budget in period t; D_t = change in debt in period t; S_t = average faculty salary in period t; F_t = number of faculty in period t; and O_t = other expenses in period t.

Notice that this can be rewritten in per-student terms to highlight the importance of the two faculty variables – S_t, the average faculty salary, and F_t/N_t, the average class size – in the evolution of costs. Since S_t has a *tendency* to grow at the same rate as wages and salaries in the rest of the economy and there is limited flexibility in the choice of F_t/N_t, unit costs have a *tendency* to rise over time. If there are no offsetting changes in P_t, G_t, E_t, M_t, or O_t, the university will find itself in financial difficulty. On the other hand, if the university manages to constrain growth in S_t, increase F_t/N_t, or adjust P_t, R_t, E_t, M_t, or O_t, financial difficulty can be avoided.

The variable S_tF_t/N_t, which economists often label unit labour cost, is critical to the story told in this section. The reader is urged to experiment with a few simple examples to see how this variable reacts to changes in S_t, F_t, and N_t. For example, suppose S_t = \$50,000, F_t = 100, N_t = 2000 (a student/faculty ratio of 20:1), O_t = 0, P_t = \$2,000, E_t = 0, G_t = \$500,000 and M_t = \$500,000. The unit labour cost, the average labour cost of educating a student over the year, will be \$2,500, the university budget is balanced, and D_t remains equal to 0. If productivity growth in the rest of the economy generates a five percent increase in wages across the board, faculty salaries increase to \$55,000 and unit labour costs to \$2,500. If the university does not react to the change in salary, a deficit of \$500,000 results. In the short run this can be financed by borrowing or running down endowments, but in the long run it is not sustainable. Hence this hypothetical university must react.

There are a number of possible reactions. First, the university could increase tuition fees to \$2,250. But this is likely to be difficult given the political process that governs prices in the university sector. The governing body of the university will include students, alumni, faculty, and other members of the general public. Students and parents have a direct interest in fees and will resist fee increases, especially given that other prices in the economy are not increasing. Representatives of the general public will likely be concerned with accessibility and they will resist fee increases for this reason. Faculty, too, will be concerned with accessibility. Thus, the simple and obvious solution will be difficult to implement.

A second solution is to increase the number of students while keeping the number of faculty unchanged. This requires admitting an additional 250 students. The student/faculty ratio rises to 22.5:1. If the increase in faculty salary is a one-time event this response is feasible, although it is likely to have an adverse effect on quality. But if there is steady growth in productivity in the rest of the economy and if faculty salaries continually increase, quality will necessarily deteriorate over time. A policy of coping with salary growth through increases in the student/faculty ratio is not sustainable in the long run.

The third solution is to secure funds from other sources such as government grants and private donations. In our example, outside funding would have to increase by \$500,000 to maintain a balanced budget.

A final option, implicitly assumed away in our example, is to cap faculty salaries at \$50,000. This is possible in the short run since faculty are not able to change employment quickly. But in the long run, the university will loose its best faculty and will find it impossible to secure replacements. Thus, capping salary growth is not a feasible long-term policy.

The simple budget-constraint version of the unbalanced-productivity-growth model clearly identifies the problems posed for universities by unbalanced productivity growth and difficulties associated with the different possible responses to these problems. It should not be surprising to observe real-world universities experimenting with different combinations of responses in different time periods.

MOUNT ALLISON UNIVERSITY: A CASE STUDY

The purpose of this section of the paper is to apply the modified Baumol unbalanced growth model in an examination of selected aspects of the financial history of Mount Allison University. The idiosyncratic events and personalities that shaped the financial history of Mount Allison do not play an active role in the story told here. Indeed, in this paper "the numbers do the talking." Fortunately, there exists a wide-ranging two-volume history of Mount Allison that not only provides an excellent survey of the major idiosyncratic events (new buildings, fires, and changes in curriculum) and influential personalities but also sets the university's history within the broader context of Canadian social history. John Reid's *Mount Allison University: A History* should be consulted by anyone interested in a more detailed examination of Mount Allison or in putting faces to the story told in this paper.[4]

The difficulties of university finance, budget allocation, and faculty compensation occupy a central place in Reid's work. This is evident in the preface to his history, where he identifies one of the organizing principles of his work:

> Mount Allison University, never a rich institution, was faced again and again with potentially conflicting demands: to maintain quality, through such means as attracting and retaining faculty members of high competence, while at the same time obeying the Christian obligation (profoundly influenced by the social gospel movement within the [M]ethodist denomination and its successor, the United Church of Canada) to make education widely available at low cost. If there is a central dynamic of Mount Allison's history, and thus an [overall] context within which the experiences of students faculty, and other participants must be interpreted, it is one of struggle to reconcile responsibilities – intellectual, moral, social – which could not easily be reconciled.[5]

The Baumol model of unbalanced growth illuminates this "central dynamic" by pointing to the underlying economic basis of "the struggle." Recall that the Baumol model emphasizes the tendency for the cost of university education to grow relative to the costs of many other goods and services provided in our economy. If the relative cost of university education had a tendency to fall over time (relatively rapid productivity growth will generate this outcome) the twin demands of accessibility and quality would not have posed such a difficult problem for Mount Allison. Increasing salaries of faculty as required to keep highly competent faculty would not have increased costs (indeed, costs may have fallen). Thus, the conflict between "responsibilities" identified by Reid is neither necessary nor inevitable. Instead, the problem of reconciling quality and accessibility was a continual challenge because the relative cost of university education had a tendency to rise over time for reasons suggested by the Baumol model.

The data used in this study were collected from annual financial reports, reports of the registrar's office, board of regents minutes, and presidents' reports covering a period from 1870 to 1987. The raw data were reorganized with the help of a senior accounting student to produce a relatively consistent set of accounts for Mount Allison University. Given the changes in accounting practices, the year-to-year variation in the information that was available, confusion over capital and operating entries, and significant institutional reorganization at Mount Allison over the period being considered, reconstruction of the financial accounts posed significant challenges. The final set of accounts that were produced provide a fairly complete picture of the operating expenditures and revenues over the financial history of Mount Allison from 1894, and they are particularly well suited for the long-term trend analysis of this paper. (Unfortunately it was not possible to construct an accurate set of balance sheets that record the evolution of assets and liabilities of the institution over its history.) No allowance is made for depreciation in the physical capital stock or in the nominal value of financial assets. Because this paper is built around the Baumol model this is not a serious problem, since the model focuses on flows, not stocks. However, it will be seen as a serious weakness by those interested in a complete financial history of the institution. It must also be recognized that even with this proviso the reconstructed accounts are far from perfect. A detailed description of the data and the methods used to reconstruct the accounts are available from the author.

Student and financial data for 1870–94 are not available in sufficient detail to summarize all developments in this period.[6] Nonetheless, it is possible to identify several important features that had an important impact on the long-run evolution of the institution.

The first development was the Province of New Brunswick's elimination of financial assistance to religious educational institutions in 1873. As a result, Mount Allison, a Methodist college, was forced to turn exclusively to fees and fund raising within the Methodist community to finance operations and for capital. Since that time Mount

Allison has continually been involved in some type of fund-raising drive. The success of these efforts were heavily influenced by the prevailing economic conditions.

The relative importance of fees and gifts and other endowment income can be seen from data for 1894, the first year we were able to reconstruct a reasonable set of accounts. In that year student fees (including room-and-board payments) accounted for almost two-thirds of revenue, gifts and endowment income making up the remainder.

The 1894 accounts also illustrate the relative importance of the different expenditure items in the operating budget. Faculty salaries are the largest single item, accounting for almost two-thirds of the expenditures, followed by residence operations. Administrative functions were carried out by teaching faculty, including presidential duties. Thus, the cost of administrative and student services are almost entirely allocated to faculty salaries.

The most important variable in the Baumol model is the salary variable, s_t. It is possible to follow the changes in this variable over the 1870–90 period. The cost of university education per student rises in the highly abstract world of the Baumol model because s_t rises at the same rate as wages and salaries in the economy as a whole while the student/faculty ratio remains constant. In the real world in which Mount Allison operated, faculty salaries might not grow as fast as wages and salaries elsewhere. In the abstract world of the model, wages and salaries grow at the same rate because labour is perfectly mobile across occupations. In the real world labour is not perfectly mobile. Faculty may not leave their jobs even though their relative wage is declining because (1) they have a strong commitment to their profession, institution, or place of residence; (2) their skills are not easily transferred to new occupations; and (3) they might believe the wage reduction is temporary and things will improve in the future. Thus, faculty may implicitly subsidize their students and thereby counteract the tendency for unit costs to rise. The subsidization of students by faculty can be identified by comparing faculty salary increases with those occurring on average in the economy.

Between 1870 and 1890 real wages in the economy as a whole grew by fifty-four percent. Over the same period real output per person hour grew by forty-seven percent. Significantly, faculty salaries at Mount Allison seem to have kept pace with wage and productivity increases in the rest of the economy.

In this period Mount Allison was an extremely small school with faculty teaching both secondary- and post-secondary-level courses. The board of regents reviewed contracts annually and decided whether or not to rehire on the basis of economics and teaching performance. In

Table 1
Salaries of Three Mount Allison Faculty Members, 1870–90
(in current dollars)

Year	*D. Allison* *President until 1877*	*J. Inch* *President: 1877–90*	*A. Smith*
1870			.
1871	1000	850	600
1872	1000	950	600
1873	1000	950	600
1874	1000	950	900
1875	1000	950	900
1876	1000	950	900
1877	1200	1200	1000
1878	1320	1320	1150
1879	1320	1320	1150
1880	.	1350	1150
1881	.	1350	1150
1882	.	1350	1150
1883	.	1350	1150
1884	.	1350	1150
1885	.	1350	1150
1886	.	1350	1150
1887	.	1350	1150
1888	.	1350	1150
1889	.	1350	1150
1890	.	1350	1150
	.	1350	

Source: Board of Regents Minutes, 1870–90.

one case the board decided not to rehire a Mr Gray, teacher of painting, "his salary being greater than the profits yielded to the institution financially."[7]

The board also set salaries. It is interesting to note that in the years prior to 1874, faculty collected fees directly from students to supplement their salary income. These supplementary fees amounted to a relatively small proportion of salary (approximately one hundred dollars in a good year). Faculty also lived in the college free of charge.

Table 1 follows the salary increases of three senior faculty members over the twenty years from 1870 to 1890. The nominal salary increases over this period varied significantly between faculty members. J. Inch enjoyed a fifty-eight percent increase in nominal salary while Smith experienced a ninety-one percent increase. Adjusting for inflation is unnecessary since prices at the end of the period were approximately equal to prices at the beginning of the period (see the estimate of the implicit price index for this period in Green and Urqhart).[8] Given that part of the increase received by Smith was due to experience, it seems reasonable to conclude that faculty salaries did not fall behind in this period and that they grew at approximately the same rate as productivity growth.[9]

Over the same period the number of students at the college/university rose from seventeen to sixty-two. Although it is impossible to determine the exact increase in class size over the period, there was undoubtedly an increase in the size of college classes. But it is impossible to determine from existing information whether this increased the revenue productivity (the additional revenue generated by an individual faculty member's teaching load) of faculty.[10]

Between 1890 and 1914 the experience was very different. Salaries of faculty with at least seven years' experience were fixed at $1,250 from 1891 until 1912. A severe recession in the mid-1890s actually resulted in deflation and, thus, increases in real faculty salaries. But by 1896 the Canadian economy had turned around and prices rose relatively rapidly.[11] Between 1900 and 1913 real faculty salaries declined by more than ten percent. Meanwhile the impact of the "wheat boom" was felt in the rest of the economy. Firestone estimates that productivity (output per person hour) grew by almost fifty percent over this period.[12] Bertram and Percy find that real wages grew by over fifteen percent.[13] Thus, real faculty salaries at Mount Allison fell by almost twenty-five percent relative to the average elsewhere.

The squeeze on faculty salaries seriously impaired the university's ability to attract new high-quality faculty and its ability to keep faculty then on staff. Several key faculty members left during this time but others decided to stay out of loyalty to the institution and the region. Those who chose to remain "enjoyed" growing class sizes and the loss of research and study trips that had traditionally enabled faculty to travel to major universities in Britain and Germany.[14]

But despite reductions in real faculty salaries and a rise in the student/faculty ratio, the university still experienced financial difficulties. In part this was a consequence of slow revenue growth. Tuition fees were held low to keep education accessible to the relatively poor Maritime Methodist community the university served. Gifts and bequests did not grow rapidly due to the poor performance of the Maritime economy. In part, the difficulties were due to growth in student numbers (from sixty-two in 1890 to 155 in 1914) and necessary expansion of residence facilities and a major fire, which resulted in significant capital expenditures to replace the underinsured physical capital.

Thus, on the evidence, it is impossible to argue that the Baumol problem of rising faculty salaries relative to faculty revenue productivity was responsible for the university's financial difficulties in this period. Indeed, far from being "responsible" for the problem, faculty helped keep the university going by indirectly subsidizing students and the institution. However, faculty cannot subsidize students and the institution indefinitely since the old "loyalists" eventually retire and it becomes increasingly difficult to attract strong faculty.

By 1918 the annual salaries of senior faculty had risen to $1,700 (a nominal increase of thirty-six percent). But over the same period prices had risen by fifty percent. Consequently, real faculty salaries again declined. (Real salaries at Mount Allison in 1896 were higher than they were in 1918, twenty-two years later.) Between 1914 and 1918 the average real wage in Canadian manufacturing also declined by 10.4 percent.[15] Thus, faculty at Mount Allison experienced another decline in salary relative to those received elsewhere over this period.

In 1920 members of the Massey Foundation Commission on Methodist Schools in Canada visited Mount Allison.[16] The commission offered "a resounding call for better terms and conditions of work for the faculty."[17] Its report explicitly recognized the growth in teaching loads that accompanied growth in student numbers (which reached 173 in 1920) and called for more faculty and a raise in salary to at least $2,500. This raise would have given faculty a hundred percent cumulative increase over salaries in 1901. Given that the average manufacturing wage had increased by two hundred percent over this period, the Massey Commission recommendation would not have restored Mount Allison faculty to their relative position in 1901. But at least the raise would have generated a real improvement in faculty living standards. Alas, the university could not even afford this increase and faculty continued heavily to subsidize the institution and, indirectly, its students.

It is important to note that the implicit subsidization of university operations by faculty was not passed on directly to students through low tuition fees. In 1904 the typical student was paying thirty-four dollars in tuition fees. By 1914 this had risen to forty-four dollars and fees reached eighty-eight dollars by 1924. The increases in fees more than covered the general rise in prices over the period and the increase was almost sufficient to maintain simultaneously faculty relative-salary position in the Canadian labour market, the student/faculty ratio, and the ratio of tuition fees to university operating costs. This is illustrated in Table 2.

Table 2 indicates that Mount Allison increased fees fast enough to assure adequate faculty salaries (at least, fast enough to maintain Mount Allison faculty's relative salary) and a constant student/faculty ratio. However, student/faculty ratios rose over the period, increasing

Table 2
Actual and Hypothetical Average Tuition Fees

Year	*Actual tuition fee*	*Real tuition fee constant at 1904 level*	*Tuition fee required to simultaneously maintain relative salary position, student/faculty ratio, and fees/operating costs ratio at 1904 levels*
1904	$34	$34	$34
1914	$44	$43.50	$44.50
1924	$80	$65	$85.20

faculty's revenue productivity and workloads and, perhaps, reducing the quality of education provided by the institution. Thus, both faculty and students assumed a larger share of responsibility in financing university operations at the time. Much-reduced income from gifts and endowments accounts for part of the shift in financial responsibility in this period. The diversion of revenues to expand the physical plant and replace a major building lost to fire were also significant.

Mount Allison's financial position did not improve during the late twenties. The economies of the Maritime provinces never recovered from a serious recession in 1921 and, unlike most of North America, depression conditions persisted throughout the 1920s. Revenues grew very slowly and expanding enrolment required a heavy investment in recruiting. The university responded by running short-term deficits, which they hoped would be covered by gifts and bequests when the economy improved.

By 1933 the worldwide depression was well established and Mount Allison's financial problems were even worse than in the twenties. Gifts and bequests could not be expected under such depressed conditions and interest charges on debt accumulated during the late twenties was pushing Mount Allison towards bankruptcy. Fortunately, a new bond issue of almost half a million dollars to cover maturing debt and the current deficit allowed the institution to survive the immediate crisis. The bond issue did not, however, solve the fundamental financial problems of the university and a variety of actions were taken to "get the house in order."

One measure was the liquidation of a number of assets (largely real-estate holdings). Another was a cut in faculty salaries (by five percent in 1933 and by a further five percent in 1934). Retiring faculty were not replaced and the board of regents asked for the resignation of others. The executive-committee minutes note that "with regret it was recommended that we ask for the resignation of Professor Selfridge. It is felt that a suitable lady teacher be found for his position at approximately half the salary."[18] The failure to replace retiring faculty resulted in a substantial increase in the student/faculty ratio (an increase of over fifty-eight percent between 1924 and 1934).

Although Mount Allison was forced to take relatively drastic action, including wage cuts, to cope with the Depression, faculty fared relatively well. Between 1924 and 1934 the average earnings of Canadian workers fell more than Mount Allison faculty salaries, thereby improving faculty's relative position in the wage distribution. However, after 1934, average earnings in the Canadian economy began to grow while average faculty salaries at Mount Allison continued to decline.[19] By 1944 the starting salary for university faculty at Mount Allison actually fell below the average earnings of Canadian production workers.

The squeeze on faculty salaries in the late 1930s and early 1940s was a consequence of declining enrolments due to the Depression and the war and a disastrous fire on campus, which forced the university to cope with a necessary but unplanned capital expenditure. Again, faculty had to subsidize university operations indirectly to assure the continued existence of the institution.

The experience between 1870 and 1945 at Mount Allison does not provide much support for the predictive version of the Baumol model of unbalanced growth. One of the critical assumptions that underlies the model – that salaries of faculty will grow at the same rate as the wages of production workers in the manufacturing sector – is not consistent with experience. Faculty did not move to sectors experiencing high wage growth and it was still possible to attract new faculty despite the offer of relatively low wages. The tendency identified in the tautological version of the Baumol model never did manifest itself in a financial crisis. Instead, the financial problems were a consequence of other, exogenous, factors.

At the end of the war the demand for university education rose throughout the country. Between 1945 and 1954 the number of students at Mount Allison increased from about six hundred to one thousand. In part, this was due to a new cohort of young men who were not drawn to the military and young women who could no longer find industrial employment. In part, the growth in enrolment occurred because returning veterans drew on the federal government's Veterans Rehabilitation Act, which provided bursaries covering tuition and board costs. Significantly, this legislation also provided direct grants to universities in recognition of the fact that student fees accounted for only forty percent of revenue. This additional funding helped Mount Allison cover the fixed-interest costs incurred as a result of earlier fires and deficits.

The return of Canadians from overseas also had an impact on faculty salaries. Not only did the inflow of funds from the federal government provide needed cash but also the Mount Allison board of regents

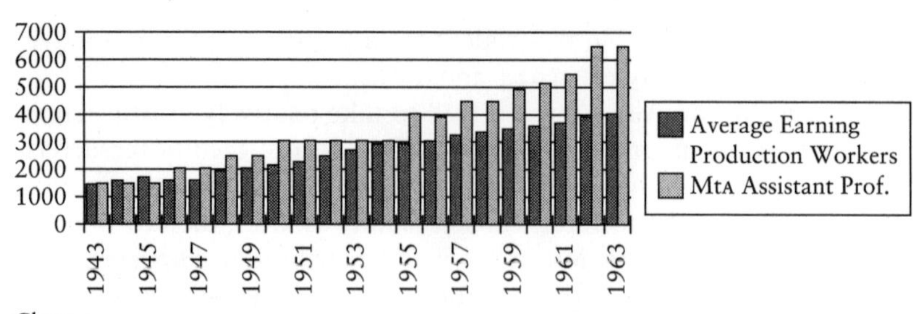

Chart 1
Mt Allison Faculty Salaries

believed that a salary increase was necessary in recognition of the participation of a number of junior faculty members in the war effort overseas.[20]

Chart 1 illustrates the evolution of faculty salaries between 1943 and 1963. It is clear that the relative gains slowly eroded between 1948 and 1954. This was a consequence partly of reduced veteran enrolment and partly of capital expenditures needed to adjust to higher overall enrolments. It is also important to note that student/faculty ratios rose by over thirty percent between 1948 and 1954. Thus, faculty revenue-productivity growth covered much of the increase in wages.

It is also clear from Chart 1 that faculty salaries at Mount Allison began to grow, absolutely and relative to the average production worker, much more rapidly after 1955. The dramatic growth in salaries in this period followed the introduction of federal and provincial programs to support universities, which in turn were supported by general growth in the economy as a whole and in government tax revenue. In 1943 there was no direct government support (as a private denominational university, Mount Allison was ineligible for provincial funding); by 1954, thanks to changes in provincial legislation and the introduction of federal post-secondary education funding, government was providing approximately fifteen percent of total revenue; by 1963 government was accounting for almost twenty-five percent of revenue.

The growing importance of highly skilled scientific, technical, and managerial workers in the post-war economy simultaneously generated an increase in demand for university spaces, new career options for existing and potential university faculty, and the appearance of universities on the public-policy agenda. Significantly, the emergence of government funding eased the financial crisis that seemed perpetually to characterize the university sector as a whole, and increased competition for highly skilled manpower forced universities to use some of the increased revenue to increase salaries.

The increased flow of funds from government did not, however, allow the university to decrease faculty teaching loads. Faculty continued to

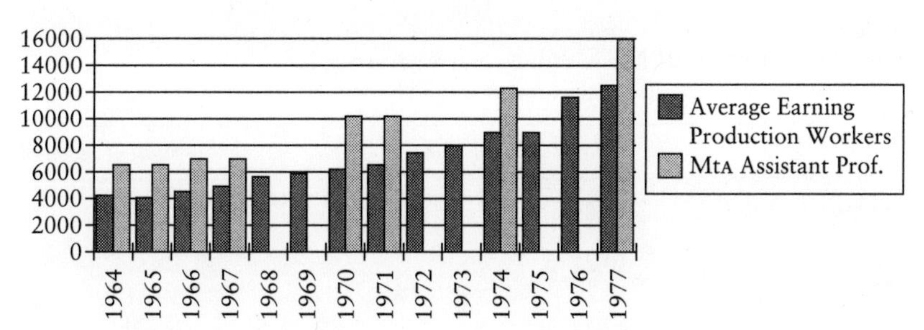

Chart 2
Mt Allison Faculty Salaries

teach four or five courses as well as regular Saturday classes. The student/faculty ratio also continued to rise, reaching its highest point in Mount Allison's history in 1963. It is interesting to note that the increasing student/faculty ratio resulted in a serious debate among Mount Allison faculty about the future of the university. Not surprisingly, the committee struck to examine "the idea of excellence at Mount Allison" recommended a cap on enrolment and a curriculum that would allow faculty more time for research and creative activity, while also providing more personal interaction between individual students and individual faculty.

The recommendations of the committee were never explicitly acted upon. However, the economic environment of the mid- and late sixties and the early seventies did provide a base for a period of unprecedented prosperity at the university. Government funding rose from about half a million dollars (twenty-five percent of total revenue) in 1963 to over three million dollars (almost fifty percent of total revenue) in 1973. Tuition fees rose slightly from $460 in 1963 to $635 in 1966 and remained constant at that level to 1975. Although enrolments grew from about 1,238 in 1963 to 1,363 in 1973, the rate of growth was significantly less than in the Canadian university system as a whole. Indeed, student/faculty ratios at Mount Allison declined by one-third.

Chart 2 illustrates the growth in faculty salaries from 1964 to 1977. It can be seen that faculty salaries kept pace with average salaries in the wider economy.

The expansion of government programs supporting post-secondary education between 1946 and 1975 countered any tendency to financial crises at Mount Allison. Indeed, government funding and healthy endowment income (made possible by donations and bequests received during this relatively prosperous period) allowed Mount Allison simultaneously to hold down tuition fees, reduce student/faculty ratios, and increase faculty salaries at about the same rate as in the economy generally. Revenue growth also enabled the university to improve facilities through the purchase of new laboratory equipment, new

Table 3
Expenditures on Central Administration and Student Services
(per dollar spent on academic departments, the library, and the Office of the Deans)

Year	*Central Administration*	*Student Services*
1943	$0.33	$0.08
1953	$0.28	$0.95
1963	$0.27	$0.11
1972	$0.23	$0.11
1983	$0.34	$0.10
1987	$0.30	$0.10

teaching tools, recreational facilities, and new buildings. The university was able to expand its course offerings and a number of new departments were created while others expanded. New administrative and support functions also appeared with the introduction of a variety of offices, staffed by full-time professionals rather than by volunteer faculty, including a registrar's office, an admissions office, a business office, a personnel office, and an athletics department with professional coaches.

Remarkably, the expansion of service and administrative functions did not result in dramatic changes in relative expenditures. Table 3 records the expenditure (for every dollar spent on the academic side of the university) on central administration (the president's office, registrar and admissions, the business office, purchasing, personnel) and on student services (dean of students, athletics, chaplaincy).

As long as government funding grew at a rapid rate the university was able to avoid serious problems. But when the rate of growth in government funding fell and interest rates rose in the late 1970s, the university began to run into trouble. The first response was to maintain programs by running down endowments, in real terms (no allowance was made for the impact of inflation on financial assets and the university financed a growing deficit through borrowing). In addition, the university allowed enrolment to rise and increased faculty revenue productivity by increasing student/faculty ratios. Between 1973 and 1989 enrolments rose from 1,354 to almost 2,000, while the student/faculty ratio grew by twenty percent.

Faculty salaries also suffered in the late seventies and early eighties. As Chart 3 illustrates, the earning differential between the Mount Allison assistant professor floor (the base for the salary schedule) and the average production-worker salary fell between 1970 and 1982. But after 1982 Mount Allison faculty recorded some relative gains. Faculty unionization in 1981, the relatively low salaries (throughout its history Mount Allison's faculty were among the poorest paid in the country),

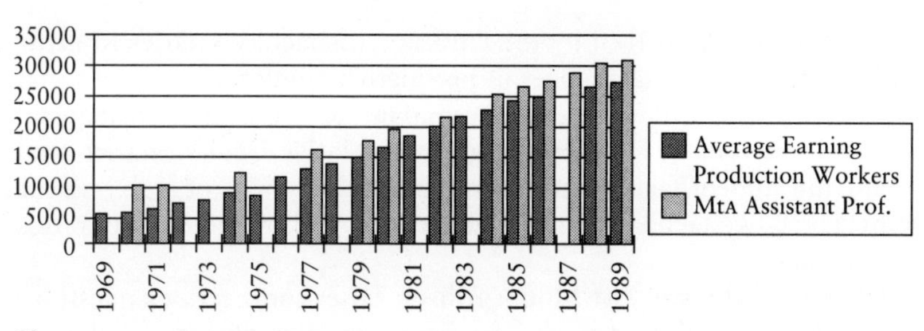

Chart 3
Mt Allison Faculty Salaries

and the university's desire to keep strong faculty combined to generate these relative gains despite the general financial troubles.

By 1987 it was clear to the university that it could no longer finance operations by running down endowments. New accounting and budgeting systems were introduced, the university reduced discretionary spending, leaving faculty were not replaced, and numerous *ad hoc* measures designed to reduce costs were implemented. The university also declared "financial exigency," which opened up the possibility of laying off tenured faculty members and eliminating entire departments. In the end, the university administration did neither, but its actions clearly indicated the seriousness of the situation. Likewise, in its 1992 contract negotiations with the Faculty Association, the university administration asked for a two percent wage cut. This negotiating stance generated the first faculty strike in Mount Allison's history. The resulting collective agreement held real wages constant.

The policies to control financial problems reduced the perennial operating deficit and the university finally achieved a balanced budget in 1992. This should not, however, be seen as the end of the university's financial difficulties. Government funding will almost inevitably decline as government struggles to cope with extremely high debt loads and students, parents, and governments struggle to keep tuition fees from rising. As a consequence, faculty at Mount Allison, like public-sector workers generally, should not expect rapid salary growth. Faculty will also face considerable pressure to increase productivity in the nineties through new teaching techniques, especially through computer-assisted instruction methods.

CONCLUSION

This paper applied a model of unbalanced productivity growth in an examination of the financial history of Mount Allison University in Sackville, New Brunswick. This examination did not suggest that financial crises are driven by the tendency for faculty salaries to grow without accompanying changes in productivity. Indeed, it suggests that revenue growth is the critical determinant of a university's financial health. In periods of low revenue growth, relative faculty salaries tend to fall and student/faculty ratios tend to rise. In periods of high revenue growth, relative faculty salaries tend to grow and student/faculty ratios tend to fall.

The financial history of Mount Allison raises some serious questions about the applicability of the predictive version of the unbalanced growth model. Faculty salaries and slow productivity growth do not drive the university to financial crisis. Instead, salaries and productivity seem to change in response to revenue growth and other "exogenous" factors (such as major fires, capital expenditures, and interest-rate changes). This finding is consistent with Bowen's arguments that revenue is the main determinant of unit costs at American universities.[21]

Still, it is impossible to dismiss the unbalanced-growth model completely. Faculty salaries did grow over time and the student/faculty ratio (the measure of the revenue productivity of faculty) remained relatively stable. Consequently, the unit cost of university education had a tendency to rise. Although the Mount Allison experience suggests that relative faculty salaries do not grow as fast as salaries elsewhere, the relatively steady growth in salary expenditures did play an extremely important role in determining the overall cost of running the university. This growth is likely to continue in the future, and meeting the faculty salary bill will remain one of the most significant challenges facing the university.

NOTES

1 W.J. Baumol, "Macroeconomics of Unbalanced Growth: An Anatomy of Urban Crisis," *American Economic Review* 57, no. 3 (1967): 415–26; W.J. Baumol, S.A. Batey-Blackman, and E.N. Wolff "Unbalanced Growth Revisited: Asymptomatic Stagnancy and New Evidence," *American Economic Review* 75, no. 4 (1985): 806–17; L. Osberg, E.N. Wolff, and W.J. Baumol, *The Information Economy: The Implications of Unbalanced Growth* (Halifax: Institute for Research on Public Policy, 1989).

2 R.M. Spann, "The Macroeconomics of Unbalanced Growth and the Expanding Public Sector: Some Simple Tests," *Journal of Public Economics* 8, no. 3 (1978): 397–404.

3 See J. Johnes, "Unit Costs: Some Explanations for Differences Between UK Universities," *Applied Economics* 22, no. 7 (1990): 853–88, and C.D. Thorsby, "Cost Functions for Australian Universities," *Australian Economic Papers* 25, (Dec. 1986): 175–90.

4 J.G. Reid, *Mount Allison University: A History to 1963*, 2 vols. (Toronto: University of Toronto Press, 1984).
5 Ibid., vol. 1, viii.
6 Even when some data are available, it is impossible to allocate revenues and expenditures to the three constituent parts of Mount Allison: the academy, the Ladies' college, and the college.
7 Mount Allison University, Board of Regents Minutes, 1873.
8 Green and Urqhart, "New Estimates of Output Growth in Canada: Measurement and Interpretation," in *Perspectives on Canadian Economic History*, ed. D. McCalla, (Toronto: Copp Clark Pitman, 1987), 182–99.
9 O.J. Firestone, *Canada's Economic Development 1867–1956* (London: Bowes and Bowes, 1958), offers estimates of wage and productivity growth that are based on relatively poor data. These can be used to give a very general picture of what was happening. The conclusion drawn in this paper is based on the fact that the increases are quite similar.
10 Because faculty often taught classes in more than one of the Mount Allison institutions (the college, the Ladies' College, and the academy), it is extremely difficult to determine the teaching loads of the college professors. It is clear that faculty numbers did not grow as rapidly as student numbers in any of the institutions. Thus, it is possible to conclude that student/faculty ratios in general increased in this period. But because undergraduates were increasingly hired to teach courses in the academy, college faculty were freed to concentrate more and more on university teaching and enjoy the smaller classes at that level. Consequently, it is impossible to reach unambiguous conclusions about teaching loads of the college faculty.
11 Although the Canadian economy experienced significant intensive and extensive growth between 1896 and 1912, the economies of the Maritime provinces performed relatively poorly. This exacerbated the financial problems at Mount Allison since students were unable to afford higher tuition fees and gifts and endowments from people in the region were difficult to secure.
12 Firestone, *Canada's Economic Development.*
13 G. Bertram and M. Percy, "Real Wage Trends in Canada 1900–1926: Some Provisional Estimates," *Canadian Journal of Economics* 12, no. 2 (1979), 310.
14 Reid, *Mount Allison University*, vol. 2, 40.
15 Bertram and Percy, "Real Wage Trends in Canada," 309.
16 Reid, *Mount Allison University*, vol. 2, 38.
17 Ibid., 39.
18 Mount Allison University, Executive Committee Minutes, 1933.
19 The decline in average salaries of Mount Allison faculty occurred for two reasons. First, starting salaries were reduced each year between

1933 and 1937 and were held constant until 1945. Second, the university replaced relatively expensive faculty with relatively cheap faculty.

20 Mount Allison University, Executive Committee Minutes, 15 May 1945.

21 H. Bowen, *The Cost of Higher Education: How Much Do Colleges Spend Per Student and How Much Should They Spend?* (San Francisco, CA: Jossey-Bass, 1980).

CHAPTER ELEVEN

Helping the Student to Learn: Special Assistance to Undergraduates

JANE DROVER, BRIAN MCMILLAN, AND ALEXANDER M. WILSON

At Mount Allison, the "special" qualities of all students are recognized and fostered. However, for the purpose of this chapter, the term "special populations" will refer to two groups of students who, in the university setting, are at risk and need help to meet the demands of studies at this level: those with a learning disability, and those inadequately prepared for the transition from secondary to post-secondary education. It was largely in an effort to meet the needs of these special populations that Mount Allison established a centre to serve as a focal point for the activities of both students and service providers. Known for several years as the Centre for Learning Assistance and Research, it was renamed the Meighen Centre for Learning Assistance and Research in 1994 in recognition of a substantial grant from Themadel Foundation of St Andrews, New Brunswick.

In September 1987 the senate of Mount Allison University, on the recommendation of a special committee, approved a written policy on learning-disabled students that set out the process for admitting students with learning disabilities and established general guidelines for the academic staff who might become involved with them.[1] This support from the university community and the addition to the education department of another faculty member with expertise in the area of learning disabilities greatly facilitated the establishment of the centre. In the later 1980s, the founders of the centre had become aware through their professional activities that students with learning problems were being better served by the public schools and would therefore be in a position to want, and to qualify for, post-secondary education. A clinic at Mount Allison to serve university students with special needs would benefit those students, the faculty and student teachers of the education department, and those faculty who were pursuing research in this field.

Since its inception in 1987, the centre has been guided by the following goals:

1 to provide support to university students with learning disabilities so that they may reach their full potential academically, socially, and personally;
2 to carry out research with university students, particularly in the areas of learning disabilities and academic enhancement;
3 to develop resource materials and curricula for students with learning disabilities;
4 to develop learning-strategies/study-skills resource materials for adolescent and adult learners;
5 to disseminate information about the Academic Enhancement Program (AEP) and the ongoing work with university students with learning disabilities to secondary, post-secondary, and other interest groups;
6 to develop and implement in-service training programs for personnel working with adolescents and adults with learning disabilities; and
7 to monitor and evaluate the effectiveness of student services provided by the centre.[2]

During the past seven years, the centre has undertaken a number of initiatives: the establishment of a program for students with learning disabilities; the provision of support for the certificate program in special education for students and teachers enrolled in the Bachelor of Education program at Mount Allison; the development of a learning-strategies program for incoming students; the implementation of research projects in related areas; and the initiation of efforts to establish a regional resource centre for college students with a learning disability.

A PROGRAM FOR STUDENTS WITH A LEARNING DISABILITY

Once established, one of the centre's first initiatives was the development of a program to support university students with learning disabilities as defined by the Learning Disabilities Association of Canada:

> Learning disabilities is a generic term that refers to a heterogeneous group of disorders due to identifiable or inferred central nervous system dysfunction. Such disorders may be manifested by delays in early development and/or difficulties in any of the following areas: memory, attention, reasoning, coordination, communication, reading, spelling, calculation, social competence,

and emotional maturation. Learning disabilities are intrinsic to the individual and may affect learning and behaviour in any individual including those with potentially average or above average intelligence. Learning disabilities are not due primarily to visual, hearing, or motor handicaps, mental retardation, emotional disturbance, or environmental disadvantage, although they may occur concurrently with any of these. Learning disabilities may arise from genetic variations, biochemical factors, events in the pre- to peri-natal period or any other subsequent events resulting in neurological impairment.[3]

In plain terms, learning disabilities affect how an individual processes information. They produce a pattern of uneven abilities in students of average or above-average intelligence as the disability may affect many areas of performance or only one. In addition, there are often striking contrasts between latent abilities and actual level of achievement. The condition is permanent and can affect the individual's ability to listen, read, speak, write, reason, perform mathematical operations, and function socially. Unfortunately, it remains a "hidden disability" since, unlike a physical impairment, it cannot be seen except by its effects on the academic, personal, and vocational lives of the students.

However, it must be remembered that in spite of their effects on an individual's performance of various skills, learning disabilities are not intellectual disabilities. Nor are they the result of an identifiable cause such as poor academic background, emotional disturbance, problems with vision or hearing, any other physical handicap, or any lack of motivation on the part of the individual affected.

Nonetheless, these disabilities can create devastating problems.[4] The students may read very slowly and have great difficulty understanding and retaining the material they read but not material that is presented orally. In writing, there may be errors in grammar, sentence structure, punctuation and spelling, poor handwriting, and difficulty in copying correctly from the board or overhead. On the other hand, the problems may be oral: students may find it difficult to concentrate on speech, or they may speak poorly and be unable to sequence events and express ideas that they seem to understand. Faced with mathematics, they may confuse or reverse numbers and operational symbols or copy problems incorrectly; they may have difficulty reading and understanding word problems, or they may have trouble with reasoning and abstract concepts. Memory may also be affected, so that they are unable to retain basic facts.

These students typically show poor organization of themselves and of their materials and do not manage their time well.[5] They may miss or misunderstand directions or instructions and often need extra time to complete assignments and to write tests and examinations. They may also be disoriented in time or space, getting lost easily or losing track of time. In addition, they may have poor social skills and be unable to interpret subtle messages from others, missing the cues offered by tone of voice and body language.

An estimate by the Learning Disabilities Association of Canada indicates that ten percent[6] of the population is affected by a learning disability. Such students are at risk of failing or of dropping out of school if their special needs are not met. Recently, increased awareness of and provision for their needs at the elementary and high school levels has meant that many of these students are now contemplating further education at the post-secondary level.[7] It is at this point that students with a learning disability become truly "at risk." Organized support services are limited at this level and assistance is often given with good intentions but with little empirical evidence to support what should be done.

It is recognized in the literature that a program at the post-secondary level for students with learning disabilities should encompass many areas.[8] First, it should provide assessment and diagnostic services to determine individual learning problems. Then, the student must be helped to become a self-advocate, able to explain the nature of the disability and the kind of assistance that will be needed. In addition, there must be consultation involving the individual student and his or her instructors to ensure that they all understand the problem and their role in achieving academic success. Remedial assistance in the form of tutoring and help with developing learning strategies is another essential component of a comprehensive program. Students with learning disabilities need guidance in areas such as time management, reading, notemaking, writing, critical thinking, exam preparation, and test taking. Finally, an awareness and education component is necessary for professionals who work with students with learning disabilities. These professionals must become better informed and more effective in their dealings with these particular students.

Mount Allison's support services program for students with learning disabilities begins with the admissions process. The policy adopted by the university senate in 1987 provided for the admission of students identified as having specific learning disabilities and established procedures for the admission process. Section 3.02 of the university's calendar reads:

> In special circumstances, a student lacking the specified requirements may be admitted. Applications from students identified as having specific learning disabilities are considered individually. They must include an assessment from

the high school made within the previous year, detailing the type of learning disability, the techniques used to compensate for it, and the special requirements or considerations requested from the university. Students admitted under these conditions may be required to take a reduced load.[9]

Students who identify themselves as having a learning disability on the regular Mount Allison application form are automatically sent a supplemental admissions form. Coordinating and processing these applications has become a joint effort between the admissions office and the Centre for Learning Assistance and Research. To identify the needs of students and make an informed decision about each applicant it is necessary to collect additional information. Therefore, applicants are required to submit a recent comprehensive psychoeducational assessment and a sample of writing completed without assistance in their own hand. In addition, three letters of recommendation are required: one from an English teacher, one from a resource room teacher or tutor, and one from another source such as teacher, coach, or employer.

Mount Allison University is currently able to provide support services to only a limited number of students identified as having a specific learning disability. Therefore, such students are advised to identify themselves and submit their supplemental application form as early as possible to be considered for support services. Students who might choose not to identify themselves are cautioned that they might later find the services of the centre restricted or inaccessible. In practice, no student with a learning disability who is in need of help is turned away, but resources are being stretched to accommodate the number of students asking for help.

During the academic year the centre receives additional referrals for service in two ways: first, students with a learning disability who are already attending Mount Allison but have not identified themselves make self-referrals when they realize that they need help; and second, Mount Allison faculty members consult increasingly with the centre and refer students.

The centre can provide full psychoeducational assessments for its students once they are accepted. However, the decision to carry out the assessment is based on an initial interview and background information. If required, the process includes both standardized tests of learning aptitude and achievement, and informal educational assessments.

After an assessment, centre staff meet with each student to review the results in detail. Students are encouraged to ask questions until they have a thorough understanding of their individual learning strengths and weaknesses.

FACILITIES AND RESOURCES

Students who receive support for learning difficulties require special facilities. To this end, the centre has computers and printers available for student use, as well as tape recorders, calculators, and hand-held spell checkers. There is also a test library/workroom that serves as a testing, counselling, and teaching facility, and one additional office that functions as a workspace for students and staff.

The human resource team at the centre consists of two faculty members who are registered psychologists teaching in the education department and one full-time resource specialist. Because the faculty members are able to provide support services on a part-time basis only, the resource specialist is responsible for coordinating the day-to-day activities of the centre. In addition to this staff, various individuals have been employed on short-term contracts in the capacity of research assistants on several occasions. Student and adult volunteers also provide tutoring to students seeking assistance. To help volunteers become an integral part of the services to students, a peer-tutoring program has been established. Participants receive in-service training on how to help people with learning disabilities apply learning strategies to improve their academic performance.

A major curricular resource for the centre is the Academic Enhancement Program, which will be discussed later in the chapter. This comprehensive ten-week learning skills program is open to anyone with a learning disability. In addition to having students participate in the program, AEP learning activities are often adapted and used as part of the students' ongoing support programs while attending Mount Allison. The centre also has a modest resource library that is supported by the university's main library.

One of the centre's philosophical goals has been to have students become self-advocates; this is an essential skill for them to acquire if they are truly to become life-long independent learners.[10] To this end, all students receive counselling. The two major goals of the counselling process are for students to be able, first, to clearly articulate the nature of their learning disability, and second, to identify what accommodations are required for their academic success. For many, this represents a considerable challenge as they have always had their parents or significant others (e.g., relatives, teachers, and counsellors) represent them during their educational experiences. Hence a considerable amount of time is directed towards helping them speak for themselves. Fortunately, the small size of Mount Allison tends to foster a relationship between professor and student that is close and direct. Further, the university's emphasis on good teaching and its traditionally supportive attitude towards its students work to facilitate the student's task of self-advocacy.

Personal[11] and academic[12] counselling are recognized as valuable aspects of a student support program and are available to all students from several sources at Mount Allison. For students with a learning disability, staff at the centre also provide personal and academic counselling. In addition to counselling, students with a learning disability may need specific help with specific courses; hence the centre's peer-tutoring program, begun in the fall of 1992. The volunteer tutors are Mount Allison students who have taken or are currently enrolled in the course where tutoring is needed. As noted above, they are trained by centre staff in both learning disabilities and learning strategies.

To help auditory learners and those with reading problems, the centre is able to supply books on tape to students with a documented learning disability through a service called Recording for the Blind (RFB).[13] The catalogue for this service lists over 75,000 books and textbooks. There is a small once-in-a-lifetime fee for this service, and special tape recorders required to play these tapes must be purchased from RFB by students.

Many students with a learning disability prefer to work on computers.[14] Mount Allison has a Macintosh computer lab on campus for use by all Mount Allison students. There is also a well-equipped personal-computer lab available for student use. Self-help information is available directly on the computers and through written material in the labs. Students requiring additional information can receive help through the centre.

Sometimes the nature and effects of a learning disability are such that individual arrangements must be made to enable the students to demonstrate their learning.[15] With the support and cooperation of faculty members, the centre is able to offer test- and exam-writing accommodations to students with a learning disability at Mount Allison. The specific accommodations that a student may receive are determined on an individual basis by the centre staff after meeting with the student and considering information from the psychoeducational report. While staff give consideration to the type and severity of a student's learning disability, the specific course content and the type of test being given are also taken into account.

One of the accommodations used by many students is the opportunity to write their tests and exams at the centre, where they may receive extra time to write as well as the opportunity to write in a quiet environment without distractions. Several students use computers with word-processing and spell-checking software to complete their tests. Other students are allowed to use hand-held spell checkers and simple calculators. When necessary, students may be allowed to go over the exam orally and clarify responses with the faculty member concerned once the written part of the exam has concluded. Finally, students may have exam questions read aloud to them for clarification before they begin to answer them.

Improving both student learning and faculty teaching has always been one of the centre's goals, and in fact the activities of the centre appear to have had a positive effect on teaching within the Mount Allison community. Although the university's policy does exist and could be forced on faculty, the centre has always preferred to educate and persuade rather than demand compliance. Congenial collegial relations and physical proximity to faculty offices have helped to make this possible. On a small campus, lines of communication are open and direct. Through informal meetings and conversations with centre staff, faculty members have become more aware of different learning styles and teaching methods. This enhanced knowledge no doubt benefits all students, not only those with learning problems. In their efforts on behalf of students with learning disabilities in their classes, faculty members have raised their personal level of awareness and increased their knowledge about learning disabilities. This has been demonstrated in the increased number of referrals to the centre by faculty members. Presently, forty percent of the students coming to the centre are self-referrals, thirty-five percent are referred by the admissions office, twenty percent are referred by the faculty, and five percent by their parents.

The total number of students experiencing learning difficulties who are being served by the centre has grown over the past seven years. Each year the number of students served has increased, from four in 1987–88 to forty-five in 1993–94. Approximately seventy-five percent of those seen to date have learning disabilities. Since the publication of Mount Allison's policy on learning disabilities in the university calendar, the number of enquiries about the centre's services and the number of applications from students with learning disabilities has increased.

The success of the centre may be seen in its graduates. As of May 1995, thirty-six students receiving its support have graduated, and another five are expected to graduate this year. These students have been very successful academically and have contributed to student life at Mount Allison in the areas of fine arts, music, drama, student government, and athletics.

The presence of the centre has also been of benefit to the student teachers in the Special Education Block Program at Mount Allison.[16] The test library contains a wide variety of assessment instruments to which the students have access. As well, the audio, visual, and printed resources of the centre are shared with the Bachelor of Education students. The experience of centre staff in the area of learning disabilities is also shared with students in the education program.

As a result of its work with post-secondary students with learning disabilities, the centre has taken part in outreach activities at many levels. Once it had developed its own program, it was in a position to look beyond its walls to regional, then to national needs.

At the local level, staff have provided in-service training for faculty, student services staff, and admissions staff at Mount Allison and to teachers in the local public school district. They have also acted as external consultants to the local schools in the area of assessment of learning disabilities.

Provincially, the centre has been actively involved in a series of workshops on learning disabilities for instructors and counsellors from the community colleges through the Department of Advanced Education and Labour, and for ACCESS Centre personnel through the federal-provincial Youth Strategy Initiative. It has also provided consultation to the New Brunswick Community College, Saint John, on its Learning Disabilities Project with the country of Jordan, and to the ACCESS centres and Canada Employment and Immigration in the area of assessment of learning disabilities. The centre also presented a brief to the Department of Education's Excellence in Education initiative, met with one of the authors, and received a citation in the final report.[17]

Regional demand for the services offered by the centre demonstrates both the need for such services and a recognition throughout Atlantic Canada of the centre's expertise. Assessments and consultations regarding students with learning disabilities have been done for several Maritime universities. There have also been site visitations to Mount Allison from most universities in the region. Workshops have been held for Canada Employment and Immigration staff at their request.

In the fall of 1992, the centre cooperated with Acadia University to plan and organize Atlantic Canada's first meeting of people who provide services to students with learning disabilities. It was held at Acadia in November 1992, with a follow-up meeting at Mount Allison in early 1993. These gatherings enabled service providers to meet each other and exchange ideas and information about what institutions were doing for students with learning disabilities. The informal group thus formed as the "Atlantic Post-secondary LD Network" hosted a symposium on learning disabilities at the Nova Scotia Teacher's College in May 1993, where service providers and interested government officials met and discussed some of the challenges facing the field. A handbook for service providers was released at the second conference held in May 1995 at Dalhousie University.

On a national level, the centre, in partnership with the Learning Disabilities Association of New Brunswick and with the financial support of the Department of the Secretary of State, undertook a study to determine what service providers at post-secondary institutions across Canada perceived to be their greatest needs regarding provision of services for students with learning disabilities.[18] Other goals of the study were to target future national initiatives for enhancing the overall delivery of such services, and to determine the degree of interest in a national network for those providing services to students with learning disabilities at post-secondary institutions. The sixty-five percent response rate to the survey questionnaire indicates that needs have been identified at the national level.

This survey, published in 1993,[19] produced a number of recommendations based on its findings, all supporting an increase in programs and services to students with learning disabilities and greater cooperation among service providers.

Although satisfactory progress has been made to date in the provision of support services to post-secondary students with learning disabilities, several challenges remain. One is to educate faculty to accept the existence of a disability that they cannot see. Having once understood the nature of a learning disability, they will be better able to accept that it is necessary for them to make accommodations for persons with such disabilities as readily as they would for persons with a visible physical disability.

In addition, faculty must be educated to remember that students with learning disabilities are in all other respects typical young adults. Occasionally, therefore, they are likely to display behaviours common to their age group, including those that are less desirable; not because they have a learning disability, but because they are young.

The students themselves need help to understand and accept that they have a learning disability and that the disability is lifelong. They must also realize that normal but irresponsible behaviours such as missing classes and submitting assignments late may adversely affect the positive relationship with faculty that they particularly need to establish and maintain.

As with most organizations today, acquiring adequate funds to provide a reasonable program of support for persons with learning disabilities presents a significant challenge. To accomplish its financial goals, the centre has had to identify and approach a variety of potential funding sources. It has received funding from the following external and internal sources: the Leonard Ellen, Harold Crabtree, and Themadel Foundations; Employment and Immigration Canada through Job Strategy and Challenge grants; Department of the Secretary of

State; New Brunswick Department of Labour; Social Sciences and Humanities Research Council; and, at Mount Allison, the Senior Administrative Group, Student Administrative Council, Dean of Students Office, and the Department of Education. Without the support of these groups, it would not have been possible to provide services to approximately two hundred post-secondary students over the past six years. Efforts to generate external funds continue as the centre aims to become financially self-sufficient by the year 2000.

Lastly, the staff at the centre face a challenge that exists for all service providers: to find answers to research questions about learning disabilities that have yet to be addressed. As more is learned about this relatively new field, the centre will be in a better position to help people with learning disabilities to achieve greater academic and personal success.

A PROGRAM FOR STUDENTS IN TRANSITION: THE ACADEMIC ENHANCEMENT PROGRAM

The Academic Enhancement Program is a one-term, non-credit course aimed at teaching the students specific skills that will enhance their ability to study effectively in any discipline and may help them to function better in their personal and later professional lives. The program is based on longstanding evidence that deficient study skills can become a barrier to academic success,[20] whereas students who draw on good study skills experience higher levels of achievement on learning tasks.[21] Fortunately, the skills needed to learn most effectively can themselves be learned,[22] and all post-secondary students can benefit from the skills and learning strategies that the AEP presents.

The need for a program of this type at Mount Allison was originally suggested by an examination of the academic needs of students with learning disabilities. The study of their unmet needs in turn identified the specific skills that are required for success in studies at the university level, and that might be usefully taught to these students.

However, it is not only students with learning disabilities who arrive at post-secondary institutions with inadequate study skills and learning strategies; the problem is common, especially among first year students.[23] Traditionally, educators have regarded the development and application of appropriate learning skills as an intuitive process; hence they have emphasized the teaching of course content in the elementary and secondary schools and almost entirely neglected equally important instruction in how to study and learn.[24] It is not surprising, therefore, that there is substantial dissatisfaction with post-secondary students' study skills among faculty[25] and students[26] alike. This dissatisfaction was evident at Mount Allison.

Since, as already noted, research has indicated that students who apply study skills do learn better, it is again no surprise that some universities have developed programs to help their students. The first programs were designed as self-help: inventories of procedures that the students could apply on their own, without any formal instruction. However, it was soon found that direct instruction in how to apply the study skills produced greater improvement than mere access to the information.

Current learning-skills programs are based on knowledge of cognitive processes and accommodate the individual differences of students, particularly their individual learning styles. Students are encouraged to understand and monitor their own thought and learning processes and to select and adapt the strategies that are best suited to each learning task.

The Academic Enhancement Program (AEP) at Mount Allison is based on sound learning principles and has been developed to enhance and complement a student's academic program. Because the active involvement of the student is essential, student participation has been important and influential from the beginning. Students helped to choose, design, and develop the individual modules and had an opportunity to recommend changes to the program in its pilot stages.

However, the instructor/student interaction is an essential part of the AEP. The program was not designed as a "self-help" or independent program of study that could be used on its own. To reap the rewards of the program, students must attend classes faithfully and take an active part in the learning exercises and discussions.

Therefore, both an instructor's and a student's manual have been prepared. The student's manual contains brief explanations of learning skills and strategies and activities to reinforce them. In contrast, the instructor's manual provides a detailed plan for each lesson. It gives a thorough explanation of each learning skill and strategy, objectives for the lesson, suggestions for set induction, activity, and discussion exercises, sample extended activities that the instructor might wish to use, and the overhead masters to use with the lesson.

One goal of the program is to lead students to recognize and then apply their own personal learning style. Students not only need to know their own personal learning style but must also be able to adapt it to the instructor's teaching style when necessary. One entire lesson is devoted to the subject of learning style, and the idea of learning style permeates every lesson.

Another significant component of the Academic Enhancement Program is the use of metacognitive strategies within each learning-skill module. Students are made aware of the processes required to complete a task and are taught that they must become adept at regulating and monitoring their own behaviour if they wish to become better learners. In other words, they need to have a plan for learning and be able to adapt their plan when necessary.

The Academic Enhancement Program includes the following six modules: time management, listening and notemaking, critical reading, critical thinking, writing, and test taking and exam preparation.

Time management. Through awareness of time-management techniques, students can become responsible for managing their own time effectively. In this module, students must first establish their goals, set priorities, and make decisions about the specific components and time requirements for each task. Students learn to recognize problems and try to solve them using processes suited to their individual learning style. They then apply these learned strategies to situations that require time management, both inside the classroom and out.

Listening and notemaking. Being able to listen and to make notes is essential to academic success at the post-secondary level. In this module students examine the role that listening plays in academic performance, come to understand the types and levels of listening, and develop effective listening strategies. They then learn to become proficient in functional notemaking skills by practising a specified notemaking system and employing a cognitive strategy to record relevant information from lectures. Finally, students learn how to use metacognitive processes to enhance their listening and notemaking skills.

Critical reading. Effective reading involves both active and interactive processes on the part of the reader. Readers must understand the meaning intended by the writer but also make their own contribution through interpretation, evaluation, and reflection on that meaning. In this module, students improve their ability to derive meaning from what they read. Using materials from current first year textbooks, they learn to apply their skills to understand textual functions and writers' styles, to read with a purpose, and to apply specialized reading study strategies.

Critical thinking. At the university level, it is not enough merely to understand material. The student must also be able to make a rational evaluation of what has been read or heard. In this module students are taught to identify different types of thinking, evaluate claims, check inferences and implications, and analyze arguments, as well as to present and defend organized responses to specific materials. They learn to employ strategies based on their own learning style that will allow them successfully to apply fundamental critical thinking concepts to both academic and everyday situations.

Writing. Writing is a method of learning. As students write, they not only become actively involved in learning subject matter but they are also forced to think critically and to continually evaluate their topic. This module teaches students appropriate metacognitive strategies for pre-writing, writing, and rewriting. By employing these strategies while keeping their own learning style in mind, students will become more competent and confident with the writing process and with themselves as learners.

Taking tests and examinations. In addition to knowing their material, students must become "test wise" to succeed at writing tests and examinations. They can be taught the basic skills of test preparation and test taking and can learn to improve their overall performance on tests and examinations. Students in this module students learn strategies that they can apply before, during, and after different kinds of tests and examinations. Using sample test formats, they apply their strategies to real testing situations and evaluate the results.

The AEP evolved as follows. During the 1988–89 academic year faculty members were asked what learning skills they deemed important to first year students. Once their views were collected, a pilot program of learning skills was designed and put into effect with a sample of incoming students. Included in the program were time management, listening and notetaking strategies, and critical reading. Phase 1 of the AEP concluded by assessing the proficiency of first year students in terms of their learning skills and by evaluating the program itself.

Phase 2 of the Academic Enhancement Program (1989–90) saw the development of three new modules. These included critical thinking, essay writing, and taking tests and examinations. The three new modules were piloted with first year students and again the program was evaluated.

Phase 3 of the project (1990–91) involved the rewriting of both the student's and instructor's manuals for the six modules that were field tested during Phases 1 and 2. As well, a thirteen-week course was prepared and offered during the fall semester of the 1990–91 academic year. These first three phases were taught by the developers of the program, as "expert" instructors. Phase 4 (1991–92) presented all six modules and introduced one novice instructor as a field test of the instructor's manual. In 1992–93 and 1993–94, the program was presented in a more condensed form, including four selected modules: time management, listening and notetaking, critical reading, and taking tests and examinations.

At the end of each program, students are tested on the skills they have been taught and are asked to evaluate various aspects of the program. They always show improvement in all skills and perceive themselves to be more efficient, more competent, and more confident as learners. Some also see themselves as having earned higher marks as a result of being involved in the program. When asked whether they would recommend the AEP to their friends, eighty-three percent say that they would.

Analysis of the data gained from these evaluations suggests several points. First, direct instruction in learning skills speeds up their acquisition. Second, it may take some time for the skills to become really useful to the student after they are presented and first practised; hence there is good reason to begin instruction early in the first year of studies. Third, the program appears to enhance the students' perceptions of themselves as learners and achievers; this is another reason to present the program early in their university careers. Finally, it appears that learning-skills instruction is a need not just for a few but for a majority of post-secondary students.[27]

In conclusion, of the original goals set for the centre, all have seen at least some degree of success. However, a great deal remains to be done. The findings of the National Needs Survey indicate a great need for assistance both to students with learning disabilities and the service providers who work with them, and to first year students. With its seven years of evaluated experience in the field, the Meighen Centre is in an excellent position to build on what has already been done and become a leader in the development and delivery of programs that meet the requirements of post-secondary special-needs students.

NOTES

1 Minutes of the Senate, Mount Allison University, 16 September 1987, Mount Allison University Archives.

2 Centre for Learning Assistance and Research, *Faculty and Student Handbook* (Sackville, NB: Centre for Learning Assistance and Research, Department of Education, Mount Allison University 1992), 9.

3 Legislative Task Force, Learning Disabilities Association of Canada, *Making the Most of the Law: Education and the Child with Disabilities* (Ottawa: Learning Disabilities Association of Canada, 1993), xii.

4 Pamela Adelman and Debbie Olufs, *Assisting College Students with Learning Disabilities: A Tutor's Manual* (Columbus, OH: Association on Handicapped Student Service Programs in Post-secondary Education, 1990), 8.
5 Donna McPeek, "Developing Organization and Time Management Strategies with Adolescents and Adults," *Support Services for Students with Learning Disabilities in Higher Education: A Compendium of Readings, Book 3* (Columbus, OH: Association on Higher Education and Disability, 1993), 97–103. (First published in *Pulling Together: Selected Proceedings of the 1991 AHSSPPE Conference* (Columbus, OH: Association on Handicapped Student Service Programs in Post-secondary Education, 1992).
6 Cathy Smith, *For You: Adults with Learning Disabilities* (Ottawa: Learning Disabilities Association of Canada, 1991), 18.
7 Loring C. Brinckerhoff, Stan F. Shaw, and Joan M. McGuire, *Promoting Post-secondary Education for Students with Learning Disabilities: A Handbook for Practitioners* (Austin, TX: Pro-Ed, 1993), 2–3.
8 Loring C. Brinckerhoff, "Establishing Learning Disability Support Services with Minimal Resources," *Journal of Post-secondary Education and Disability* 9, nos. 1 and 2 (1991): 182–96.
9 *Mount Allison University 1994–1995 Academic Calendar* (Sackville, NB: Mount Allison University, 1994), 10.
10 Smith, *For You*, 53–78.
11 Barbara Scheiber and Jeanne Talpers, *Unlocking Potential: College and Other Choices for Learning Disabled People, A Step-by-Step Guide* (Bethesda, MD: Adler and Adler, 1987), 171–8.
12 Ibid., 85–9.
13 Ibid., 97.
14 Ibid., 110–15.
15 Ibid., 96–104.
16 *Education at Mount Allison: 1994–1995 Program Handbook* (Sackville, NB: Mount Allison University, Department of Education, 1994, p. 27).
17 New Brunswick, Commission on Excellence in Education, *To Live and Learn: the Challenge of Education and Training: Report of the Commission on Excellence in Education* (Fredericton, NB: Policy Secretariat, 1993, p. 18).
18 Jane Drover, Lorraine Emmrys, Brian McMillan, and Lex Wilson, *Serving Students with Learning Disabilities at Canadian Colleges and Universities: A National Needs Survey of Post-secondary Service Providers* (Sackville, NB: Centre for Learning Assistance and Research, Department of Education, Mount Allison University, in partnership with Learning Disabilities Association of New Brunswick, 1993).

19 Copies of the full report or the executive summary are available from the authors.

20 M.J. Baldwin, "Studies in Development and Learning," *Archives of Psychology* 12 (1909): 65–70.

21 Brinckerhoff, Shaw, and McGuire, *Promoting Post-secondary Education*, 253–4.

22 Ibid., 253.

23 Martha Maxwell, *Improving Student Learning Skills* (San Francisco, CA: Jossey-Bass, 1979), 1–11.

24 D. Durkin, "What Classroom Observation Reveals about Reading Comprehension Instruction," *Reading Research Quarterly* 15 (1978–79): 143–8.

25 Lucy Cheser Jacobs, *Faculty Perceptions of the Basic Skills of University Freshmen* (Bloomington, IN: Indiana University Bureau of Evaluations, Studies and Testing Division of Research and Development, 1981).

26 Edward A. Holdaway and Karen R. Kelloway, "First Year at University: Perceptions and Experiences of Students," *Canadian Journal of Higher Education* 17 (1987).

27 Information on the development of the Academic Enhancement Program is available from the authors.

CHAPTER TWELVE

Technical Innovation and Liberal Education

PAUL CANT, ROBERT HAWKES, AND NANCY VOGAN

It is commonly agreed that formal and informal interaction between students from different disciplines is one key advantage of the small liberal arts university. In this paper we will argue that microcomputer-enhanced learning can play a major role in fostering cross-disciplinary interactions among undergraduate teachers and students, as well as lead to more effective communication between teachers and students. We will start with an account of a typical day in the Macintosh learning laboratory at Mount Allison. A description of the nature of the laboratory setting and the networking will show how these interactions can be promoted. At the same time, the traditional division of subject matter into courses of study exerts an influence on the nature of the computer-assisted instruction that is delivered. One successful example (a computer-mediated lectureless physics course) will be examined in detail, first from the teacher's point of view, and then from the student's perspective. This will show how such a new and rich learning environment can be used to improve the operation of a typical university course.

However, the emphasis on local production of learning materials raises serious questions about electronic publishing and the setting of a curriculum. The potential dangers with instructor-produced learning materials will be addressed, in particular the lack of external review. We look to the Internet to play a role in promoting exchanges of course materials and as an effective review and quality-control mechanism. We conclude with a summary of suggested implementation guidelines based on our experiences for those considering the establishment of technology-enhanced instruction in a liberal arts university.

THE COMPUTER LABORATORY AT MOUNT ALLISON

A typical evening in the Macintosh computer laboratory at Mount Allison includes a number of students from a variety of disciplines engaged in course assignments or individual study. In one corner of the room two first year physics students study explanations, animations, and examples for a lectureless physics course. In another corner several education students prepare a HyperCard-based presentation for a class.[1] A psychology student uses the scanner to enter images for a computer-based class assignment, while other psychology students watch simulated rats "learn" for a learning and memory course. An astronomy student uses a desktop planetarium program to "discover" relationships in apparent star positions and rising times as viewed from different locations on the Earth, while another examines images downloaded over the Internet the previous week from the Hubble Space Telescope. A music education student examines a new theory program for high school students; a second explores the Performing Arts Series stack to see what works will be performed at the next event. A first year German student learns basic vocabulary applicable to images from the actual German House residence at Mount Allison. Other students run simulations, write essays, perform statistical analyses, read key lecture notes, and so on.[2] Meanwhile, in the main library where a CD-ROM jukebox is attached to a Macintosh computer, students in an introduction to music course do their listening assignments by using an interactive HyperCard stack to control the playback of an audio CD recording.

Similar activities occur at most universities. However, we think that several features distinguish the approach taken at Mount Allison. First, the integrated laboratory (as opposed to discipline-specific microcomputer clusters) leads to natural liberalization of the educational experience. All materials are accessible to all students, therefore students can and do explore materials from a course other than their own. In addition, the physical arrangement of the laboratory is conducive to informal interaction, which is futher encouraged by the fact that students with very different educational backgrounds often share similar application programs. HyperCard is common to most of the computer-assisted instruction. Other commercial software is used by students in different programs. For example, both music students and students taking a fourth year physics course in signal processing use SoundEdit, a digital sampling-and-analysis program. Students may learn about a variety of campus resources such as the Deutsches Haus, the Owens art collection, or the Performing Arts Series because of the appearance of these materials on the campus file servers. From the same access point, students are increasingly using World Wide Web browsing and search tools to obtain information from the growing host of online sources. In this sense the modern computer network serves some of the roles of the traditional library, including encouragement of the sort of intellectual browsing that is a vital part of the educational experience.

A second distinguishing feature of the laboratory is the degree to which the course materials have been locally created. The use of HyperCard, which is versatile, relatively easy to use, and inexpensive, has facilitated this. Instructors from fields as diverse as biology, physics, music, German, psychology, and education have come together to share techniques. While commercial products and resources in the public domain are utilized, the emphasis is on the use of locally produced materials. In a real sense the instructor speaks to the student through these materials.

A third distinguishing feature of the laboratory is the degree to which students play a role in the authoring of instructional materials. Conventional seminar presentations have been replaced or expanded through computer-based materials. For example, music education students prepare reviews of several band methods that they then put in HyperCard format for use by their fellow students; students in advanced physics courses have used digitized images and video to present such topics as the physics of dance or karate; and psychology students have worked cooperatively on the production of a stack on famous psychologists. One advantage of this approach is that students from one year can benefit from the ideas and experiences of a previous class. In the same way that instructor-authored materials are simply a new way for the instructor to "speak to students," student-authored materials represent a new way for students to exchange ideas.

THE COMPUTER AS MEDIUM OF INSTRUCTION

The effectiveness of the teaching materials that have been produced for use by students has inevitably led to a major change in course delivery in some instances. One of us (P. Cant) has eliminated the lecture component of the introductory physics course entirely, replacing it with computer-based learning modules. The structure of this course and its advantages from the point of view of student and teacher are described below.

The course organization is much like the traditional one. HyperCard stacks direct the students to read specified pages in the textbook, study certain concepts presented electronically, try problems (frequently with hints or complete solutions available electronically), and observe animation sequences. Conventional tests and laboratory work are retained as part of the course structure. The text and pictures presented by HyperCard essentially constitute an electronic textbook, to be read in a simple linear sequence. The student is expected to study approximately one hundred screens of illustrated text per week of the course. However, the animations and simulations possible in electronic texts have advantages over printed textbooks for the teaching of a subject such as physics. Furthermore, since the material is locally authored, the instructor can better integrate all components of the instruction in the course and indeed promote integration across different courses within the university.

The role of the professor is not diminished by the computer presentation of materials, and we believe it will not diminish as electronic resources and the materials available through them reach higher levels of refinement. Just as textbooks need regular revision to reflect current trends and knowledge in the discipline, electronic course materials will need similar constant revision.

In some fields, and especially in physics, much of the literature is difficult. Undergraduates cannot be expected to make frequent use of the research journals as sources of digestible information. The process of gaining an understanding of one or two printed pages such that their content relates well to one's existing state or structure of understanding might require a week or more of study. Such efforts are exactly what is demanded of the graduate student. For the benefit of the undergraduate, however, those who teach must continually assess current ideas and then interpret, organize, and present them by means of a suitable medium. Until we see the effective implementation of the electronic "intelligent agent" that will know what we have seen and read, what we understand, and what we desire, the professor will continue to play the primary role in assessing the state of each student's understanding of a group of concepts and in providing students with the most appropriate study materials to link most effectively with their current partially formed picture of a problem or topic. Gradually students learn to decide for themselves when and where to find the paths to further enlightenment through thought and study.

The small university provides an environment in which ideas and methods can be continually refreshed and revised. The operation of the open computer lab allows the professor to watch a student at work, casually inquire how she or he is progressing, recommend files or programs to explore or new ideas and portrayals to watch, and identify obstacles to understanding. Computer materials can then be rapidly adapted to the perceived needs and continually shaped for optimum performance.

Our experience has demonstrated that students want to learn this way. A survey of students in the autumn of 1991 revealed that the computer was their most important source of information in the Physics 1011 course. Two-thirds said that they were attracted by the idea of a lectureless course and there have been no complaints since the course was implemented.

From the students' point of view, the greatest advantage to computer presentation of course materials is that they can work at their own speed. For many students lectures are often too rapidly paced, and in sequential subjects such as physics, misunderstanding of early concepts interferes with subsequent learning. Self-pacing also benefits the gifted student, or those with particularly strong backgrounds, since they do not have to proceed at a rate suitable for the average student. It also allows more flexibility. For example, in one term a student was absent for some weeks when her child was born, but she was able to catch up all of the work upon her return and obtain a very good mark in the course.

Students approach the computer materials in different ways. Initially, some students view them as they would a lecture. They sit at the screen and make detailed notes, mainly copying the textual portion of the multimedia material. Most students, however, quickly learn to work interactively with the materials, making few if any notes. In effect, then, the HyperCard materials have directly replaced the transmission of knowledge by lecturing. The computer becomes the blackboard that does not get erased after class or the overhead projector that does not get turned off. From that perspective, computer-based presentation is quite superior to the more traditional lecture format.

Students prefer the depth and breadth represented in the computer-based materials. Typically the material is somewhat more detailed than that covered in a typical lecture but much less broad than a conventional textbook. Traditional textbooks, which seem to grow ever longer, appear endless to many students. The breadth of the material presented sometimes interferes with clear enunciation of critical concepts. The computer-based materials are a much smaller set, which present a less-daunting initial view of a subject.

Learning requires effort, which in turn requires psychological preparedness. While poor computer-assisted instruction can lead to very passive learning, we feel that there is potential in these technologies for more meaningful student activity. The very act of choosing when and how to use the materials encourages the notion that it is the students who direct their own learning. The self-paced aspect means that fewer students feel hopelessly out of touch with the class level. Whatever the reasons, based on our experience, we find that computer-based learning at the undergraduate level works. Students come to realize that to learn, it is they who must do the work, not the teacher.

PROBLEMS OF TECHNOLOGICAL EMPOWERMENT

With most enabling technologies there are both advantages and disadvantages. In this section we will consider desktop publishing and desktop courseware authoring, including potential problems and opportunities.

In many disciplines, textbooks have defined the curriculum of the modern university. Whether deliberately or subconsciously, many of us have decided that a given topic should or should not be included in a particular course according to the emphasis given to that topic in the common textbooks. In a broader way, we would argue that, fairly often, our curriculum decisions regarding division of material into specific courses is driven by the divisions reflected in texts, rather than the converse. There have always been some who refuse to use "textbooks," instead drawing together collections of locally produced materials, or directing students to use the library in a broad, flexible manner. The locally produced materials have gradually become more "professional" in appearance, but until the last few years they could not usually be described as a truly unified body of material with full graphic support, indexing, use of publishing features such as sidebars, etc. That has all changed – now everyone has the power to produce a text that will begin to rival "commercial texts." There is even a trend among university bookstores to encourage and support this "personal publishing" industry. However, it does not stop with desktop text publishing. Through products such as ToolBook and HyperCard the individual faculty member can develop courseware support materials. In addition, through presentation programs such as Microsoft PowerPoint, Aldus Persuasion, or ClarisWorks, we do not need to depend upon the publisher to provide the "in-class" enhancements such as standard overhead transparencies included in textbook-adoption packages. Increasingly, through technologies such as Kodak Photo CD, inexpensive video-digitization cards, and local CD pressing, we can develop personal multimedia collections of CD-based images or video clips. Instructors are now using Web pages to make these items available to students who access them with net browsers such as Netscape.

Most of us have probably at one time or another used texts that were very similar to our teaching style and viewpoint, and others that contrasted sharply with our preferred approach. The extreme case of a "comfortable" text is one that we write ourselves. Naturally, we as teachers are quite at ease in that circumstance, and it is probably fair to say that the students are also more comfortable, since there is coherence and unity between the text and the other components of the course. However, the words comfortable and effective should not be interchanged in the context of teaching and learning. Indeed, some would argue that a fairly high degree of intellectual dissonance or discomfort is the necessary first step for effective learning of new concepts.[3]

Another potential concern regarding the use of teacher-authored computer materials or textbooks is that they have not gone through a formal review or evaluation process. While misconceptions appear even in standard textbooks, the professional review process guards against major errors. Another effect of the standard review process that is not as positive is the tendency to compare all new writing to the current standards. This works against the evolution of the curriculum and the development of new ideas in the teaching of concepts or sequencing of topics.

The Internet opens up avenues for communication in a global teaching community. As an example, we posed the question regarding positive and negative effects of "self-authored" texts and course materials to the Society for Teaching and Learning in Higher Education's Internet-based electronic forum (STLHE-L). Within several days, this generated extensive discussion, suggestions, and opinions.[4]

Internet-based electronic exchange mechanisms have altered the manner in which discussion and, in some cases, even research regarding teaching takes place. It has enabled teachers at small institutions to discuss and collaborate with others around the world. Somehow electronic discussions can be more frank and honest than is often the case with face-to-face communication.[5] Through electronic forums, newsgroups, listing services, and electronic sharing of documents and software, both teachers and students increasingly share a much larger university. It will be our challenge as teachers in the undergraduate curriculum to make the most of these opportunities to remove potential barriers imposed by small departments and institutions, without losing sight of those attributes that make learning in the small liberal arts university both more effective and more enjoyable.

Perhaps also within the Internet umbrella lies a resolution of the dangers of teacher-authored materials. If such materials are regularly deposited to standard electronic sites so that they can be easily shared among faculty, and if this is coupled with an electronic mechanism such as a mailing list or newsgroup that fosters discussion for the teaching of that particular discipline, one can have an effective review process for teacher-authored materials. Indeed, this review process can in principle be far more effective (due to a larger number of participants) than the standard textbook reviews. It also offers the advantage of continuous interchange of ideas and improvement of teaching resources, whereas textbooks tend to be revised in a discrete series of steps.

THE MOUNT ALLISON APPLE CENTRE FOR INNOVATION[6]

Having used computers in education for the past twenty-five years, Mount Allison was in a good position to expand this field of activity. Recently it established computer labs and received assistance from the Apple Canada Educational Foundation to set up the Mount Allison Apple Centre for Innovation (ACI). The initial projects were successful in producing teaching materials for music, psychology, German, physics, fine arts, biology, and astronomy. A second grant of equipment early in 1993 led to progress with QuickTime movie production and a general increase in the graphics capabilities available to the participating courseware developers. Continued advancements in innovative music instruction were also well supported. HyperCard stacks, movies, and other forms of software are continually being placed on electronic file servers to be accessed by students in various courses at all levels and across a number of departments. Access to the newer materials and development tools is provided in the library and music department and in an ACI room with fast computers, while regular student usage occurs in the MacLab and on individual machines on and off campus. The residential network[7] increasingly provides individualized access points to the same materials. The state of development of the materials and the expertise of the faculty were two strong points that ensured success as proposals were made to offer credit courses remotely by TeleEducation New Brunswick. The same computer and multimedia learning materials that are used to assist students on campus are now being used to bring educational opportunities to students who cannot attend in person. On- and off-campus courses are more highly integrated than in many distance-education ventures, which benefits both sets of clients.

COMMENTS ON IMPLEMENTATION OF TECHNOLOGY-ENHANCED INSTRUCTION

In this final section we wish to draw together some of the themes of this paper. We have listed below a number of conclusions we have reached on the basis of experience so far with technology-enhanced undergraduate instruction.

(1) The development of a formal or informal structure was important for the sharing of approaches and techniques across different disciplines. Perhaps as important as equipment was the fact that instructors in a variety of disciplines collaborated in the design of instructional materials and the effective delivery of computer-assisted instruction. Through this common enterprise, we have shared views and ideas both about our disciplines and about effective teaching. This interchange has enriched the resultant course materials in the true tradition of the liberal arts university.

(2) An open, campuswide computer lab encourages interaction and promotes feedback. While individual access points (such as the Mount Allison residence network) and departmental computer clusters can certainly play a role in the delivery of computer-based instruction, we believe that there will always be a role for open-access computer laboratories. These are the places where students share ideas and experiences (and help each other use the computer-based materials most effectively); at the same time they provide the physical space for instructor-student interaction and feedback.

(3) Instructional systems should evolve in a dynamic way and, in general, be directed by the instructors and students rather than by administrative design. There certainly is a place for administrative planning and vision with respect to technology-based education. However, we believe that the most effective instructional systems are driven by the people directly involved in the educational process: teachers and students. That has certainly been the case at the Mount Allison Apple Centre for Innovation, where the entire effort was an evolutionary process propelled by our interests and feedback from our students. Just as effective research can only be planned down to a certain level, effective courseware should evolve in a dynamic way, rather than by a one-shot global plan.

(4) A significant core of instructor-produced, or at least instructor-modified, course materials is important. In general we learn most effectively when we feel that there is a personal link between the teacher and the student. If the student can feel that the teacher is speaking to that student through the computer materials, the instruction will be

far more effective. Furthermore, locally produced materials are more readily modified and adapted to meet individual needs and to complement other components of the course. The requirement for local involvement in construction of computer materials means that careful thought should be given to the medium. We have chosen HyperCard because it is inexpensive, flexible, and relatively easy to learn. This is not to say that there are not other good choices for courseware authoring (and the success of others has proven this). However, we would caution readers against involvement with systems that, either because of cost or technical complexity, will discourage a broad base of liberal education faculty from direct involvement in production of course materials.

(5) Computer-based materials can most effectively replace or supplement the lecture component of traditional courses. Some of the same traits that characterize a good lecture should be present in effective computer-based materials. We argued earlier that this mode of computer-assisted instruction in essence replaces the lecture component of traditional courses and has the advantages of a self-paced, more richly illustrated, and permanently (over the length of the course) recorded presentation. Some of the same traits that distinguish a good lecture must be found in effective computer-based learning materials. For example, there should be a logical progression of ideas and a clear and well-conceived conceptual structure. Most of the ACI authors use humour, from time to time, in their computer-based materials, just as they would in their conventional lectures. In most disciplines it is more important to use a careful selection of material, rather than an eclectic collection of loosely related ideas, concepts, and applications.

(6) Computer-based learning replaces only certain aspects of traditional courses and should be complemented by other learning modes such as laboratory or field work, discussion, individual guidance, and student-based inquiry.

(7) Students must not be left with the impression that the computer-based materials form a complete view of the subject. Rather, one hopes that the computer-based exploration will encourage them to do further searching, through electronic or conventional learning modes.

(8) Students should be involved wherever possible in the preparation of electronic materials. We encourage students to use the computer media to present their own syntheses or assemblies of ideas and conclusions. Following examples set by us and others in writing and illustration, graphical animation and musical composition, organization and exposition of concepts, and the linking of thoughts into a coherent whole, the students can participate increasingly in this large and important facet of the educational experience.

(9) Computer-based instructional resources should be shared electronically between universities. The development of Web pages has established networks that facilitate collaboration and provide effective review of instructor-authored learning materials. Not only does this lead to more efficient production of resource materials (by reducing duplication of effort) but, perhaps more importantly, the dangers inherent in a single view of a subject will be kept in check.

While some may think of educational technology as contrary to the aims of liberal education, we firmly believe that it provides new opportunities that are consistent with the goals of liberal education. It is evident that this whole thrust towards technological solutions must necessarily involve a redirection of effort towards the art of teaching. What form of liberal education results from this? Choosing between the rhetorical and the philosophical lines as presented in the article by J. vanderLeest,[8] one might say that the computer-based activity constitutes a reversion to a Ciceronian emphasis on the organizational and presentational approaches to dealing with subject matter. Students are expected to develop the necessary skills to use the new forms of communication so that in their undergraduate years and in later life, they can make their arguments with clarity and success no matter what subjects they have studied. But now the components, the preface, the narrative, the classification, have given way to the file arrangement, the topic menu, the submenus, and the sound and video segments of the new multimedia. And the venues for delivery are not the senate and courts of Rome but rather the classroom, the corporate boardroom, and the Internet with its millions of participants. There are welcome signs that the extreme compartmentalization and rivalry accompanying the emphasis on research success are now being moderated by a degree of interdepartmental cooperation in the planning of public computer laboratories and the implementation of server and software training infrastructure that makes it possible for students to immerse themselves in the new way of learning. Thus, while the use of computers does not restore the old ideal of a core curriculum, it does generate a certain commonality of attitude and method. With care, we can make this a time for a marked improvement both in the effectiveness of learning and in the degree of satisfaction that students take from their own journey along the paths of a liberal education.[9]

NOTES

1 HyperCard is a versatile Macintosh program based on the metaphor of a set of library index cards, each of which is able to contain a wide mix of text, graphics, sounds, etc. In addition, there are dynamic links (buttons)

that allow one to flip sequentially through cards, or to go to specific locations. The buttons can also be used to cross reference different stacks, or to initiate external picture, digitized video, or application windows. HyperCard has played a central role in the educational software developed for the Macintosh platform at Mount Allison.

2 For a more detailed overview of different computer-assisted instruction projects, see the booklet *Hypercard and Other Macintosh Instructional Software at Mount Allison*, ed. S. Walker (Sackville, NB, Mount Allison University, 1993), 19 pp.

3 This concept of cognitive dissonance as a key component of science teaching has been championed by professors such as the late Tik L. Liem; see his *Invitations to Science Inquiry* (Lexington, MA: Ginn Publishing, 1981).

4 "All this talk about correct texts leads me to think of good old William James, who, in his no doubt exemplary teaching of psychology, said that he always used Spencer's book because it gave him something to argue against. Learning is often enhanced to a greater degree by negative examples than by kowtowing to the correct. Should we add 'academic correctness' to the vocabulary?" (Graham Skanes, St John's, Memorial University of Newfoundland, Society for Teaching and Learning in Higher Education Electronic Forum, 17 May 1995; available from listserv@unb.ca in file STLHE-L LOG-9305). "You make an interesting point: using a text you don't particularly like could lead to some interesting discussions. But I think that you romanticize the publishing industry and all the 'reviews' that texts undergo. From my perspective in English, it seems that whatever looks saleable gets the nod. Right now we have anthologies, like the Heath, that are driven by a particular orthodoxy. As books, like schools, try to be all things to all people, they get bigger and bigger. Any book that you can't comfortably read in bed is not worth assigning." (Jim Ventola, Massasoit Community College, Brockton, MA, Society for Teaching and Learning in Higher Education Electronic Forum, 18 May 1995; available from listserv@unb.ca in file STLHE-L LOG-9305).

5 This point, as it relates to student-faculty communication, is addressed in R.L. Hawkes, "Computers, Mail and Teaching," *3M Teaching Fellowship Journal* 2 (1991): 18–20, 31.

6 Aspects of computer-based instruction at Mount Allison and the Mount Allison Apple Centre for Innovation are given in a collection of articles published in the *Mount Allison Record*, no. 44 (Winter 1994): 6–10.

7 All rooms in the main university residences are equipped with Ethernet-based connection to the campus computer networks. For a small connection fee students who own computers can access all learning materials, most commercial software, and Internet services such as electronic mail, file transfer protocol (ftp), newsgroups, and Web browsers directly from

their rooms. More limited services are offered to students not living in residence through modem connections.

8 See chapter 1.

9 The innovative instructional developments described in this paper would not have emerged without the technical expertise and driving force of Stewart Walker, the coordinator of the Mount Allison Apple Centre for Innovation. We would also like to stress that the authors of this article are just three of a team of faculty, staff, and students who have developed the approaches and courseware described in the paper, and we acknowledge their support and help. In addition, we would like to thank those students who have provided the encouragement and ideas that have driven the evolution of the learning materials. The Apple Canada Educational Foundation provided funds for this work, while the Macintosh Laboratory was supported by the Mount Allison Universitas Campaign. Current developments in several areas are being funded by program-development grants under the New Brunswick/Canada Cooperation Agreement administered in conjunction with TeleEducation New Brunswick. We acknowledge the assistance of instructional-technology developers Cameron Bales and Christopher Mackay, who are currently working on the Mount Allison TeleEducation Project.

Contributors

MARK BLAGRAVE is associate professor of English and director of Drama at Mount Allison. He is an active playwright and director, with research interests in Maritime theatre history and dramatic literature, and in Restoration drama.

PAUL A. BOGAARD is a professor of philosophy at Mount Allison University. Along with publications in the history of philosophy and the philosophy of science, he has edited *Profiles of Science and Society in the Maritimes prior to 1914*. He is currently working on a comprehensive study of the Canadian scientific professoriate up to 1945.

BRIAN CAMPBELL is an associate professor in the Department of Sociology and Anthropology at Mount Allison University. His main research and teaching interests are in the sociology of science, technology, law, expertise, and education.

PAUL CANT has taught physics at Mount Allison University since 1964. He has used computers for modelling, animation, and instrument control to assist with research and instruction throughout that time. His main research interests have been in the fields of nuclear magnetic resonance and the analysis of tides and waves. At Mount Allison's Apple Centre for Innovation he has produced course materials for local use and for New Brunswick's TeleEducation Network.

JANE DROVER is the coordinator of the Meighen Centre at Mount Allison University. Her work involves providing assistance to students with learning disabilities and actively managing the day-to-day operations of the centre. She is active in several organizations associated with the field of learning disabilities and involved in the in-service training of educators at the post-secondary level.

BERKELEY FLEMING is head of the Department of Sociology and Anthropology at Mount Allison University. He has published books on the history of social theory, rental housing markets in Montreal, and French second-language educational opportunities in Canada. He is currently conducting a comparative analysis of the growth of French as a Second Language (FSL) programs in Nova Scotia and New Brunswick.

VIRGIL HAMMOCK is head of the Department of Fine Arts at Mount Allison University where he has taught since 1975. He is a well-known art critic and the author of several monographs on European and Canadian artists and numerous articles on contemporary art in various publications. He has served as president of both the Universities Art Association of Canada and the Canadian Section of the International Association of Art Critics.

ROBERT HAWKES teaches physics at Mount Allison University and conducts research into the nature and atmospheric ablation of small meteoroids. His teaching excellence has been recognized through regional and national teaching awards. In recent years he has been active in the use of computers to enhance educational experiences, and he was a key figure in the Apple Centre for Innovation at Mount Allison and in curriculum develolopment through New Brunswick's TeleEducation Network.

BRIAN McMILLAN is currently seconded to the Department of Indian and Northern Affairs from his teaching position in Mount Allison's Department of Education. However, as codirector of the Meighen Centre, he has maintained his affiliation with the centre and continues his work there on a weekly basis. Brian is active in the Association of Higher Education and Disabilities and is chair of the Canadian Special Interest Group. His research interests are in the areas of learning strategies and learning disabilities.

MARK PARENT is presently the minister of the Pereaux United Baptist Church, Nova Scotia, and an honorary research associate at Acadia University. He has taught at Mount Allison University, NB, Atlantic Baptist College, NB, and Queen's Theological College, Queen's University, ON. He holds a PHD in Religious Studies from McGill University.

CHRISTINE STORM is a professor of psychology at Mount Allison University and former director of Research Administration. She has published articles in the areas of psycholinguistics and developmental psychology in addition to her higher education research.

TOM STORM taught psychology at the University of British Columbia for many years. Since retiring from UBC he has been a visiting professor at several Maritime universities and a consultant on survey and evaluation research for Health and Welfare, Canada. He has published articles and books in the fields of alcohol and drug use, social psychology, and language. He is currently a private scholar.

FRANK STRAIN is associate professor and head of the Department of Economics, Mount Allison University. Dr Strain's research interests include Atlantic Canadian economic history, public-sector economics, labour economics, and education.

MICHELLE STRAIN has been a part-time lecturer in both the Economics Department and the Commerce Department at Mount Allison University. Her published work includes a paper in the *Urban History Review.*

J. VANDERLEEST is a member of the Department of Classics at Mount Allison University. His main areas of research are in the fields of archaeology, Roman history, and historiography. He has served as secretary of the University senate and as a member of the senate's Academic Matters Committee, and in those roles he has been active in the development of the curriculum and the approach to liberal education at Mount Allison.

NANCY VOGAN is a professor of music and education at Mount Allison University and coauthor (with J. Paul Green) of *Music Education in Canada: A Historical Account.* She is active in many associations and has been honoured for her contributions to music education in Canada. As a member of the Apple Centre for Innovation she has been exploring the use of computers in music instruction in both her music-education and music-history courses.

ALEXANDER M. WILSON teaches special education in Mount Allison University's Department of Education. He is also codirector of the Meighen Centre for Learning Assistance and Research. His primary research interests are in the fields of learning disabilities and neuropsychology. He is coeditor of a recent book, *Serving Postsecondary Students with Learning Disabilities: A Resource Book for Service Providers.*